PUBLIC
FINANCE

PUBLIC FINANCE

Jack Ochs

University of Pittsburgh

Harper & Row, Publishers

New York   Evanston   San Francisco   London

Sponsoring Editor: John Greenman
Project Editor: Carol E. W. Edwards
Designer: Emily Harste
Production Supervisor: Robert A. Pirrung

PUBLIC FINANCE

Library of Congress Cataloging in Publication Data

Ochs, Jack, 1940–
    Public finance.

    Includes bibliographies.
    1. Finance, Public. I. Title.
HJ141.034   336   73–13302
ISBN 0–06–044885–7

CONTENTS

PREFACE

This book has evolved out of a series of lectures that I prepared when I was first asked to give a course in public finance several years ago. Having had an interest in various aspects of political economy, but no formal training in the area of public finance, I was to be my first student. In reading the textbooks and journal literature in the field, I was impressed by the differences in emphases, and even analytic framework, between the recent literature, which focuses upon both positive and normative analyses of expenditures, nonmarket decision making, and various aspects of regulatory taxation and control, and the topic coverage of then-extant texts, which emphasized the normative and positive dimensions of tax policy and stabilization policy. The purpose of my first lecture notes, therefore, was to establish for myself and my students a course outline that gave greater emphasis to the directions in which research in public finance was moving than I could find in the then-available texts.

This effort to present an outline of the field as it currently stands has been carried over from those first notes to the present manuscript.

My second purpose was to describe and explain those economic principles that the student must grasp if he is to understand the content of contemporary literature in public finance. To this end, this text emphasizes theory and its application rather than institutional description.

It is my belief that a textbook should be more than an exposition of principles, it should also be a self-teaching device. It is by their application that the student learns the principles. Therefore, an integral part of this text is the questions for discussion at the end of each chapter. Some end-of-chapter questions are meant to link discussions in different chapters, either anticipating points not yet formally developed or to reinforce the meaning of points raised earlier. Other end-of-chapter questions serve as guides to recent literature which incorporates principles discussed in the text. The reader who wishes to reinforce and extend his understanding of the text should attempt to answer most, if not all, of these questions. Answers to many of these questions are contained in the last section of the book. References to articles dealing with several other questions are also given.

I have made an attempt to make this text self-contained, providing definitions for terms and illustrations of concepts whenever they are first introduced. In principle, anyone could understand this work. However, in practice, a prior knowledge of the language and techniques of microeconomics and macroeconomics, at least at the level of the more rigorous principles texts, such as Samuelson's *Principles* or Lipsey and Steiner's *Economics*, is probably necessary for reading at least some of the chapters. The intended audience is, therefore, upper-class undergraduates and first-year graduates with some training in formal economic analysis.

INTRODUCTION

As the saying goes, "There is nothing in life which is certain except death and taxes." Like death, the existence of taxation has provoked all manner of speculation among philosophers, scientists, and the general public from time immemorial. Yet we still have not acquired a full understanding of the causes and consequences of taxation.

Taxation is an instrument of government. In order to understand why taxation exists, one must first conceive a rationale for government activity. In a democratic society, this requires some understanding of the objectives individuals seek when they participate in a political process. There are as many different perspectives to be brought to this task as there are social sciences. This book reflects the perspective (some would call it bias) of an economist.

The economist views economic activity as processes of resource allocation. He is concerned with giving an account of "how," "what," and "for whom" the production and distribution of commodities take place in a society. A basic assumption in the analysis of any economic process is that individuals participate in the process in order to improve their own circumstances. Most economic theorists have restricted their analyses of economic activity to free market processes of resource allocation. For our purposes, there are two distinctive features in the analysis of a market process. First, the basic decision-making units in market processes are assumed to have a well-defined objective which governs each unit's decisions. The outcome of market activities is the result of individual choices and is not governed by any collectively determined objective. Secondly, individuals are not directly bound by decisions that they deem opposed to their own interests. The political economist must go beyond the market. He views political processes as an alternative mode by which individuals may seek to affect the allocation of resources (that is, as a form of economic activity). Unlike market processes, a political decision to change the allocation of resources reflects a collective choice to which all members may be bound regardless of how they individually perceive that decision as affecting themselves. In providing a rationale for government activity, therefore, the political economist must try to explain the circumstances under which individuals will generally prefer to bind themselves to collective agreements on resource allocation rather than seek their own interests by dealing with the market.

In Chapter 1, we seek to show how pressure for collective action will be generated by the failure of markets to adequately reflect the value that individuals attach to certain kinds of goods. Such market failure leads to an imbalance in the allocation of resources, too few resources being devoted to some activities, and too many resources being devoted to others relative to the most efficient pattern of resource allocation. In Chapter 2, we explore several manifestations of this imbalance in the forms of pollution, congestion, and blight. Our purpose is to understand why market processes fail to adequately reflect the value individuals place on various dimensions of their environment and why such conditions are likely to persist in the absence of collective action.

For many years, economists have recognized the territorial claims of the political scientist to the analysis of political processes. Undoubtedly, both disciplines have gained as the result of such specialization of labor. If the economist is to understand the demand for goods created by collective action, however, he must have an understanding of the process that leads to the decision to express these demands. In the past two decades, a small but growing literature has developed which brings an economic perspective to bear upon the political decision-making process. In Chapter 3, we discuss various attributes of voting processes in which economists have shown interest. In particular, we shall be concerned with whether a voting system will necessarily produce decisions that improve the allocation of resources relative to what could be accomplished without such a system.

Because the formulation of proposals takes place prior to making choices among proposals, the character of the final decisions will depend on the character of the process by which proposals are produced. The proposals in which the economist is most interested are those contained in the budget, that is, those that involve the expenditure of money and the use of resources. Economists have been active in attempts to reform the budget process so that the proposals contained in the budget reflect an "appropriate" accounting of their benefits and costs. In Chapter 4, we review some of the literature of cost-benefit analysis and its impact on the budgeting process.

While the economist is treading on somewhat alien territory when he discusses the character of the political process, he is on more familiar grounds when he analyzes how government activity affects the circumstances that shape individuals' market behavior. How will the way in which government activities are financed influence market decisions about the supply of labor, the direction of investment, the supply of savings, and the distribution of income? These are standard questions in the theory of public finance to which we address ourselves in Chapters 5 through 8.

The spending and financing decisions of the government affect not only the pattern of economic activity, but also its volume. In the decades since the Great Depression of the 1930s, this aspect of government activity has been much stressed in both popular and professional circles. The role of the government in sustaining full employment is the topic of Chapter 9.

Government is distinguished from other social institutions by virtue of its monopoly of the powers of coercion. People look to government to use its power to establish and enforce rules that govern private behavior. In the economic domain, government has been called upon to regulate the behavior of firms which might otherwise act in ways inimical to the interests of those who seek such regulation. An important class of regulated firms are those who have secured a natural monopoly in their markets by virtue of the economies of scale implicit in their technology. In Chapter 10, we discuss the controversies that have developed with respect to government regulation of these natural monopolies.

Finally, the organizational structure of government is itself a reflection of the pressures for collective action. The allocation of tasks among federal, state, and local governments has undergone significant shifts. New forms of political organizaton such as authorities and regional compacts, which have cut across historic political boundaries, have been created to achieve a measure of coordination not otherwise achievable. In our concluding chapter, we analyze some of the economic forces that shape the organizational structure within which the pressures for collective action are expressed.

Every author accumulates many debts in the process of developing a manuscript. In this respect I am no different. First, I wish to thank the many students who bore the burden of studying from early versions of the manuscript. I have benefited from many discussions with my colleagues Edgar Hoover, Arnold Katz, George Schieber, Morton Schnabel, Michael Spiro, and Jerome Wells on various points raised in the text. Gail C. A. Cook, University of Toronto, Charles Metcalf, University of Wisconsin, Ray Whitman, University of Maryland, and Colin Wright, Northwestern University provided valuable comments, which, I hope, led to many improvements in the text. Naturally, whatever shortcomings this text may have remain my sole responsibility. Only those who read the initial draft of my manuscript could fully appreciate the efforts of my wife, Phyllis, to simplify the language and clarify the arguments in the text. If some of the arguments still are stated in cumbersome language, it is because of my inability to state them more succinctly without the use of mathematics. I am also grateful to Mrs. Esther Zavos, who not only typed but also edited the many versions of this work. Finally, I wish to express my gratitude to my parents, to whom this book is dedicated.

Jack Ochs

1

THE RATIONALE FOR GOVERNMENT ACTIVITY

Modern views about the role of government have been forged out of the experiences of the transition from a feudal to an industrial society. In the medieval age, society was essentially static. Institutional change was imperceptibly slow, and individual roles were well articulated. Each individual had "his place" described by virtue of custom and law. The scope of individual decision was highly circumscribed by a set of obligations binding upon both serf and lord. Society was viewed as a family with a hierarchical, paternalistic structure. The entire social fabric appeared preordained and independent of the will of any individual.

As long as society remained static, such a world view seemed natural. But the growth of trade and the rise of cities created social pressures which rent the fabric of medieval society. A serf who left the field for the city left behind not only the protection of his lord, but also his obligation to him. Voluntary contract replaced the obligations of heredity. The scope of individual choice widened, and class conflict was widespread. As a result, the conception of government changed. No longer were men governed by custom and stable social order. The power of the state could be (and was) wielded to serve particular interests of those who controlled it. The opening of society to dynamic forces of individualism paved the way for tyranny and social mobility. This left those who experienced this change with a profound fear that a government, which was a tool of men, would be controlled by the few to the disadvantage of many. Almost two centuries before President Eisenhower spoke of the danger of a military-industrial complex, Adam Smith warned of the power of monopolists who "like an overgrown standing army, . . . have become formidable to the government, and upon many occasions intimidate the legislature."

If the breakdown of the feudal order impressed men with the danger of a government of men, it also convinced them that the direction of society was not preordained. In a dynamic world, government would inevitably play a role which was dictated by the desires of individuals. The practical political problem was to structure the processes by which social decisions were made so as to make them reflective of the interests of the many and not merely of the few.

From this perspective, a free-market system, in which competition limited the power of any individual to exact an advantage from any other individual, seemed an ideal form of social organization. Each individual was free to pursue his own interests. But the achievement of his purposes required that his actions benefit others as well as himself. Gradually, the view developed that competition made the consumer sovereign and that competition was sufficient to guide the use of society's resources into a pattern that best served the general welfare.

If the consumer is to be sovereign, then the general welfare requires that resources be allocated in accordance with consumer preferences. Within this context, what role should government play in the process of resource allocation? This is the question to which this chapter is addressed. We shall proceed to answer this question in the following way. First we shall discuss criteria and methods for making social comparisons of different patterns of resource use. Then we shall discuss the manner in which various idealized market economies that are free from active government participation would operate, and we shall explore the circumstances under which such economies could achieve an optimal allocation of resources. We shall learn that such conditions are very stringent and are unlikely to be met in any actual society. The role of the government in the economy can then be viewed in terms of what is required to compensate for the failures of the market mechanism.

WHAT IS THE GENERAL WELFARE?

● In a democracy, the welfare of the community is not distinct from the welfare of the individuals of the community. Rather, it must be defined in terms of their welfare. Moreover, it is assumed that the individual is the best judge of his own welfare. This does not mean that each individual, no matter how ignorant, is capable of deciding whether a particular policy is likely to promote his welfare, for it may take special knowledge to determine what the consequences of a policy will be. But it does mean that once the consequences are known, each individual is to be the judge as to whether these consequences serve his own interests. To assume otherwise is to assert that the values which some people hold are superior to the values of others. But such a view presupposes some objective standard by which the values of different individuals can be compared. If such a standard existed, then one could, in principle, know whether a policy promoted the general welfare without asking anyone how they viewed the consequences. However, no one has discovered such a standard, and the practical significance of asserting that one person's values are better than another has been to justify the suppression of popular sentiment by an elite.

MEASURING THE GENERAL WELFARE

● If the general welfare is to be expressed in terms of the preferences of individuals, then how can you tell if the general welfare of the community is better in one state of the world than in another? Without an answer to this question, it is clearly not sensible to speak of conditions for a socially optimal allocation of resources. If the community were composed entirely of like-minded persons, the answer would be simple: Ask any one of them which state of the world they preferred; since everyone has the same preference, it would be reasonable to say that the community's welfare is greater in the state that our representative citizen prefers than it is in the state that he considers inferior. Once one allows a variety of preferences into the community, however, the notion of a "representative citizen" vanishes, and the problem of measuring the general welfare in terms of the preferences of the individuals who compose the community becomes more complex. If some people say they prefer situation A to situation B while others prefer situation B to situation A, how is it to be determined whether the general welfare is larger in B or in A? Clearly, the process of making a *social* valuation of A relative to B involves attaching social significance or weight to the preferences of the individuals who compose the community and then deciding how those weights are to be added or aggregated.

Counting Votes

One such aggregation procedure is to distribute votes among the populace according to some rules of enfranchisement (children's opinions don't count; college professors receive a half-vote, and so on)

Table 1.1

	Individuals		
	1	2	3
Preference rank	A	B	C
highest to	B	C	A
lowest	C	A	B

and then to make social comparisons by adopting a decision rule such as bare majority or two-thirds majority to decide which alternative is socially preferable. The economist is not, by virtue of his profession, in any special position to state just what choice of enfranchisement and decision rule the community *ought* to make. These are ethical decisions for which he has no special qualifications. But, as we shall discuss more fully in Chapter 3, it is not always possible to make choices among sets of more than two alternatives by a majority decision rule. A simple example can illustrate the problem. In Table 1.1 we record the preferences of three individuals, 1, 2, and 3 among three alternatives, A, B, and C. Note that in this example, there is no alternative that is preferred by a majority to the other alternatives. Moreover, if a vote is taken on each pair of alternatives (A, B), (A, C), and (B, C), we find that while a majority prefer A to B and a majority prefer B to C, it does not follow that a majority prefer A to C. Given a choice between A and C, two out of three of our individuals would choose C. What this example shows, therefore, is that if we use majority rule as an index of general welfare, then our index will have the paradoxical property of being able to say that a change from situation C to situation B improves welfare, a change from situation B to situation A further improves welfare, *and* a change from *A back to the original situation C improves welfare.* Because of the possibility of such paradoxical behavior, many people feel that majority rule cannot always be used as a guide to the relative social merits of alternative situations.

Counting Utils

In the nineteenth century, economists conceived of another method of aggregating individual preferences into an index of social welfare. At that time, economists spoke of individuals as if they were vested with a "pleasure center" or biological mechanism common to all men.

This mechanism would allow the physical measurement of the "utils" of pleasure, which an individual could derive from any given situation. If such a mechanism existed, then it would be possible, at least in principle, to compare the levels of satisfaction produced by a given state of the world in different individuals by a common scale. The existence of such a scale would provide a "natural"[1] alternative to a voting procedure for producing a social ranking of alternative states of the world. Since one person's "util" was like any other's, one could define the social welfare of a given situation as the sum over all individuals of the utils that particular situation would produce. The "only" requirement for carrying out such measurements was to find a device to measure the "utils."

The Principle of Diminishing Marginal Utility: A Digression

The "pleasure center" has never been located. Nevertheless, economists once believed[2] that the market behavior of individuals provided indirect evidence about the nature of such a center. Specifically, they observed that, other things being equal, individuals tended to buy more of a given commodity when its price was low than when it was high. This is the law of demand. To explain this observation, they constructed a theory of consumer behavior based upon three axioms:

1. Consumers attempt to spend their income to maximize the utility they can derive from their purchases.
2. Within limits, the more of a commodity an individual could have, other things being equal, the more utility he could receive.
3. Each additional unit of a commodity yielded a smaller increment in utility than its predecessors.

The third axiom, called the principle of diminishing marginal utility, assumes that it is possible to measure an increment of pleasure or utility. Taken together, these assumptions imply that individuals will respond to price changes in the way in which they are actually observed to respond.[3]

Since the principle of diminishing marginal utility is consistent with the law of demand, evidence that supported the law of demand was taken to confirm that the "pleasure center" responded with a diminishing increment of pleasure to the additional consumption of any one commodity. Classical economists conjectured that if the "pleasure center" responded with diminishing intensity to increments of consumption of any one commodity, it would do so when consumption of *all* commodities were expanded simultaneously. Such an expansion could only take place when income increased. This conjecture implied that income was subject to diminishing marginal utility. The notion that income is subject to diminishing marginal utility has important implications for evaluating changes in the distribution of income. If one man's utils are like another's, and if the social welfare is improved when the total number of utils in the community increases, then if income is subject to diminishing marginal utility, a redistribution of income from the rich to the poor will increase the social welfare. (Why?) The concept of diminishing marginal utility of income, therefore, seems to give support to an egalitarian ethic.

Is Income Subject to Diminishing Marginal Utility? The claim that increases in income yield diminishing increments of satisfaction was not based on direct measurements of changes in satisfaction. Rather, it was inferred by a chain of reasoning from the observed law of demand. The chain of reasoning was attacked by later economists in several ways. First, they pointed out that the assumption of the diminishing marginal utility of income did not logically follow from the assumption that each good was subject to diminishing marginal utility, *holding quantities of other goods constant.* The value an individual would attach to an extra set of tires may well depend on how many cars he has and if he has the gasoline to drive them. Evidence supporting the law of demand did not, therefore, necessarily support the principle of the diminishing marginal utility of income. Economists pointed out even if the law of demand did provide indirect support of the principle of the diminishing marginal utility of income, it would not support the assumption that the loss of utility of a rich man from having his income reduced $1 was likely to be less than the gain in utility of a poor man whose income was increased by $1. For one cannot estimate the pleasure an individual derived from expending a given income by observing the pattern of expenditures he makes. Two individuals with the same income may derive different levels of satisfaction from the same expenditure pattern.

The third line of attack was to derive the law of demand from assumptions about individual preferences, which did not require the assumption of a measure of satisfaction or mechanism to record "utils." By providing such an analysis of consumer behavior, these later economists deprived adherents of the principle of measurable utility of the claim that evidence in support of the law of demand provided indirect support for the existence of a biological mechanism, which registered the "utils" of pleasure derived from different circumstances. On the basis of these attacks, most economists now agree that programs of income redistribution cannot be justified by reference to economic arguments. Rather, an appeal must be made to notions of equity when judging income distributions.

The Principle of Pareto Superiority

Returning to our discussion of the problem of constructing an index of social welfare, we see that both the principle of majority rule and the principle of highest aggregate utility are designed to cope with the problem of ranking social alternatives when individual evaluations of those alternatives differ. These are conflict situations. Any *comprehensive* index of social welfare must tell us how to resolve a conflict of individual interests. Unfortunately, the paradox of majority voting and our inability to measure utility on a scale common to all individuals eliminate these methods as acceptable methods of building a comprehensive index of social welfare.

Happily, not all choices among possible alternatives necessarily raise the issue of conflicting individual preferences. Many acts of resource reallocation are essentially private transactions, which materially influence only the two parties directly involved. As long as the grocer is willing to sell to me on the same terms as he does to my neighbor, and does not set these terms according to the volume of goods my neighbor purchases, I may be indifferent with respect to whatever exchanges are made between my neighbor and the grocer. But my neighbor and the grocer are not indifferent. They only engage in trade if they find it mutually advantageous. If some people are better off after the exchange and no one else is worse off, then it would seem natural to say that the exchange had improved the general welfare. More generally, whenever some people prefer situation A to situation B while no one prefers B to A, we shall say that A is *pareto superior* to B and that any situation, A, which is pareto superior to another situation, B, is *socially preferred* to B.

The notion of pareto superiority gives us one criterion by which to evaluate alternative systems of resource allocation. If system A produces an allocation of resources that is pareto superior to the allocation produced by system B, then system A would be judged better than system B as long as the merits of the systems are measured only in terms of the results that they produce. Of course, people may be concerned about the processes by which the end result is reached as well as with the end result itself. Even if an economic system in which all decisions were made by a dictator produced a final allocation of resources that everyone preferred to the final allocation achievable by a process that let everyone make some decisions, it would not necessarily follow that people preferred the dictatorial system to the non-dictatorial system. Pareto superiority is one criterion by which to compare systems, but it is not the sole criterion.

Pareto Optimality

In engineering, the performance of one machine relative to another is judged in terms of an abstract standard called the "efficient" machine. If a machine is efficient, it converts all of its energy input into useful energy output. The larger the percentage of energy input a machine converts into useful energy, the more nearly efficient it is. The performance of one machine relative to another can then be expressed in terms of the ratio of their respective efficiency coefficients. In economics, the notion of pareto optimality is akin to the engineer's notion of efficiency. The law of conservation of matter assures us that no machine can have an efficiency index greater than 1; that is, the best any actual machine can do is to be as efficient as an efficient machine. Similarly, the concept of pareto optimality is defined as a limiting concept. No allocation of resources can be pareto superior to an allocation which is *pareto optimal*.

We can illustrate the concept of pareto optimality by means of a simple example involving the allocation of fixed quantities of two goods, x and y, between two individuals, Crusoe and Friday.

In Figure 1.1, the length of the line AB corresponds to the total amount of good y, which is to be divided between Crusoe and Friday. Similarly, the length of AC represents the total quantity of x, which is to be divided. Each point within the box represents a particular allocation of the goods between the two men. Crusoe's share of y in a given allocation is measured by the perpendicular distance from the point representing that allocation to the bottom of the box; Friday's share of y in that allocation is measured by the perpendicular distance from the point to the top of the box. Similarly, Crusoe's share of x in a given allocation is measured by the perpendicular distance from the point representing that allocation to the left side of the box, and Friday's by the perpendicular distance to the right side. For example, in Figure 1.1, point W represents an allocation in which Crusoe gets VW units of x and RW units of y, while Friday gets SW units of y and TW units of x.

Let us suppose that both Crusoe and Friday are *egotists* who rank alternative allocations solely in terms of the goods that they themselves would possess in each allocation. Suppose that all goods were completely *private*, in that no attribute of any good would give satisfaction to anyone who did not actually possess it. Given these assumptions, we can then map the preference rankings of Crusoe and Friday onto our diagram. (It is important to remember that the concept of pareto

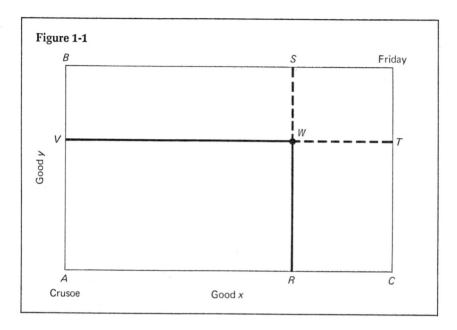

Figure 1-1

superiority does not imply that individuals are egotists or that goods are purely private. We make these assumptions both for expository convenience and to set the stage for an analysis of the optimality or nonoptimality properties of a free market system.)

In Figure 1.2, we have drawn portions of the preference-ranking maps of Crusoe and Friday on our box of feasible allocations. Crusoe's ranking is represented by the indifference curves labeled C_i. Since the lower-left corner of the box represents an allocation in which Crusoe gets nothing, the further one of his indifference curves is from the lower-left corner, the higher the preference-ranking points on that curve have. Similarly, Friday's indifference curves are oriented toward the upper-right corner, the point at which he receives nothing. The further one of Friday's indifference curves, labeled F_i, is from this origin, the higher the index number it carries.

Friday's most preferred state is Crusoe's least preferred, and conversely. Neither cares for the welfare of the other. Nevertheless, their interests are not always strictly opposed when one state of the world is compared with another. Starting from a given allocation, there may be a set of alternative allocations that both Friday and Crusoe prefer. Such a situation is illustrated in Figure 1.3. In this figure, point W lies on the curve through all of the points to which Friday assigns a preference index rank of 30. All of the points to the left of this curve are

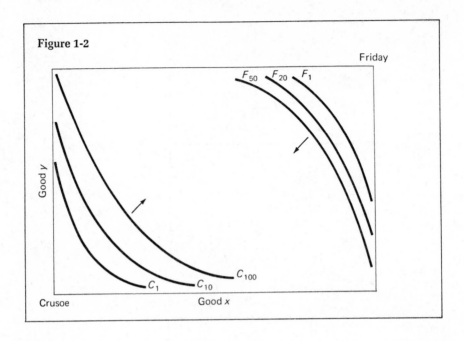

Figure 1-2

Friday

F_{50} F_{20} F_1

Good y

C_{100}

C_{10}

C_1

Crusoe

Good x

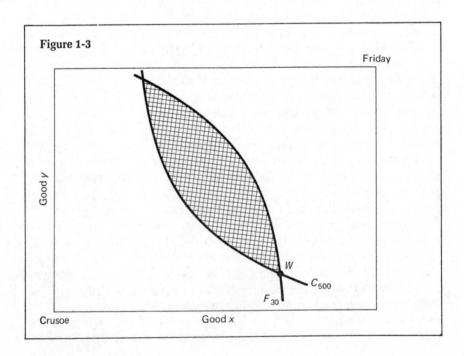

Figure 1-3

Friday

Good y

W

C_{500}

F_{30}

Crusoe

Good x

better than W from Friday's point of view. Similarly, W lies on the curve through all of the points to which Crusoe assigns a preference rank of 500. All of the points to the right of this line are better than W from Crusoe's point of view. All of the points in the crosshatched area, or lens formed by the intersection of the two indifference curves through W, are, therefore, preferred to W by both Crusoe and Friday. That is, all of the points inside the lens are pareto superior to W.

From a social point of view, all the allocations inside the lens formed by the intersection of the two indifference curves through W are better than W. But not all of them are equally good. In Figure 1.4, we have denoted four points inside this lens, W_1, W_2, W_3, W_4, all of which are pareto superior to W. If we compare W_2 with W_1, we see that W_2 lies inside the lens formed by the intersection of the indifference curves through W_1. Therefore, W_2 is pareto superior to W_1. Similarly, W_3 lies within the lens formed by the intersection of the indifference curves through W_2. Therefore, W_3 is pareto superior to W_2. Notice that at W_3 the indifference curves are just tangent to each other. Therefore, their intersection does not form a lens or, in other words, contain any point other than W_3. This means that any point Crusoe considers better than W_3, Friday considers worse, and conversely. (Why?) Consequently, there is no point which is pareto superior to W_3. Therefore, W_3 represents a *pareto optimal* allocation.

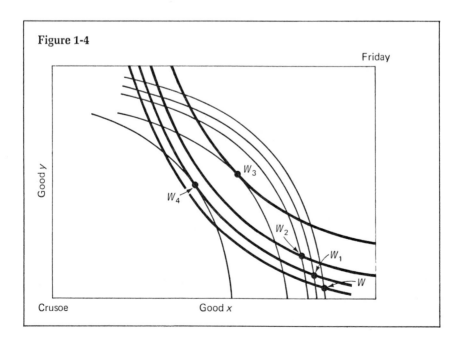

Figure 1-4

Efficiency and Equity

If, among all possible allocations, only one allocation were pareto optimal, then that allocation would be preferred from a social point of view to all other allocations. Unfortunately, life is not so simple. As we can readily verify, in Figure 1.4, allocation points W_3 and W_4 are both pareto optimal allocations. Indeed, if the two goods represented in the diagram are infinitely divisible, then it can be shown that there are an infinite number of points inside the diagram that satisfy the conditions for pareto optimality. Therefore, the fact that an allocation is pareto optimal is not sufficient to identify it as the best attainable allocation from a social point of view.

In Figure 1.5, the curve AA' represents all of the pareto optimal allocations. By definition, if Crusoe prefers pareto optimal allocation C to pareto optimal allocation D, then Friday must prefer D to C. If we are to say that C is socially preferable to D, therefore, we must apply some standard of fairness, or equity in judging each allocation. If C is considered a more equitable distribution than D, then very probably allocation Z, which is very close to C, would also be considered more

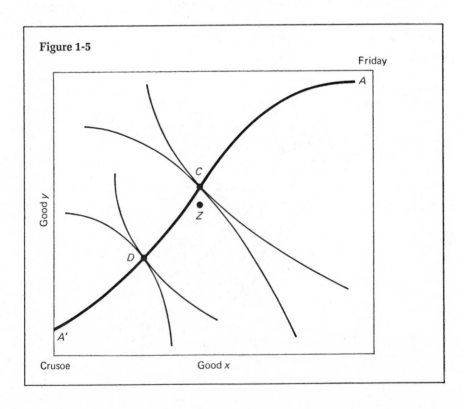

Figure 1-5

equitable than D. On these grounds, if an outside observer were asked to choose between Z and D, the allocation with the higher social welfare, he might choose Z in spite of the fact that D is pareto optimal, while Z is not. However, because Z is not pareto optimal, there must be some point on the CC' curve that is pareto superior to it. For this reason, if our outsider were asked to choose *from among all of the allocations* the one with the *highest* social welfare, he would not choose Z, or any other nonpareto optimal point. That is, pareto optimality is a *necessary* condition for social welfare maximization even though it is not a sufficient condition.

In the theory of exchange, the AA' curve is sometimes called a contract curve, since as long as the allocation is off the curve, the parties will have a mutual interest in contracting trades to reach some point on it. Once some point on the AA' curve is reached, however, no mutually profitable trades can be arranged. In other words, a pareto optimal allocation represents the limit of mutually profitable reallocations. It is in this sense that an economic system that reallocates resources until a pareto optimal allocation is reached may be termed efficient. An efficient system does not stop short of producing all *reallocations* that can be mutually profitable. We emphasize the word *reallocations*, because the limits upon the possibility of mutually profitable exchanges are dictated by the *initial* allocation of goods or distribution of income. Consequently, an efficient system of exchange, which starts from an inequitable distribution of wealth, may not produce as socially desirable outcome as an inefficient system, which starts from a more nearly equitable distribution. No proof of the efficiency of a slave system could convince many persons that slavery was desirable even if every other economic system could be shown to be inefficient.

MARKET EQUILIBRIUM AND PARETO OPTIMALITY

● The concept of pareto optimality is a natural standard of efficiency by which to judge free market systems of resource allocation. If a particular system tends to reallocate resources until a pareto optimal state is achieved, it will do all that can be done in the absence of coercion.

There are many possible kinds of economic systems in which the government plays no active role beyond establishing a legal framework and adjudicating disputes over property rights. In these systems, economic activity is comprised of voluntary exchanges between buyers and sellers. The basic rules governing such systems would prevent any buyer from being coerced to pay more for a product than he would willingly pay or any seller from selling a product at a price he would not voluntarily accept. Under such rules, no participant in the exchanges that comprise economic activity can be knowingly made worse off than he would be if he did not participate.

Welfare economists are interested in studying the properties of various free market systems. An important question to which they have addressed themselves is to determine whether particular free market systems do, or do not, tend to equilibrium allocations that are pareto optimal. The importance of this work is that if it can be shown that system A leads to a pareto optimal allocation but system B does not, then it can be argued that the government should adopt policies that make the economy perform like A rather than like B. For example, suppose system B were a system where producers of widgets were free to form a monopoly. This would not violate our basic ground rules—no one would be forced to buy a widget if he didn't wish to pay the monopoly price, and no firm would agree to the merger unless it could increase its profits by doing so. In fact, we know from price theory that each firm could gain by joining the monopoly and that the monopoly price would be higher than a competitive market price. The gains to the firms come at the expense of its customers. We may or may not like the distribution of wealth associated with the monopoly structure of the market. This is a problem in equity. (What if poor blacks or Indians or any other group you wished to help owned the widget factories?) Nevertheless, if a competitive market system tends to a pareto optimal allocation while a system in which the widget industry is monopolized does not, then starting with the allocation implied by the monopoly equilibrium it would be to everyone's advantage to switch to a competitive system. To make such a switch may require a change in the legal framework within which firms operate so as to prohibit collusion among, or mergers of, firms that are potential competitors. If the basis of the monopoly is technological then it may be necessary for the government to take over the industry or to subject it to special regulation. In the latter case, the question arises as to what rules or regulations will lead to an improvement in the efficiency with which the economic system operates.

Another dimension of the study of the optimality properties of free market systems has been the identification of conditions under which no system of free market trading will tend to produce a pareto optimal allocation. The fact that such conditions exist, as we will demonstrate later in this chapter, means that individuals must act outside the market—perhaps through the government—to accomplish reallocations that they would find mutually profitable but practically impossible to accomplish via free market activity. However, before turning to these general failures of free market systems, we must get some appreciation for the relationships that exist between market equilibrium conditions and the conditions for a pareto optimal allocation of resources.

Perfect Competition and Pareto Optimality

The most fully developed theory of a free-market system is of a system comprised of perfectly competitive markets. In this section, we shall show that this system produces an equilibrium allocation of commodities among individuals that is pareto optimal.

In a competitive system, each individual is assumed to act as if the prices at which he trades are beyond his control. Given the prices that he faces, the individual is assumed to place orders for the sale and purchase of commodities so as to change his initial endowment in a way that will maximize the personal value he can derive from his wealth. For trade to take place, there must be two parties who agree to the trade. This means that the market system must produce a set of prices that will bring the parties into agreement that the quantities which one wishes to sell the other wishes to buy. We can illustrate the way a competitive system might operate by means of the following example. Suppose that before any trade takes place, the division of the total stock of x and y between Mr. Smith and Mr. Jones was represented by point A in Figure 1.6. At point A, Mr. Smith and Mr. Jones place different personal valuations upon another unit of y relative to x. This is indicated by the difference in the slopes of their respective indifference curves passing through A. Both may, therefore, gain from trade if some suitable price ratio, or terms of trade, were found at which they could balance their offers of sale and purchase.

The setting of prices is to be outside the control of either man. We, therefore, introduce an "umpire" or "auctioneer" who announces a tentative rate of exchange of y for x (that is, P_x/P_y). Suppose that the initial exchange rate he calls out is equal to the slope of the line AA'. Each individual takes these prices as given and submits his purchase and sales orders. Smith would like to move up the trading line AA' to point B, since B represents the best allocation he could achieve given his initial endowment and the proposed market prices. He offers to sell BB' of x and to purchase AB' of y. Jones would like to move along AA' to point C, since C would be the best he could achieve given his initial endowment and the proposed market prices. Jones, therefore, offers to sell AC' of y and to purchase CC' of x. These respective offers of Jones and Smith are inconsistent with each other. At the prices

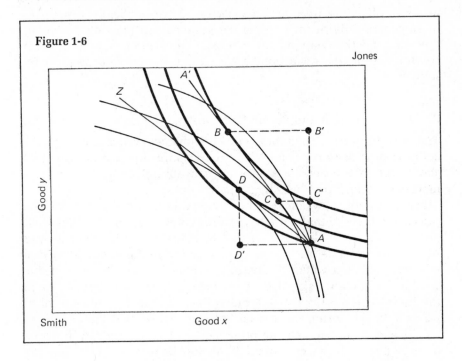

Figure 1-6

implied by the slope of AA', Smith wishes to sell more x than Jones wants to buy, and he wants to buy more y than Jones wishes to sell.

In competitive markets, the price of those goods in excess demand is assumed to rise, and the price of those goods in excess supply is assumed to fall. By this type of adjustment, the parties will come to an agreement. When an agreement is reached (no excess demand or supply in any market), the process has attained its equilibrium. Since AA' generates excess demand for y, the umpire must call out new prices, raising the price of y relative to x. This will make the trading line less steep. Suppose the new relative prices are represented by the slope of the line AZ. At these prices, Smith would like to move up the trading line AZ to D. He would offer to sell AD' of x and to buy DD' of y. Facing the same prices, Jones would offer to sell DD' of y and to buy AD' of x, for he would also wish to move to D. The prices implied by the slope of AZ would, therefore, be an equilibrium set of prices relative to the initial allocation, A. They will lead each participant to just offer for sale the quantities that the other participant wishes to buy.

Note that point D, the allocation which represents the competitive equilibrium, is a pareto optimal point. *This is not an accident.* Given the assumptions underlying the construction of the box diagram, namely, that individuals are egotists and goods are purely private, the competitive exchange process described must always lead to a pareto optimal allocation. This correspondence of competitive equilibria and pareto optimality stems from the fact that if an individual is maximizing his utility subject to a given set of prices, he will choose that bundle of goods for which his rate of substitution of one good for another is equal to the rate at which he can exchange them in the market. In the competitive equilibrium, all individuals face the same set of prices and, therefore, the same rates of exchange of one good in terms of another. But if every individual's rate of substitution of good y for good x is equal to P_x/P_y, then they must all have the same rate of substitution of y for x. Since mutually profitable trade is possible whenever two individuals have different rates of substitution, equality of rates of substitution is a necessary condition for pareto optimality as well as for a competitive equilibrium.

It must be emphasized that this correspondence results from all individuals adjusting to the same set of relative prices. If, for example, the government were to tax the purchase of x but not y, or to tax x and y at different rates, then buyers of x (who are sellers of y) will be facing a different set of prices than the sellers of x (buyers of y), because the buyer sees the price as including the tax, while the seller is interested in the price net of tax. But if different individuals are adjusting to different sets of prices, then in the equilibrium allocation, not all individuals will have the same rates of substitution between given pairs of commodities. Such taxes will, therefore, tend to reduce the efficiency with which a competitive market system can allocate resources. We shall discuss this problem more fully in Chapters 5 and 6.

Monopoly and Pareto Optimality

Adam Smith attempted to demonstrate that monopolies were inconsistent with promoting the general welfare whether created by government or by the collusion of producers. The principal difference between a monopoly and a competitive market is that in the monopoly market, one individual sets the terms at which the others may offer to buy the good he has for sale. If the monopolist must offer all individuals the same price, then ne has a *simple* monopoly. In this system, the monopolist sets the price that will maximize his gains from trade, while the other parties adjust their endowments to the terms he sets so as to maximize their gains from trade given the price the monopolist has set.

Figure 1.7 illustrates how an individual will adjust his endowment to various possible terms of trade the monopolist might present. His pretrade endowment is point A. Suppose the monopolist offered terms

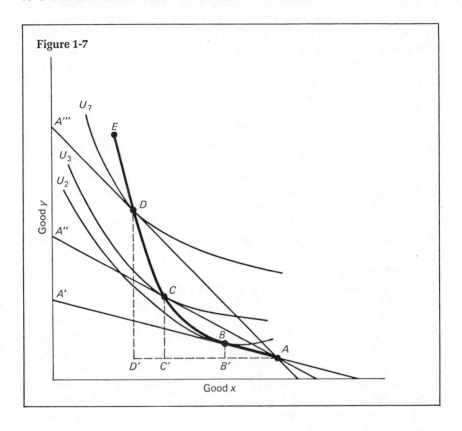

Figure 1-7

of trade such that starting from A this individual could attain any allocation on the line AA'. The slope of AA' would then represent the rate at which the monopolist would exchange y for x. If this were the terms offered, the best our individual could do is offer B'A of x in exchange for B'B of y. If the monopolist lowered his asking price for y so that starting from A this individual could attain any allocation along the line AA'', then the best he could do would be to exchange AC' of x for C'C of y. By rotating the terms of trade line through point A, we trace out in this manner a set of points like B, C, D, E, each of which represents the best this individual could do if the terms of trade line through A passed through them. Such a curve is called this individual's offer curve, because it represents the quantities of x and y he would offer to trade at different possible terms of trade.

In Figure 1.8, Smith's offer curve is represented by the curve OO'. Jones, who has a monopoly in y, can choose any terms of trade of y for x that he desires. Wishing to maximize his own gain from trade, Jones

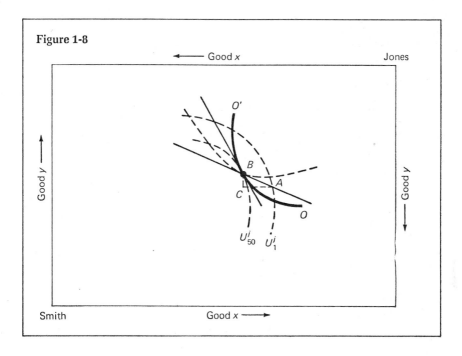

Figure 1-8

will seek that point on Smith's offer curve that is just tangent to one of Jones's indifference curves. In the diagram, B is this point. In order to induce Smith to choose point B, Jones must set his price of y in terms of x equal to the ratio of BC/CA. By construction of the offer curve, Smith's rate of substitution of y for x at point B is just equal to BC/CA. Notice, however, that Jones's indifference curve has a slope at B, which is greater than BC/CA. This implies that the terms of trade that yield the monopolist his largest gains, *given that he can only set the price and must accept the quantity that the buyer wishes to purchase at that price*, does not lead to the exhaustion of all mutually profitable trades. For if at B the monopolist's rate of substitution of y for x is greater than his customer's, then starting at B both could gain from further exchanges. However, since B is the equilibrium state, this implies that simple monopoly trading is not efficient.

What constrains the monopolist from further trading with the representative buyer if, at the simple monopoly equilibrium B, both he and the individual represented could be made better off by further trading between themselves? It is the fear of the monopolist that if he sold to one individual at a lower price than to others, he would find the low-price buyer undercutting him in trades he tried to arrange with other buyers. It is this potential competition that gives the monopolist the incentive to set a common price and forego what would otherwise be profitable trades.

Discriminatory Monopoly Pricing

If the monopolist sold a product which the purchaser could not resell, then the monopolist would be free to arrange separate trades with each customer on an all-or-nothing, take-it-or-leave-it basis. We illustrate such a system in Figure 1.9. Let A represent the initial allocation, U_s^1 the indifference curve of the first individual, and U_m^1 the indifference curve of the other who has a monopoly in the sale of good y. The best the monopolist can hope to do is get the first individual to accept a trade that leaves the first individual no worse off than he is at A. Of all the possible trades that leave the first person no worse off, an offer to exchange $A'C$ of y for AA' of x is the trade that most improves the monopolist's position. The equilibrium allocation, C, being a point of tangency between the monopolist's indifference curves and U_s^1, the indifference curve of the first individual, is also pareto optimal. This not only illustrates that there is more than one system of exchanges whose equilibrium outcomes are pareto optimal, but also reminds us that efficient systems may be regarded as highly unethical. Most

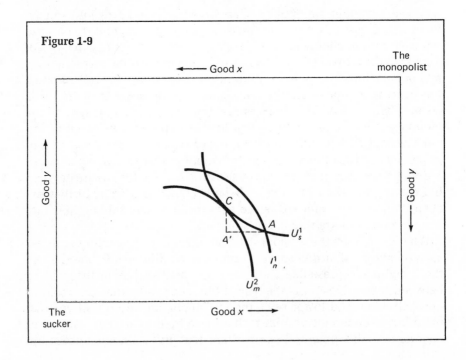

Figure 1-9

people dislike being gouged by a monopolist; they may resent even more deeply having to pay a higher price for some service than one of their neighbors. But it is just this latter kind of "injustice" that allows discriminating monopolists to exhaust all mutually profitable trades.

Monopoly and Government Regulation

Every businessman would like to be a monopolist. The firm whose market is shielded by competition can secure a larger share of the total gains from trade than would be possible if his customers had the option of purchasing his product from other producers. A monopoly position is not only attractive to the firm that has it, its profits are also likely to be attractive to other producers who are not earning as large a yield on their investments elsewhere. Therefore, if a monopoly position is to be sustained, the monopolist must work under conditions that create a barrier to the entry of other firms into his market.

In some cases, the barrier may be institutional in origin (for example, craft union membership regulations, tariffs against foreign-made goods, and so on), and efficient competitive pricing could replace the monopoly system if social policy broke down these institutional impediments. In other cases, however, the monopoly is derived from the technological advantages of large-scale operation. In these cases, competition cannot be fostered by a change in social policy. Rather, the industry must be subject to public operation or control as a *public utility*. Since simple monopoly pricing is inefficient and competitive pricing not possible in such circumstances, public utilities require a set of operating rules of their own if they are to operate in the public interest. The problem of establishing such rules is discussed in Chapter 10.

PRODUCTION AND PARETO OPTIMALITY

● Up to this point, we have only been concerned with the problem of distributing a given volume of commodities among several people so as to increase their social value. The analysis of the problem has allowed us to focus upon the important distinction between equity and efficiency and to indicate how taxation and monopoly pricing may lead to an inefficient allocation of resources. But the distribution decisions represent only one set of problems a society faces in managing its resources. A second set is to decide *what* to produce, and a third set is to decide *how* to combine the resources it has so as to produce the outputs it desires. In judging the efficiency of an economic system, therefore, we must evaluate these production decisions as well as the distribution decisions.

We introduce the following definition of production efficiency: *Any allocation of inputs to outputs that could not be changed so as to increase the output of one good without reducing the output of any other good is producer efficient.* Producer efficiency is clearly a necessary condition for pareto optimality. If an allocation were not producer efficient, then it would be possible to produce more goods from a given set of inputs than were being produced. With more goods, it would be possible to make at least one person better off without making anyone else worse off.

We can illustrate the conditions that must be satisfied for producer efficiency by means of a production-possibility box diagram, Figure 1.10. In this figure OA represents the total amount of resource i available, and OB represents the total amount of resource j available to be divided between the production of goods 1 and 2. A given quantity, say α units of good 1, can be produced by a variety of combinations of i and j. These possibilities are represented by isoquant I_α^1 drawn in the production-possibility box. The isoquants I^1 represent two physical laws. First, because you can't get output without input, point A', which gives more of input i and no less of input j to 1 than point A'', lies on a

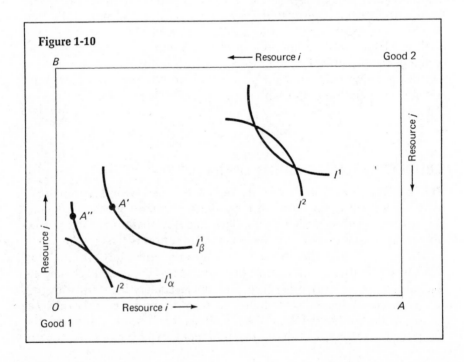

Figure 1-10

different isoquant than point A''. Every point on isoquant $I_\beta{}^1$ represents a greater production of good 1 than any point to the left of $I_\beta{}^1$. In general, the further to the right the isoquant, the greater the quantity of good 1 which is represented by the isoquant. Secondly, the isoquants are strictly convex to reflect that increasing the proportion of one input to another tends to reduce the additions to output attainable from incremental increases in one input holding the other constant. This is the law of variable proportions. (If this were not so, it would be possible to grow all of the world's food supply in a small window planter.) The isoquants I^2 are constructed under the same assumptions, but are oriented toward the northeast corner of the production-possibilities box. Each point in the box lies at the intersection of two isoquants and, therefore, represents a possible division of the resources between the production of goods 1 and 2.

Except for its physical interpretation, Figure 1.10 is equivalent to the box diagram shown in Figure 1.2. Any allocation point at which the intersection of the isoquants through that point forms a lens of positive width cannot be producer efficient. Points in the interior of the lens represent production of more of both goods than the point of intersection. Producer-efficient points are, therefore, characterized by tangency of isoquants. The slope of an isoquant at any given point represents the rate at which one input must be substituted for another so as to maintain the same rate of output of the good represented. Therefore, *if an allocation is producer efficient, the marginal rates of input substitution for any two goods that use the same inputs must be equal.*

The curve OO' in Figure 1.11(a) passes through all of the producer-efficient points. Each point on this curve represents a different combination of outputs just producible from the given inputs. Transforming the production possibilities into output space, as in Figure 1.11(b), the set of producer-efficient points for a given set of inputs defines the boundary of the production-possibility set. This boundary is called the production-transformation function. It represents the maximum quantity of one good available to society given fixed quantities of all other goods. The slope of the transformation curve at any point represents the reduction in output of one good required to release enough resources to produce one additional unit of the other. We, therefore, say that the slope of the transformation curve represents the rate of product transformation (RPT).

Integrating the production and distribution decisions, we can now describe a state of the world by a particular distribution among individuals of a particular set of outputs produced by using a given set of inputs. If a state of the world is pareto optimal, then starting from

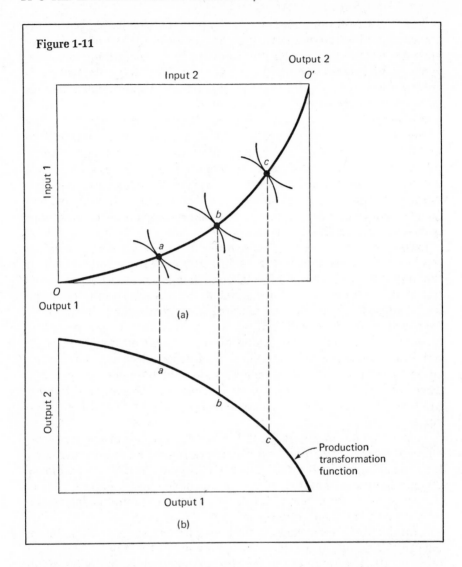

Figure 1-11

(a)

(b)

that state, there must be no combination of exchanges and physical transformations that can result in making at least one person better off and no one worse off. If all of the goods are purely private in the sense defined earlier, then a pareto optimal state must satisfy three conditions.

1. The output point must be on the boundary of society's production-possibility set; that is, the allocation of inputs to outputs must be producer efficient.
2. The outputs must be distributed among individuals so that each individual

has the same rate of substitution in consumption for every pair of commodities as does every other individual. This is the exchange-efficiency condition developed in the earlier sections.

3. Each individual's rate of substitution in consumption for every pair of goods must equal society's rate of production transformation of one element of that pair into the other. We can prove this by contradiction. Suppose that in a given state, Jones were willing to substitute 3 units of x for 1 unit of y. If society could take the resources released when production of y is reduced by 1 unit and produce more than 3 units of x, then Jones could be made better off without anyone being made worse off by the transformation. Similarly, if x could be transformed into y at a rate less than 3 units of x to 1 unit of y, then by reducing the production of x by enough to increase the production of y by 1 unit, Jones could again be made better off without harming anyone else. Therefore, as long as the rate of production transformation of x into y differs from some individual's rate of substitution in consumption of y for x, the allocation cannot be pareto optimal.

PRODUCTION, PERFECT COMPETITION, AND PARETO OPTIMALITY

● The introduction of production into the economy does not change the nature of the correspondence between competitive equilibria and pareto optimality. For if the input markets are competitive, each producer will face the same set of prices for inputs. At those prices, each producer finds that his cost of producing any given level of input is minimized when his rate of input substitution of input i for input j is equal to the ratio of the price of j to the price of i.[4] Since all producers adjust to the same set of prices, all producers using the same inputs will choose productive techniques with the same rates of input substitution. A competitive equilibrium is, therefore, producer efficient.

Price theory also tells us that competitive producers adjust output until the marginal cost of production equals the price in the market. On the production side, therefore, $MC_x/MC_y = P_x/P_y$. Now if the marginal cost of x were $3 and that of y $2, then a one-unit reduction in the output of x would release enough resources to produce $3/2$ units of y. This means that the ratio of marginal costs can be interpreted as the rate of product transformation of x into y. The conditions for a competitive equilibrium, therefore, imply that the rate of product transformation of x into y be equal to the ratio of the price of x to the price of y. In addition, as we noted on page 17, consumers adjust to given prices until their rate of substitution of y for x equals P_x/P_y. Therefore, the competitive equilibrium conditions imply an equality between the rate of product transformation and the rate of substitution in con sumption for all pairs of commodities for all individuals. Together, therefore, the competitive equilibrium conditions imply that the necessary conditions for pareto optimality are also satisfied.

DECENTRALIZED DECISION MAKING

● The attractiveness of an economy in which all activity is organized in competitive markets does not lie simply in the optimality characteristics of the equilibrium of such a system. Other systems may also satisfy the conditions for pareto optimality. An equally important feature is the economy of resource use a competitive system affords in the transmission of information and incentives necessary to coordinate the activities of very large numbers of people. Consider the information required to devise an economic plan which would efficiently allocate resources in an economy composed of over 50 million households and 50,000 commodities and factors of production. The preference structure of each household would have to be recorded. All of the possible techniques for producing various products would have to be entered in a "recipe" file. A description of the available stock of every input would have to be in the central file. All of these files would need to be continuously updated as new resources and new techniques were discovered and as tastes changed. Given these files, it would be a purely (monumental) computational task to identify all of the pareto optimal states available to society. But as F. A. Hayek said,

> The peculiar character of the problem of a rational economic order is determined precisely by the fact that the knowledge of the circumstances of which we must make use never exists in concentrated or integrated form, but solely as the dispersed bits of incomplete and frequently contradictory knowledge which all the separate individuals possess. The economic problem of society is thus not merely a problem of how to allocate "given" resources — if "given" is taken to mean given to a single mind which deliberately solves the problem set by these "data." It is rather a problem of how to secure the best use of resources known to any of the members of society for ends whose relative importance only these individuals know. Or, to put it briefly, it is a problem of the utilization of knowledge not given to anyone in its totality.[5]

The beauty of a competitive system is that there does not need to be any central institution to collect and process this vast amount of information in order to guide the economy. Decision making is highly decentralized, with the coordination of these decisions guided by the transmission of price information to which each individual responds.

No decision maker receives more information than he needs in order to adjust his behavior to a change in society's opportunities. The baker does not need to know the details of a change in farming technology, or even the change in the total volume of wheat that will be produced in order to adjust his production plan. He need only know the change in price of wheat, which records in a very summary fashion the impact of developments which he possibly could not otherwise easily interpret. There is no central plan, only the planning of myriad individuals coordinated by an information-feedback system, which transmits data in a form those individuals can easily interpret.

The use of markets to generate and transmit the information necessary to guide resources from lower- to higher-valued outputs is not dependent upon any particular form of ownership. In response to the argument that a socialist system could not develop production plans that would be responsive to the preferences of consumers, Oscar Lange wrote a brilliant essay describing how a central planning agency could, by specifying decision rules for firms and varying prices in response to bids which it would receive from consumers and firms, simulate the operation of a competitive marketing system. In this way, a socialist system could achieve the same economy of information and decentralization of detailed planning as a capitalist, competitive system.[6] In recent years, much of the thrust of economic reforms in socialist countries has been to replace aspects of central planning with a market structure which could transmit information to guide the production decisions.[7]

INTERDEPENDENCE, EXTERNALITIES, AND CONSUMER INTERRELATEDNESS

● Up to this point, we have assumed that each individual's valuation of different states of the world was determined completely by the goods assigned to him and was independent of the property assigned to others. This assumption of independence is crucial to maintaining the efficiency properties of a decentralized system of resource allocation, since it implies that all of the impacts that any one individual's decision will have on anyone else will be recorded by changes in prices to which the affected parties can respond. In other words, the independence assumption assumes that the only way the interests of individuals are related is through the market. Once the initial distribution of income is given, the market then becomes a device which is fully capable of reconciling and coordinating all of their mutual interests.

Unfortunately, the independence assumption does not mirror reality. What one's neighbor does with his property is of concern to others in the neighborhood; the amount of pollution produced is a concern of the receivers as well as the emitters of pollution; people who own land above mines are concerned with the possibility of subsidence created by the withdrawal of the minerals from the mines, and so on. Given such interdependencies, usually referred to as *external economies and diseconomies*, individuals will find it profitable to use their initial endowments not only to secure a preferred pattern of their own resource use through market transactions, but also to bribe other individuals to choose a different pattern of resource use than these individuals would choose in the absence of such bribes.

For example, consider the case of a doctor and a baker who own space on either side of a common wall. The doctor observes that by using the area next to the common wall as a diagnostic room, he can increase his profits by $12. The baker observes that by moving a noisy piece of equipment next to the common wall, he can increase his profits by $10. If the baker does so, however, the doctor cannot use the area on his side of the wall because it would be too noisy. Suppose further that it would cost $25 to soundproof the wall. Clearly, the doctor could bribe the baker not to move his machinery by offering him more than $10 but less than $12 to do so. But why should the doctor do so? Instead, he goes to court to seek an injunction against the baker on the theory that the baker's equipment is interfering with the use of his (the doctor's) property. The baker replies that granting such an injunction would interfere with his (the baker's) use of his property. What is at stake is determination of who owns the right (property) to determine the amount of noise passing through the common wall. Once this property right is assigned, the greater value which the doctor places on the area will be effectively recognized by the owner of this right, and the area will end up in control of the doctor. For if the court rules in favor of the baker, then the doctor will find it to his advantage to offer to buy this right for more than the right is worth to the baker; if the court rules in favor of the doctor, then the baker will not find it profitable to offer to buy the right at the lowest price the doctor would accept.

If both the doctor and baker rented their space from the same landlord, the necessity for legal proceedings in order to facilitate the most efficient use of the space would not arise. The landlord would be able to exact a larger increase in rent from the doctor if he prohibited the baker from moving his equipment than he could exact from the baker for permitting the move. It would, therefore, be in the landlord's interest to honor the doctor's wish and not the baker's. In effect, the landlord would *internalize the externality* created by noise passing through the common wall. He would choose, in a single decision, the combination of area uses that maximized the total value producible by both areas rather than letting a separate decision be made on the use of each area. The landlord serves the same function as a market in the (property) right to determine noise through the common wall. In the absence of the landlord, such a market will function only if one party is given title to that property right and allowed to sell it like any other property.[8]

In the preceding example, if the court assigned the right to the baker, then the baker could increase his profits by getting the doctor to agree to pay him for not placing his machinery next to the wall. Sometimes, however, the owner of an asset cannot physically exclude other people from receiving services from this asset without reducing the value which his assets provide to himself. *Such assets are called public goods.* As an example of a public good, consider a garden situated between two apartment houses. The garden is owned by one of the apartment houses, but its presence adds to the value of the second apartment house. The only practical way for the owner of the garden to prevent the tenants of the other apartment house from enjoying the view is to take out the garden. But his own tenants would then also be deprived of the view. Even though others get benefits, he cannot collect payments.

A less trivial example is national defense. It is not possible to defend one subgroup against foreign attack without at the same time protecting everyone within the community. Another example is a reduction in pollution. If air pollution is reduced for some persons within an airshed, it must have been reduced for all persons within that airshed. The total quantity of a particular public good secured when each individual independently purchases some of the good for his own use is likely to lead to a nonpareto optimal allocation of resources. This is because each individual, receiving no compensation from others, has no incentive to consider how his holdings yield services to others. No one is likely to purchase the services of an army on his own even though each would be willing to make a payment toward a jointly owned army. Similarly, the cost of reducing pollution levels by 15 percent in an airshed may run into the tens or even hundreds of millions annually. If there are several million people affected, each may receive a sufficient gain so that the sum of the gains exceed the cost of such improvements in air quality, although no one individual or firm may find it profitable, acting independently, to incur such a cost.

Individual action can also lead to too much of a service being produced. For instance, measles is a contagious disease. Therefore, the probability of any uninoculated member of a group contracting measles is inversely related to the percentage of the group that has been vaccinated. In the absence of any joint decision on the percentage of the group to be inoculated, it is likely that each individual will buy the vaccine in order to protect himself. Suppose that the same level of individual protection might be secured by having only 99 percent of the group receive the vaccine. A joint decision would have achieved the same result at lower total cost.

As the above examples indicate, when interdependencies of preferences exist, economic systems, which allow for joint or collectively made decisions, are capable of producing resource allocations that are pareto superior to those that could be achieved in the absence of such decisions. What we mean by this is that the *logical* possibility exists for collective action to improve the allocation of resources. Collective action implies the operation of some political process by which decisions on the provision of public goods are reached. If the logical possibility is to be translated into an actuality, then the political process must get people to reveal their true evaluations of public goods. In the marketplace, consumers reveal their true preferences by paying the price demanded by the seller. No buyer can enjoy the benefits of wearing a coat unless he has paid for it. But public goods are, by definition, not subject to this *exclusion principle*. This makes the question of determining the appropriate public expenditure on various public services a most difficult one. We shall treat this question more fully in Chapter 4.

PUBLIC GOODS AND PARETO OPTIMALITY

● The possibility of using society's resources to produce public as well as private goods requires a modification in the statement of conditions an allocation must satisfy if it is to be pareto optimal. A whole group of individuals benefits from the production of another unit of a public good. Therefore, it is possible to divide the sacrifice of private goods that the production of additional public goods entails over the whole group of beneficiaries. As long as each individual values the additional public goods more than the fraction of the private-goods sacrifice he must make, everyone could be made better off by redirecting resources from private to public goods. Formally, this implies that if the sum of the affected individuals' marginal rates of substitution of a public for a private good is *less* than society's rate of product transformation of the private into the public good, the allocation cannot be pareto optimal. This is because, under the condition stated, a unit reduction in private goods could be divided among all of the affected group, so that the resulting increase in the public good more than compensated each of them for their sacrifice. Conversely, if the sum of the marginal rates of substitution were *greater* than society's marginal rate of transformation, the allocation cannot be pareto optimal. For, in this case, it would be possible to divide the extra private goods producible by a unit reduction in the public good so that everyone was more than compensated for the loss of the public good. A necessary condition for pareto optimality, therefore, is that *the sum of the affected individuals' rates of substitution of public for private goods equal society's rate of transformation of the private for the public good.*[9]

In markets that reflect only individual exchanges, even if they are perfectly competitive markets, this summation condition will only be satisfied by chance. Individual, independent action fails to produce a pareto optimal allocation, because each individual will extend his purchase of public goods only if the benefits he alone derives exceed their total cost. But the criterion for pareto optimality requires that such purchases be extended as long as the *sum* of the benefits exceeds this cost. To achieve a pareto optimal allocation, therefore, individuals must come to some agreement on the division of the costs of producing public goods. Using governmental institutions is one method of producing such an agreement. It is in this sense that government can help people to do collectively that which they individually desire but cannot achieve by independent actions.

SUMMARY

● Our survey of welfare economics points to several roles that government might play in the economic affairs of a free society. As we saw in the doctor-baker example, the functioning of free markets presupposes a judicial role for government. In deciding whether the doctor or baker has the right, the court has no basis for assignment other than one of equity. This question of equity extends beyond such neighborly disputes over particular pieces of property to property in general. Who is to decide whether you or I have the right to use or trade any particular piece of property? Ultimately, whoever has the power to enforce his will. Carl Sandburg put the issue nicely in the following poem, entitled "Private Property."

"Get off of this estate."
"What for?"
"Because its mine."
"Where did you get it?"
"From my father."
"Where did he get it?"
"He fought for it."
"Well, I'll fight you for it."*

Most of us would be willing to have this power wielded by the state rather than by the physical conflict of one individual with another, provided only that the state acted fairly. A government that supported the claims to property of individuals whom many believed to have come by those claims unfairly would lose popular support and would not rule by the consent of the governed. From a democratic point of view, therefore, a well-ordered economy presupposes that government acts so as to maintain an equitable distribution of claims to property.

The second role of government that emerges from the discussions of this chapter is as an institution through which individuals can make collective choices which would improve the efficiency of resource allocation once the distribution of wealth had been determined. It is within this context that one looks to government for the control of activities which would otherwise become monopolized, for the provision of public goods, and for the establishment of controls which will confront individual decision makers with the full consequences of their decisions when those decisions lead to external economies or diseconomies.

There is one final basis for governmental economic activity. We have evaluated different economic systems in terms of their equilibrium states. Very often, however, an economic system is not in a state of equilibrium or even on the boundary of its production-possibility set. Experience has taught us that in the absence of governmental efforts to stabilize the economy, free-market systems can generate substantial amounts of unemployment for considerable periods at a time. Consequently, a third basis for governmental activity is to keep the economy near its production-possibility frontier at all times.

Notes

1. We place the word "natural" in quotes, since this view of measuring the general welfare assumes that welfare consists solely of pleasure, a concept many would deny. For a critique of the utilitarian view of ethics, see Nich-

* From *The People, Yes* by Carl Sandburg, copyright, 1936, by Harcourt Brace Jovanovich, Inc.; renewed, 1964, by Carl Sandburg. Reprinted by permission of the publishers.

olas Rescher, *A Constructive Critique of the Utilitarian Theory of Distribution*, Indianapolis: Bobbs-Merrill, 1966.

2. Some still do. See J. K. Galbraith, *The Affluent Society*, Boston: Houghton Mifflin, 1960.

3. Assuming that the marginal utility derived from any commodity depends only upon the quantity of that commodity, the law of demand can be derived from these axioms by observing that a necessary condition for deriving maximum utility from a fixed income is to spend it in such a way that the utility derivable from spending an additional dollar on any one commodity x be equal to the additional utility derivable from spending that dollar on any other commodity y. Of course, the utility derivable from a dollar spent on a commodity depends on the price of the commodity. The lower the price, the more units of that commodity a dollar will buy. Now, assume that an individual initially faces the set of prices P_X^0, P_y^0, and that the bundle of commodities x_0, y_0 satisfies the condition for utility maximization. If the price of x falls, the original bundle x_0, y_0 cannot yield a maximum of utility under these new conditions. The fall in the price of x has raised the utility derivable per dollar spent on x above the utility derivable per dollar spent on y. The consumer could, therefore, increase the utility derivable from his income by purchasing more of x and less of y. As he substitutes x for y, the marginal utility of y increases, while the marginal utility of x decreases. These changes in marginal utility will guarantee that small changes in prices do not lead to large changes in the composition of the bundle purchased. In this way, the theory accounts for the observations made on actual consumer behavior.

4. To see this, calculate the change in the cost of producing a given output as $P_i\Delta_i + P_j\Delta_j$, where Δ_i and Δ_j are the compensating changes in inputs which just leave total output unchanged. That is, $|\Delta_j/\Delta_i|$ is the rate of input substitution of i for j. If $P_i/P_j > |\Delta_j/\Delta_i|$, $P_i|\Delta_i| > P_j|\Delta_j|$. Suppose j is substituted for i, so that $\Delta_i < 0$, $\Delta_j > 0$. If we then subtract $P_i|\Delta_i|$ from both sides of the inequality, we find $0 > P_i\Delta_i + P_j\Delta_j$. Therefore, if $P_i/P_j > |\Delta_j/\Delta_i|$, the total cost of producing a given level of output can be reduced by substituting j for i. By a similar argument, if $P_i/P_j < |\Delta_j/\Delta_i|$ then $P_i|\Delta_i| < P_j|\Delta_j|$, and total cost can be reduced by substituting i for j. Consequently, the cost-minimizing input combination is the one for which $|\Delta_j/\Delta_i| = P_i/P_j$.

5. F. A. Hayek, "The Uses of Knowledge in Society," *American Economic Review*, Vol. XXXV, September 1945, pp. 519–530.

6. See O. Lange and F. Taylor, *On the Economic Theory of Socialism*, edited and with an introduction by Benjamin Lippincott, Minneapolis: University of Minnesota Press, 1938; New York: McGraw-Hill, 1964.

7. For a discussion of such reforms, see the papers given by Robert Campbell, George Staller, and Benjamin Ward followed by the discussions of Abram Bergson and John Montias in the Papers and Proceedings of the Eightieth Annual Meeting of the American Economic Association published in the *American Economic Review*, May 1968, pp. 547–582.

8. Notice that the market in the externality right (to control the transmission of noise) cannot be a competitive one, since there is only one possible buyer and one possible seller.

9. By "affected" we mean those who derive benefits from the existence of the public good. Notice that if a private good is defined as a public good for which the size of the affected group is one, then condition C on page 25 is just a special case of the condition just derived.

Questions for Discussion

1. Suppose that there was a mine which, if mined out completely, would yield $200 profits from the coal operation alone. If 25 percent of the coal is left unmined, there will be only $150 profit from the mining operation. If more than 75 percent of the coal is removed, the land above the mine will subside. If the land subsides, it is worthless. Otherwise, the land is worth $60.
   a. What is the pareto optimal percentage of coal to extract if Jones owns the mine and Smith the land? If Smith owns the mine and Jones the land? If both the mine and land are owned by the same party?
   b. Suppose that land and mining rights cannot be bought or sold and that Smith owns the mine and Jones the land. What is the most profitable level of extraction from Smith's point of view? From Jones's point of view?
   c. If mining rights, but not land, could be bought and sold, would this change your answers to b? If so, how?
   d. Suppose that Jones died and divided his property equally among 100 persons. Would 1 mine owner and 100 landowners (each owning 1 percent of the land) change your answer to c? If so, how?

2. Milton Friedman has argued that a capitalistic system will operate in the best interests of all of the people if the decisions of businessmen in operating their businesses are determined solely by the motive of maximizing their profits. If all markets are perfectly competitive, this objective implies that businessmen expand output to the point at which price equals marginal cost.
   In his essay on the economic theory of socialism, Lange states that managers of plants should be instructed to fix output at that level at which price equals marginal cost. This isomorphism between rules of profit maximization for capitalists operating in competitive markets and socialist plant managers is not accidental, for Lange is attempting to describe decision rules that would make a socialist system behave *as if* the decisions were being made by capitalists in a system of perfectly competitive markets.
   a. Why might a socialist want his economy to operate as if its production decisions were being made to maximize profits? That is, what social function might "profit" play in a socialist system?
   b. Do profits serve the same function in a capitalist system? Is this the only function of profits in a capitalist system?

3. Kenneth Arrow has stressed the importance of recognizing that market failures are not immutable, but rather are relative to modes of economic organization, for it is the mode of organization that determines how the individual decision makers perceive the possible alternatives open to them. In what way(s) might individual members of a consumer's cooperative, which has just taken over a former monopoly retail establishment, view their alternatives differently than when they were merely customers of the monopolist? Would the cooperative necessarily produce better results for its members than the former organization of the market?

Suggested Readings

Problem of Welfare Maximization

Bator, F. M., "The Simple Analytics of Welfare Maximization," *American Economic Review*, March 1957, pp. 22–59.

Hansen, A., "Standards and Values in a Rich Society," reprinted in Phelps, E., ed., *Private Wants and Public Needs*, New York: Norton, 1962, pp. 3–14.

Jouvenel, Bertrand De, "Efficiency and Amenity," reprinted in Arrow, K., and Scitovsky, T., eds., *Readings in Welfare Economics*, Homewood, Ill.: Irwin, 1969, pp. 100–112.

Lange, O., "The Foundations of Welfare Economics," *Econometrica*, 1942, pp. 215–28. Reprinted in Arrow, K., and Scitovsky, T., eds., *Readings in Welfare Economics*, Homewood, Ill.: Irwin, 1967.

Samuelson, P., *Foundations of Economic Analysis*, Boston: Harvard University Press, pp. 219–253.
The Lange and Samuelson readings require calculus. The Bator selection provides a concise geometrical treatment.

The Role of Markets in the Allocation of Resources

Friedman, M., *Capitalism and Freedom*, Chicago: University of Chicago Press, pp. 7–21.

Lange, O., and Taylor, F., *On the Economic Theory of Socialism*, edited and with an introduction by Benjamin Lippincott, Minneapolis: University of Minnesota Press, 1938; New York: McGraw-Hill, 1964.

The Failures of Markets and the Efficiency Role of Government

Bator, F., "The Anatomy of Market Failure," *Quarterly Journal of Economics*, August 1958, pp. 351–379.

Dupuit, Jules, "On the Measurement of Utility of Public Works," in Arrow, K., and Scitovsky, T., eds., *Readings in Welfare Economics*, Homewood, Ill.: Irwin, 1967, pp. 255–283.

Friedman, M., *op. cit.*, pp. 22–36.

Samuelson, Paul, "The Pure Theory of Public Expenditures," *Review of Economics and Statistics*, November 1954, November 1955.

General

Baumol, W., *Welfare Economics and the Theory of the State*, Harrow, Eng.: Longmans, Green, 1952.

Lerner, A. P., *The Economics of Control*, New York: Macmillan, 1946.

Musgrave, R., *The Theory of Public Finance*, New York: McGraw-Hill, 1959, ch. 1.

Pigou, A. C., *The Economics of Welfare*, New York: Macmillan, 1932.

2

THE PATHOLOGY OF MARKET FAILURE: COMMON PROPERTY, PROPERTY RIGHTS, AND EXTERNALITIES

In the last chapter, we spoke of a market system as a set of institutions for transmitting information which is necessary to guide production decisions. In a market system, those who have control over the use of resources learn of the value consumers place on having resources allocated among activities in a particular way by observing the bids buyers make for the opportunity to purchase the output of these various activities. Of course, a bid will only be recognized if it is backed by certificates, which give the bidder a claim to the use of resources (for example, money). The requirement that a bidder "put his money where his mouth is" rules out capricious bids and makes people reveal their true preferences. The sellers are then assumed to have either the incentive or the responsibility of dividing the available supply among the highest bidders.

Social pathologies develop when the value of inputs in a particular activity is not represented by bids in the input markets. In such circumstances, the resource allocation is misdirected because suppliers, observing no bid, will consider it unprofitable to set inputs aside for use in that activity. The value of inputs devoted to other activities will then bear no relation to their potential value in the unrepresented activity. Since the benefits of private goods are limited to whomever physically possesses them, brokers realize that these goods are marketable. They will, therefore, submit the necessary bids in the input markets to assure that inputs are set aside for the production of private goods. The bids a broker or firm submits will reflect the income he believes he can secure by selling the output, which will be produced from the inputs for which he is bidding. But public goods are, by their very nature, unmarketable. Individuals derive benefits from public goods even if they do not hold legal title to them. Once they are produced, public goods become common property. The benefits an individual derives from the existence of common property is independent of his share in the cost of producing it. Each individual, therefore, has an interest in minimizing his share of the cost. One strategy, which suits this interest, is to wait for others to act and then to simply enjoy the benefits of a "free ride." Of course, if there are a large number of "free riders," then no bid for the public good will be made. Consequently, as Galbraith puts it, "In the absence of social intervention, private production will monopolize all resources. Only as *something* [italics added] is done about it will resources become available for public services."[1] That *something* may either be the submittal of a bid made on the basis of a collective decision, or else a change in the tax system, or regulations that will induce suppliers to divert some resources to public use.

While public goods have the legal characteristic of common property, not all common property has the characteristics of a public good. The benefits any one person derives from a public good are not directly dependent upon the benefits others derive from them. But the benefits each person derives from commonly held property may be directly dependent on how others use the property. For example, in New England towns, a plot of land was specified as a Commons, or common property grazing land upon which everyone could graze their animals. The benefits any one person derived from the Commons were directly related to the extensiveness of his own use. But since there was only a limited area, the more extensively one person used the Commons, the smaller the benefits others could derive from it. In those situations where common property does not have the characteristics of a public good, a problem of allocating the use of the property exists. However, if the property is commonly owned, then a private market cannot serve as the allocative mechanism, since no private individual or firm has clear title to the property. Sometimes, as in the baker-doctor example, discussed in Chapter 1, the allocative problem can be solved by converting the commonly held property into private property. But other cases, like international fishing waters and city streets, require a nonmarket approach to resource allocation.

In this chapter, we shall examine several social problems that stem from the barriers that common property and ill-defined property rights create for the allocation of resources through ordinary market transactions.

URBAN RENEWAL: THE FAILURE
OF THE URBAN REAL ESTATE MARKET

● One aspect of the American scene, which has attracted the attention of many social critics, is the extent of deteriorated housing in our cities. Most "substandard" housing is occupied by poor families. This suggests that the root of the problem of urban blight rests in the poverty of these inhabitants. The obvious solution would seem to be to raise the incomes of these families, so that they could afford to purchase better housing. Implicit in this "solution" to the problem of urban blight is the assumption that if the poor were to become less poor, they would both desire and be able to afford better housing. The housing and land markets would then respond by upgrading slum property, raising rents, and increasing profits just as other markets respond to a shift in demand from lower-quality to better-quality goods and services. However, there is one set of factors that tends to "lock" resources into slums once they have been used in that way even though market conditions for low-quality housing have changed. In most slum areas, there are a rather large number of property owners. The market value of a particular piece of property depends not only on its own physical characteristics and its accessibility to places outside its immediate neighborhood, but also upon the physical and social characteristics of the area in which it is located. Two pieces of property, which are similar in all respects other than the character of the neighborhoods in which they are located, may sell at very different prices. The difference in price will reflect the effect of the difference in the general condition of the neighborhoods in which they are located. These "neighborhood effects," when combined with a multiplicity of owners in the neighborhood, may prevent the profitable conversion of a slum area to other uses in the following way.

Suppose that an individual owner is contemplating making a $500 improvement on his property. He consults a realtor, who appraises him of the following facts. Given the present condition of the neighborhood, the improvement will raise the rental value sufficiently to increase the resale value by $400. On the other hand, if there were a general improvement in the conditions of the neighborhood, that same improvement would increase the rental value sufficiently to raise the resale value by $750. The realtor, therefore, advises that he defer making the improvement until he sees what improvements his neighbors are going to make.

If each owner finds himself in the same position, then no one will be making any improvements. However, if they all made the improvements, each owner would make a profit. In one sense, it is in the interest of each to defer until the others have acted, since each loses if he acts and others don't, but cannot lose if he waits for the others. Collectively, however, waiting is a mistake, since they all gain if nobody waits.

What this example suggests is that in the absence of jointly made decisions, the interdependence created by the fact that they share a common neighborhood or environment may lead to an insufficient upgrading of slum properties when the demand for low-quality housing falls. Instead of a reduction in blight, the slum area occupancy and rental rates tend to fall as people move to other areas. Only when the vacancy rate falls low enough to warrant abandonment will land in the area be released for other uses.

To state this result in the language of the introductory section, no bids are received in the market for land currently occupied by slums from activities which would reduce blight because each potential bidder finds it strategically sensible to wait for others to place their bids. Consequently, in the presence of this kind of market failure, reduction in poverty may be a necessary, but is not a sufficient, condition for reduction of urban blight.

The perceptive reader will note that the existence of more than one owner is crucial (it takes at least two for preferences to be interdependent). He will also notice that if a single developer could buy up all of the land in the neighborhood at its current market price and then improve the entire area, he could make a profit on the deal. It would, therefore, seem that keeping an area of land in a blighted state when it would be profitable to convert it is not a stable situation in spite of the above analysis. Those potential profits should attract a single developer who would attempt to obtain ownership of a sufficient area to "internalize" the externalities (that is, neighborhood effects). If this were likely to happen, then the market system would continue to function effectively without government intervention. However, the structure of the problem is such that it is unlikely a single developer could profitably put together a large enough tract to coordinate the improvement decisions on various parcels in the neighborhood. The reason for this is that each potential seller is likely to come to realize the buyer's (developer's) objective. Consequently, each owner asks for a higher price than the current market value of his own property in an attempt to share in the potential profits of the land assembler. This problem of dividing up the profits is likely to lead to long and costly negotiations, eating up the potential profits from the land-assembly operation. A prospective developer, looking at such a possibility, is likely to be dissuaded from the attempt. Thus, the slum remains.

Urban areas, faced with these barriers to land assembly for purposes of conversion to more profitable uses, have developed quasi-governmental agencies such as urban redevelopment authorities which are invested with the power of eminent domain. These authorities are authorized to purchase properties at a "fair market value," which is determined by assessment of the current worth of the property. If the owner refused to sell at the price offered, the authority can go to court, prove that its bid is reasonable, and have the court order the owner to sell at that price. Use of the power of eminent domain, therefore, simplifies the problem of land assembly. Once the authority has assembled a tract for redevelopment, it then sells it to a private developer, placing whatever restrictions on its use the authority deems desirable.

In recent years, there has grown considerable opposition to government efforts to convert blighted areas to uses that would increase property values (and therefore the tax base of the city). The principal complaint is sometimes voiced in the charge that "urban renewal is people removal." By this it is meant that cities have attempted to take slum areas and convert them into uses other than low-cost housing. This has often forced ghetto residents to move from renewal areas while simultaneously reducing the supply of low-cost housing. This latter effect meant that poor persons displaced by the redevelopment projects often had to pay more for housing than they were formerly paying. Of course, the tenants' losses were their new landlords' gains, so that this effect did not mean that the redevelopment was inefficient—but many people did feel that it was morally indefensible. Indeed, much of the debate over the course of urban renewal efforts has centered on this conflict between improving the fiscal base of the city by fostering more efficient land use and improving the housing opportunities for the poor.[2]

Neighborhood Environment as a Public Good

It is instructive to see that the "neighborhood effects" or externalities present in the land conversion problem can be treated as a public-good problem. We can reconstruct the problem by assuming that the value of each man's property depends upon the quantity of a "good," which we shall call "environment." Environment has the character of a public good, since it is not possible for one group within a neighborhood to have it without everyone in the neighborhood also enjoying it. The problem facing the people in the neighborhood is to decide how much "environment" to purchase. By assumption, an expenditure of $500X$ (where X is the total number of property owners in the neighborhood) will yield $750 worth of benefits to each owner. While an expenditure of $500 by any single owner (no one else spending anything) will yield him only $400 in benefits. The problem, therefore, is to put together a coalition of neighbors to submit a joint bid. In order to do so, some determination must be made as to how to divide the total cost. Each owner knows that the others will make a profit as long as their individual costs are less than $750. If there are four or more persons involved, at least one of them could refuse to pay any share of the cost, and the rest would still find it profitable to submit a bid.[3] Each, of course, would prefer to be the "free rider." If they all try to be "free riders," then the bid is not made. The problem of getting an appropriate quantity of public goods produced is, therefore, very similar to the problem of resource allocation created by external economies.

INFORMATION AND THE PROVISION OF PUBLIC GOODS

● Once the land has been assembled by use of the state's power of eminent domain, information as to its highest-valued use can be secured by allowing open bidding for the site. However, it is not always possible to use market information to guide resource decisions with respect to public assets. As an example, consider the problem of determining the level of public support of education.

The historic argument for public support of education has been based on the assumption that the education of any person produces external economies. Each citizen acquires benefits from living among an educated group of fellow citizens. The argument is made, therefore, that education should be publicly financed. This argument for treating education as a public good may be granted.[4] It may also be granted that the state should use the power of taxation to avoid the free-rider problem. Yet it may be very difficult to determine the appropriate amount of public expenditure for schools simply because it is not possible to get a clear indication of the value (over and above the value of the skills created by education) each person places on living in a community of educated people. Some indication may be given by the way people vote. But as we shall discuss at length in Chapter 3, voting mechanisms do not necessarily lead to more efficient resource allocations.

Zoning and External Diseconomies

We introduced the problems created by interdependencies in Chapter 1 by treating a problem of external diseconomies—the baker-doctor example. In our analysis of that example, we came to the conclusion that, no matter which way the judge ruled, the area would end up in the control of the doctor. The reason the issue went to court was that a particular property right, which had no value when they made their initial decisions to set up business as a baker and doctor, respectively, became, with the passage of time and a change in circumstances, a valuable right to possess. Whoever had the right would be wealthier than he was without it. And, of course, dividing up property is the business of a Solomon.

Communities have long recognized the need for developing land-use patterns that clustered compatible and separated incompatible activities. The use of zoning laws to separate industrial from commercial and residential uses has a long history. Many areas of vacant land are set aside for specific purposes in an attempt to assure that eventual uses of the area are compatible. Zoning ordinances may be useful both in preventing the social conflict that is generated by neighbors who are bickering over who has the right to do what with his property and in assuring that resources are not used inefficiently until such squabbles are resolved. Nevertheless, the use of such ordinances is limited. They are generally incapable of handling problems where activities in one entire zone produce effects (such as air and water pollution) that spill over into other areas. It has been reported that smog generated in Los Angeles has affected the air quality in Palm Springs many miles away. It would make little sense to try and prevent this effect by the passage of land-use zoning laws in Los Angeles (unless those laws had the effect of reducing automobile traffic, since it is the automobiles that are the principal generators of the pollutants which comprise Los Angeles' smog).

POLLUTION

● Degradation of the quality of the physical environment is another issue that has attracted widespread concern. Although the sources and effects of different pollutants are various, all pollutants represent unwanted materials or waste generated in the process of creating wanted products. The volume of waste generated by an emitter will depend upon the cost that the emitter faces in disposing of these wastes. *Pollution problems are created when the emitter does not face the full cost of disposing of the wastes he generates.*

Suppose you could produce a product everyone valued at −$5.00 (that is, anyone would be willing to pay $5.00 to dispose of it or would only accept if also given $5.00). You would only produce that "product" if it were a necessary by-product of a process which produced other output whose value exceeded the costs of the inputs by $5.00. That is, if you sold output in a competitive market and had to compensate people for accepting your waste products, then you would only expand production of goods which are valued at positive prices to the point where the price covered not only the marginal costs of inputs but also the social marginal cost of waste disposal. To produce either more or less output (and its associated waste by-product) would be socially inefficient. (Why?) But if you were able to dump your waste on your neighbors without compensating them for the damage, then from your private point of view, the marginal cost of waste disposal is zero, and you would increase output until the marginal costs of inputs equal value generated by an increment of output valued at the *positive prices alone*. Therefore, if wastes cannot be disposed of costlessly from a social point of view, but can be from the point of view of the producers who generate them, society will tend to overproduce those commodities that generate relatively large quantities of waste as by-products and underproduce those commodities that generate little waste or convert waste into more valuable commodities. We shall find ourselves undervaluing the durability of products, encouraging the socially uneconomic substitution of commodities that may be discarded for those that would be recycled, and depleting our stores of environmental amenities.

Ordinarily, of course, you cannot dump your garbage in your neighbor's yard without his permission. The property laws give him control over the property to which he holds title. Pollution problems result, therefore, from ill-defined property rights. Since the air and water are common property, no one individual, acting in a private capacity, can prevent another from using "his" property as a garbage dump since it is not "his" but "theirs." Control of pollution is, therefore, a public rather than a private planning problem.

When a Pollution Problem Exists

In our view, a pollution "problem" is not associated with any particular level of waste generation. An air pollution problem does not necessarily exist when the SO_2 level reaches X parts per million, and a water pollution problem does not necessarily exist when the dissolved oxygen level reaches some point. Increased rates of bronchial distress and eutrophication of streams and lakes are not prime facie evidence that a pollution problem exists. To establish that a "problem" exists, there must be evidence that people would be willing to sacrifice the output of other things which would have to be foregone if changes in environmental quality were to be accomplished.

In the early part of the twentieth century, Pittsburgh was known as the Smoky City. The output of particulate matter and smoke from the city's mills, factories, and homes was so large that pictures of Pittsburgh taken at noon showed automobiles running with their headlights on and the city having the general appearance of night. In those days, the smoke and dust belching from the city's furnaces were not called pollution. Rather, the workers and merchants spoke of those effluents as "black gold," for they meant jobs and prosperity. As long as the economic future of the city seemed intimately tied to the continued expansion of the steel industry, those effluents and their injurious effects seemed a small price to pay for prosperity. Two factors changed the pollutant emissions of Pittsburgh's mills and factories from a community asset to a community liability. By the 1930s, it had become obvious that the growth in employment in the steel industry was going to proceed at a slower pace than formerly. Furthermore, the historic locational advantages of the Pittsburgh region were being weakened by the growing importance of the Midwest as both a market for steel and as a steel-producing center. Major property owners, therefore, recognized that continued growth of population in the Pittsburgh area depended upon changing the industrial base of the city. Because of its historic ties to many national industries, it was determined to make Pittsburgh a center of administrative and research activity. This could only be accomplished if the physical environment was improved sufficiently to make Pittsburgh competitive in attracting administrative and research personnel. It was to this effect that the so-called Pittsburgh Renaissance was directed. An integral part of that effort was the adoption of smoke-control ordinances. An environmental quality improvement, which was deemed too expensive during the Great Depression and detrimental to the economic growth of the region prior to the depression, became, with the growth in per capita income and a change in the factors that underlay the historic growth of the region, a social investment of major importance.

Pollution Control and Income Redistribution

Pollution abatement is sometimes called a middle-class luxury. When an area with substantial unemployment or with significant numbers of low-wage earners attempts to exclude industry which would tend to reduce the quality of the physical environment, the unemployed and the low-wage group are likely to protest and try to stop the exclusion attempt, since, *for them*, the possibility of a higher income would be adequate compensation for the deterioration in the environment. The others, whose potential income is not changed substantially by the presence of new industry (or who place a higher value on environment relative to other goods than do the poor), will perceive themselves as receiving inadequate compensation. And so, because there is no well-defined set of property rights specifying who has the right to control the quality of the environment, the battle lines are drawn between those whose positions would be improved and those whose positions would deteriorate if a pollution-producing industry were to locate in the community.[5]

Pollution problems are like the disputed common property problems typified by the baker-doctor example in that the resolution of the problem implies a determination of whose claim to the right to determine environmental quality standards will be honored. If the firm is kept out, it is unlikely that its potential workers will be compensated for their loss of employment opportunity. In effect, they will have lost their claim to trade ownership of the environment for money income. If the firm is let in, others will suffer pollution damage without compensation. In effect, allowing the firm to pollute strips this second group of their claim to ownership. Unlike simple common-wall type problems, however, resolution of the dispute over claims to ownership of the property held in common will not necessarily be sufficient to allow that property to be used efficiently. The most efficient use may still require submittal of a joint bid. In this respect, pollution problems have characteristics similar to the urban renewal and public-goods problems. To illustrate the difficulty, consider the following situation. The Ajax Steel Company is considering locating in the town of Arcadia. Several years ago, the citizens of Arcadia settled the issue of who owned the right to determine the quality of the physical environment by setting up the Ecology Corporation whose sole asset consisted of "the right to determine the quality of the physical environment in Arcadia." It was allowed to sell or lease any part of this asset. Shares in Ecology, Inc., were distributed to the residents of Arcadia by an impartial judge. Everyone agreed that the distribution of the shares of ownership in the corporation was equitable. In order to assure that the environmental resources of Arcadia were used efficiently, the manager of the corporation was instructed to sell pollution options to the highest bidders. Each option specified the extent of emissions the optionee was permitted if he exercised his option for a pollution license. The options were to be issued in sequence, and a second option could not be offered by the corporation until the first option was exercised. The Ajax Company is the first firm to ask Ecology, Inc., to accept a bid. The Ecology management advertises that bids are being accepted and invites interested parties to submit bids. The Ajax Company calculates that $1 million is the maximum bid it could make and still find it profitable to operate.

The unemployed, who see Ajax as a source of income, might be willing to add to Ajax's bid an amount equal to the difference between the change in their incomes and the change in the quality of their environment that would be produced if Ajax were given the option. Against this joint bid, a coalition of persons who see their gain in income from Ajax's location as being less than the value of the damage done to their environment might submit a counterbid. If the value of the damage Ajax would do exceeded the increase in money income its location would generate, Ajax should not be able to get the option. The "conservationists' bid" would be the highest, and Ajax would be effectively blocked from the area. In addition, those people who would have gained from Ajax's location and who are also shareholders in Ecology, Inc., will receive compensation, in the form of a distribution of Ecology's profits, for being in the losing coalition.

A moment's reflection will show, however, that this result is unlikely even under the conditions assumed. If the sum over all of the inhabitants of the damages that would be caused by Ajax's operation exceeds the gains in income, then it is *logically* possible to put together a coalition to block Ajax's bid. The problem is to get that coalition together. This is exactly the problem faced in purchasing "environment" in the urban renewal case. The likelihood is that the Ajax bid will be the highest one even though allowing Ajax to pollute represents an inefficient use of resources.[6]

While the notion of an Ecology, Inc., is useful as an expository device to show how pollution problems share similarities with both public-goods and simple external diseconomies, it is obviously not an institutional solution to the handling of these problems. (How many people *should* own shares in the "Corporation" that controls emissions into the Mississippi? How could you determine the contribution of my automobile to the level of air pollution, given the variety of variables that affect the level of emissions my car is likely to emit? and so on.) The determination of environmental quality levels will never be made in the marketplace. It requires political resolution.

Private Response to Pollution Levels

While there are some who fear that the current pollution levels are causing irreversible ecological changes on a global scale (for example, there is concern that increased CO_2 content of the atmosphere will generate a warming trend which will melt the polar ice caps and raise the ocean levels), at least some kinds of waste-disposal problems are fairly localized. SO_2 emitted in New York does not affect Des Moines; the photochemical smog in Los Angeles does not affect Seattle. This localization of the waste disposal raises an interesting question? *Why is there a presumption that pollution problems exist?* Not all areas of the country face the same levels of pollution. People are free to move. This suggests that *other things being equal,* an area with differentially high pollution levels could only retain its population if residents in that area received differentially higher incomes to compensate them for their relatively inferior environments. In a world where relocation would be a costless process, any firm which attempted to increase the pollution level in a given location would have to realize that its waste output would induce a relocation of people, reducing the supply of labor to the firm and raising its costs. Migration will continue as long as it is possible to avoid an increase in pollution by moving to a new area where the reduction in income opportunities is less than the value of avoiding the additional pollution. In such a world, the increase in wages that a polluter would have to pay would represent the full social cost of his waste-disposal activities. From our point of view, there would be no pollution problem in such circumstances — no additional pollution will be produced unless the value of the output associated with the production of pollution exceeded the social costs of waste disposal.

A casual examination of wage rate differentials does lend some support to the hypothesis that environmental differences generate pay differentials. Many corporations are reported to be paying 10 to 15 percent premiums for executives who agree to work in New York City. But it is also obvious that it is not generally possible for everybody to move from a more polluted to a less polluted environment at smaller losses in income than the differential cost of pollution. It is this constraint that forces a public response to pollution problems.

Pollution and the National Pattern of Settlement

High air pollution levels in particular areas are a result of the density of pollution-generating activities in those areas. If people were more evenly spread out over the available land surface (for example, if we increased the number of cities, reduced their sizes, and spread them over the country), the same level of pollution generated on a national scale would cause a much smaller deleterious effect on the health and well-being of the population. The current geographic distribution of cities has both historic and economic bases which individuals, acting alone, are powerless to overcome. Because transportation is costly, historically, people tend to cluster around points of maximum access to the natural resources which are necessary for production. These resources are not evenly distributed over the land surface. Therefore, harbors (for example, New York, Boston, San Francisco), rivers (Pittsburgh, St. Louis, Cincinnati, and so on), road and railroad junctions (Chicago, Atlanta), and other points of access provide natural sites for the development of cities. Even activities that are not dependent upon natural-resource inputs find cities attractive locations. The cities provide concentration of customers and the advantages of sharing from pools of highly skilled craftsmen and professional people who might be too expensive to maintain on a permanent staff. Because of these natural advantages, established metropolitan areas continue to retain and attract population, even though the increasing concentration of the population exacerbates environmental quality problems. There are vast areas of the United States in which population densities are less than four persons per square mile. The emergence of new cities in these areas might make good sense as increasing density in the established areas leads to a greater and greater diversion between the private cost and the social cost of continued population growth. But it is the private cost, the cost as the individual locater sees it, that governs his locational choice. New cities will not develop simply because people would like to avoid the environmental deterioration of the old ones. The private cost of moving from one city to another may be relatively small. But the private cost of moving from a city to a wilderness area, where a city *might* be built someday, is likely to be more than most city dwellers would be willing to bear. If new cities of substantial size are to develop in areas away from those currently populated, it is likely, therefore, that the government will have to make substantial investments to attempt to create them.[7]

CONGESTION

● A third dimension of the urban crisis, which has its roots in the failure of institutions to present individual decision makers with the full cost of their decisions, is the extreme traffic congestion of our urban streets and highways. As in the case of waste generation, the existence of congestion or an increase in congestion is not necessarily symptomatic of inefficient resource allocation. Rather, when economists speak of a congestion "problem," they mean that it would be possible, by changing the methods of control of use of the transportation network, to make everybody better off than under the current system of control. That is, the gainers from the change in the control system *could* fully compensate the losers and still be better off.[8]

Of course, if such compensations are not arranged, there is likely to be considerable resistance to a change in the control of access to the transportation network.

Airport Congestion as a Prototype Problem

Use of airport landing and takeoff facilities is controlled in the same manner as use of urban roadways—either on a first-come, first-served basis, or on that basis combined with a fee, which is invariant to the amount of traffic using the system. Because of these similarities, airport congestion can be viewed as a prototype of the urban transportation problem.

In recent years, major airports have suffered chronic "stack-up" problems caused by more planes wishing to land in a given interval than can be handled. Similarly, queues develop waiting to take off. These landing and takeoff queues are peak-hour phenomena. (Everyone wants to take a morning flight that leaves at 8:30 and an afternoon flight that arrives before 7:30.) At nonpeak hours (say 6:30 A.M. or 9:30 P.M.), the queues disappear, and excess capacity shows up. These queues are generally comprised of planes of very different sizes and operating costs. Unless a plane must make an emergency landing, the landing is made on a first-come, first-served basis. Small planes, for whom delays would entail small costs, often land before bigger planes with higher delay costs. This is obviously inefficient. There have been suggestions that small, private planes be banned from use of major airports. Owners of these planes have objected that airport facilities are built with public funds and that they, therefore, have as much right to use these facilities as anyone else. This argument would clearly be neutralized if these owners were compensated for having to move elsewhere.

Removing small planes from this queue would only partially solve the queuing problem. It is obviously cheaper to have a plane wait on the ground at its origin than to expend fuel sitting in a stack above the airport. It would also be worth more to passengers to have guaranteed takeoff and landing times so that they could better utilize their time than by spending it on planes that are sitting in queues. Of course, you can have an effectively guaranteed takeoff and landing time currently (ignoring the vagaries of weather and equipment) by traveling at nonpeak times. If the reduction in operating costs for the airline were greater than the discount passengers required to take nonpeak flights, then individual airlines would have some incentive to shift schedules out of peak time, thereby reducing the queue further.

The extent of such rescheduling motivated by the private profit calculations of the individual airlines would not, however, generate a fully efficient use of the airport capacity. The reason is that each airline will judge the effect of its rescheduling on its profits alone. But when the length of the queue is shortened, everyone in the queue profits by reduced delay costs, not simply the airline who effected the change in schedule. Consequently, there is likely to be some additional re-scheduling, which would produce a *total* reduction in costs (summed over all airlines) greater than the loss of revenue produced by lower off-peak fares which would not be profitable for any single airline to make.

The basic problem is that the airline does not own the right to a specific place in the queue. Consequently, it will not receive compensation from the other airlines for giving up its place. It, therefore, neglects to take into account the impact of its scheduling decisions on the costs of the other airlines.

A Market for Takeoff and Landing Privileges

Under the current system, each airline that schedules landings in the same interval has an equal probability of landing on time as any other airline. (And an equal probability of *not* landing on time!) The only way to exercise a claim to land at peak hour is to show up and wait in the queue. If well-defined landing rights were established, no airline would have the incentive to schedule arrivals during time intervals in which they did not have landing rights. Much of the queuing phenomena, therefore, is a direct consequence of ill-defined property rights and would disappear if property rights were assigned.

Given a well-defined set of property rights, a market in these rights could be established, and airlines, which could generate the greatest increments in revenues from shifting their scheduled arrivals from nonpeak to peak-hour times, could buy those rights from whomsoever they were originally allotted. In this way, anyone who has a right to land at the peak hour will be fully compensated if he chooses to re-schedule his flight by the airline that purchases his peak-hour landing privilege.

Establishment of a market in landing and takeoff rights will not necessarily end all queuing. Some planes may still find it to their advantage to arrive before their permitted landing times. The cost of waiting in the air may be cheaper than purchasing a later takeoff permit from the airport of origin. But it will eliminate all of the *inefficient* stack-up delays, since total profits over all airlines could not be increased by rescheduling if each takeoff and landing right were sold to the highest bidder.[9]

The Urban Transportation Problem

As we mentioned earlier, neither airport use or urban roadway use is rationed via a market process. Like airports, urban roads exhibit peak-hour congestion, while at off-peak hours there is excess capacity. Also, no one has the right to use the road at any particular time with a guarantee of specific traffic conditions being present. Similarly, the only way to exercise a claim to use of a road at a particular time is to get into the queue. Having observed how this system of control leads to inefficiency in the use of airport space, we should not be surprised to find the same result when it is applied to space on the road network.

As a social problem, the management of urban transportation facilities is much more serious than airport congestion. There are vastly more resources embedded in these facilities, and the dimensions of the social consequences are much more complex. In the view of some authors, inappropriate social policy governing the use and development of urban transportation facilities has not only led to serious congestion problems, but has also generated an uneconomic pattern of land use, contributed significantly to the political and social conflicts between central cities and their suburbs, and has changed the cultural patterns of societies in ways which many find unfortunate.[10]

The method by which use of the road system is controlled will have an important influence on both the choice of mode of travel an individual makes and the location decisions of households and firms. We shall discuss each of these aspects in turn.

Mass Versus Private Transit

Buses utilize less road capacity per passenger than automobiles. Currently, when an individual decides whether to take a bus or car, his choice is not influenced by this consideration. Neither the bus fare nor the cost of driving one's own auto is directly related to the social value of road capacity at the time the trip is taken. It is true that gasoline and license taxes do tend to vary directly with the size of the vehicle, and in some states all roads may be *financed* by such fees. But the social cost of capacity will vary with the volume of traffic. When traffic volume is light, an additional vehicle may be accommodated with no increase in cost at all. However, when traffic volume is heavy and congestion develops, additional vehicles may be accommodated only by reducing the *average* speed and hence increasing the time costs of everybody on the road. Gasoline taxes and license fees do not reflect this variability in social costs of road use. Therefore, with respect to choice of mode for peak-hour travel, the present method of control presents an uneconomic bias toward use of private automobiles. Suppose peak-hour car drivers were taxed and the revenues used to subsidize mass transit for those who gave up driving. In this way, commuters would face the full difference in the cost of using private and public modes of transportation, and both those who continue to choose the auto (and pay the tax) and those who leave their cars and take mass transit could be made better off. It is clear that anyone who chooses to switch is better off, since the switch is made voluntarily. But those who choose not to switch are also made better off, since they would not agree to pay the tax (take their cars) unless they valued the reduction in travel time caused by reducing congestion by more than the tax. (An interesting exercise with respect to this tax-subsidy scheme is: If the "road authority" wishes to set the tax rate so as to maximize the total gains summed over all commuters from inducing people to switch modes, how can it find that rate?)

The analytical purpose of combining the tax with a subsidy to former road users is to eliminate redistributive effects of changing the control system. In practice, it is not possible to identify all those who would switch modes if the control system were changed, so that any change in controls would have to be judged in terms of equity as well as efficiency.

There are several practical ways of changing commuters' decisions if the implied redistributions of income do not create political barriers. One method would be to subsidize mass transit out of general funds or vehicle tax funds. Another would be to have downtown parking garages charge a higher hourly rate for long-term than for short-term parkers, since long-term parkers are generally peak-hour commuters, and short-term parkers are not. Privately owned parking garages are not likely to structure their rates in this way without the inducement of a subsidy, since the marginal cost of serving long-term parkers is lower than the marginal cost of serving short-term parkers. A third would be to set up toll booths at critical access points to the central business district. This method seems most practical for areas like Manhattan and Pittsburgh, where bridges play an important role in the road system. New York City recently proposed using tolls generated on its bridges to subsidize mass transit. This plan was vigorously attacked by the New York Automobile Association, which argued that the answer to congestion is not to tax drivers in order to subsidize mass transit but rather to build more roads. It was not clear that the Automobile Association objected to mass transit in principle, but they did object to subsidization at the auto user's expense. Presumably, their objection was that every user of mass transit would be subsidized, while only those drivers who became mass-transit users would produce benefits for the rest of the driving public.

Transportation and the Shape of the City

It is widely recognized that a change in the scale and geographical configuration of an urban transportation system can have an important impact on the spatial organization of activity within the area. The

growth of suburban areas and the development of secondary commercial centers at or near the junctions of major expressways give
vivid testimony to the power of the transportation system to shape a
city. Changes in the transportation system imply changes in the cost
of travel between various points in the area. People respond to these
cost changes by changing their locations in order to maximize their
advantages from the change in costs. A new expressway into a relatively undeveloped suburban area makes access from that area to jobs
and other points easier and less expensive than before. Consequently,
individuals who were previously satisfied with their old locations will
now find it to their advantage to move into this area.

Changes in the control of use of the urban road network will also
change the pattern of transportation costs and consequently induce
shifts in the location of activity within the area. Congestion tolls can
be expected to make locations nearer mass-transit service and points
nearer the downtown area more attractive than before. There would
be a reduced tendency to urban sprawl. More efficient use of the current road system would also reduce pressure for expansion of the road
network and parking facilities. Since these facilities now occupy up to
40 percent of the total land in the central parts of our large cities, a
reduction in pressure for further expansion of the system may slow
down the loss in rate of growth of commercial activity in downtown
areas. By reducing the incentive to urban sprawl, it may also retard
the deterioration in the tax base of the older, established areas. This is
not to imply that a vigorous commercial center downtown is necessarily desirable or economically the most efficient spatial pattern
(although many, especially those with real estate downtown, think it
obvious), nor that the tax base of the established areas should be preserved (although mayors of large cities certainly think so). Rather, it is
only to point out that the current changes taking place are, in part,
related to the maintenance of an inefficient system of control of road
usage. If you are among those who feel urban sprawl unfortunate, and
that the tax base of the city should be preserved, then an improvement
in the efficiency of road use might have locational and distributional
effects that you would like.

The Financing of Roads

Whenever the issue of tolls on public roads is raised, the principal
argument against them is that the roads are already paid for by users
in the form of gasoline and license taxes. As we noted earlier, from
the point of view of efficient allocation of the services of the roads,
this argument is spurious. Even if, like air, the road cost nothing to

originally produce, price rationing is desirable if congestion would develop at a zero price. The argument against tolls is, therefore, an equity argument. Tolls would force off the road some people who, through other forms of taxation, had already contributed to its cost of construction.

This raises an obvious question: Why aren't roads generally financed out of tolls instead of other user charges such as gasoline taxes and license fees? In the early period of American development, most roads between distant communities were, in fact, toll roads, where access was barred by a pike which was turned by the keeper after receipt of payment. These turnpikes were generally privately owned. With the advent of the railroad, these turnpikes lost substantial business and were unable to remain profitable enterprises. The extension of roads then fell to the responsibility of the individual states who engaged in road-building activity only when the state saw a public interest in improving communication among its various communities. For the most part, railroads and canals simply replaced roads as principal intercity connecting links. Local roads were generally provided out of the localities' taxes on property under the theory that the benefits of good access were reaped by local property owners. Besides, it would be cumbersome to levy tolls on local roads, since you would need toll booths at every intersection in order to prevent avoidance of collection.

With the advent of the automobile revolution, the demand for inter- and intracity road services expanded very rapidly. Government was called upon to mobilize the enormous quantity of resources required to put together a road network to take advantage of the possibilities of mass use of automobiles and trucks. Little thought was directed toward the problems of congestion, since roads were generally built with excess capacity. In the absence of congestion problems, gasoline and license taxes were as useful in making users pay the cost of roads as tolls and were cheaper to administer—especially in metropolitan areas. It is only when severe congestion develops that tolls serve as a better control device than indirect user charges since tolls are themselves costly to administer. In recent years, there have been substantial advances made in the electronic metering of traffic. It is now possible to place devices in automobiles that respond to signals sent from devices in the road beds. These devices register a signal at a central station much as a telephone circuit is metered. Monthly statements can then be sent out, indicating charges for using various roads at various times of the day and month. It remains to be seen whether cities will be forced by the increasing demands on their space by private vehicles to adopt this type of system or one of the tax-subsidy systems discussed earlier to handle their congestion problems.

SUMMARY

● It takes information to guide the allocation of resources. The information, which is channeled through a market system, must be summarized in the form of a bid. The senseless, mechanical response of the market to bids it receives and nonresponse to bids which it does not are vividly portrayed by Galbraith.

> . . . The family which takes its mauve and cerise, air-conditioned, power-braked automobile out for a tour passes through cities that are badly paved, made hideous by litter, blighted buildings, billboards and posts for wires that should long since have been put underground. They pass on into a countryside that has been rendered largely invisible by commercial art. . . . They picnic on exquisitely packaged food from a portable icebox by a polluted stream and go to spend the night at a park which is a menace to public health and morals. Just before dozing off on an air mattress, beneath a nylon tent, amid the stench of decaying refuse, they may reflect vaguely on the curious unevenness of their blessings. Is this, indeed, the American genius?[11]

One of the functions of government is to improve the efficiency of resource allocation, by providing extramarket means of coordinating the actions of individuals with respect to commonly held property. In the absence of such means, the market fails to receive adequate information to guide resources to their most-valued uses. The nature of some goods, such as attributes of the environment and ideas, precludes private ownership. In other cases, the costs of enforcing private contracts between individuals, such as contracting for the use of urban streets, are too high to justify the attempt to make the goods involved private. In still other cases, such as the control of disease carriers, there are economies to be achieved by coordinated actions, which cannot be achieved through market transactions. In all of these cases, nonmarket institutions are a necessary adjunct to the effective working of a free-market system.

Notes

1. J. Galbraith, The Affluent Society, college edition, Boston: Houghton Mifflin, 1960, p. 310.
2. There is a very extensive literature on urban renewal. An excellent source for interested readers is James Q. Wilson, Urban Renewal: The Record and the Controversy, Cambridge, Mass.: Massachusetts Institute of Technology Press, 1966.
3. The total cost is $500X, where X is the total number of persons in the neighborhood. This cost is to be divided among $X - 1$ persons. Each person receives $750 in benefits. The requirement that each person

gain (whether he spends $500X/(X - 1)$ or nothing) can be stated as $500X/(X - 1) < \$750$. This necessary condition can be rewritten as $\$750 < \$250X$. Therefore, the necessary condition for the free rider is $3 < X$.

4. In fact, this argument is only valid if there is reason to believe that individuals would out of selfish motivation spend less than the socially profitable amount on their own educations.

5. It is not very helpful to say that the "community" or the "government" has the right or the responsibility to control environmental quality, since the community is divided on the issue.

6. In our little story, no mention was made of the possibility that Ajax install pollution-control equipment. This possibility does not change the analysis since, if it could install the equipment for less than the cost of securing the option, it would not have to bid at all.

7. For a discussion of national planning of the pattern of settlement, see the papers by L. Wingo, H. Richardson, A. Evans, C. D. Foster, W. Thompson, and E. Mills, that were presented at a joint Resources for the Future Inc./University of Glasgow Conference on *Economic Research and National Urban Development Strategies*, August 30–September 3, 1971. These papers appear as a special issue of *Urban Studies*, Vol. 9, No. 1, February 1972.

8. Judging changes in resource allocation by this *potential* for compensation is known as the *compensation principle*. We discuss this principle at some length in Chapter 10.

9. For a fuller discussion of the role of markets and prices in handling airport congestion problems, see W. D. Grampp, "An Economic Remedy for Airport Congestion," *Business Horizons*, Vol. XI, No. 5, October 1968, pp. 21–30.

10. For example, E. M. Hoover, "Motor Metropolis: Some Observations on Urban Transportation in America," *Journal of Industrial Economics*, 1965.

11. J. Galbraith, *op. cit.*, p. 253.

Questions for Discussion

1. Does the existence of externalities necessarily preclude an efficient allocation of resources through trading in competitive markets? *Hint:* Does the fact that I derive benefits from the way my neighbor cares for his yard imply that I would be willing to pay him to take better care of it than he actually does?

2. Some communities have no fire departments; others have volunteer departments; and still others have publicly financed departments. Furthermore, the type of fire-protection service available seems to be directly related to the size of the community. How do you account for this pattern? Why don't you observe fire departments being run as private enterprises?

3. Suppose you owned a forest. What factors would determine the number of

trees you would cut down in any given year? Would you determine your cutting rate in the same manner if you were only one of many loggers working a public forest? (Assume there are no public controls on these operations.) If all forests were publicly owned, how could the government determine the optimal number of board feet to cut each year?

4. Suppose that a community could achieve the same level of pollution reduction by either adopting a set of emission standards that everyone must meet (hence everyone achieves the same rate of emission reduction) or by levying a tax per unit of emission (allowing some people to reduce their emissions by less than others). Suppose, furthermore, that the administrative costs were equal.
   a. Would you wish to choose a different target level of reduction if you used taxes than if you used standards to achieve your target?
   b. Why might you prefer taxes to standards?
   c. How would you determine the optimum target level?

5. Which goods should be made common property? If one person's use of a commodity or facility in no way affects the ability of any other person to use that same commodity or facility, then efficiency requires that use of the commodity or facility be made free of charge. That is, such commodities and facilities must be treated as common property if they are to be utilized efficiently. One example of such a facility is a bridge in a rural area, where traffic is so light that the bridge is never crowded. Other examples are the works of authors and inventors. Rural bridges are almost always treated as common property. The works of authors and inventors are usually given the legal status of private property. What is the rationale for this difference in legal status?

Suggested Readings

Bator, F. M., "The Anatomy of Market Failure," *Quarterly Journal of Economics*, Vol. 72, August 1958, pp. 351–379.
A classification of the causes of market failure.

Buchanan, J. M., and Stubblebine, W. C., "Externality," *Economica*, N.S., Vol. 29, November 1962, pp. 371–384.
Develops the distinction between externalities that are relevant to social policy decisions and externalities that do not lead to market failure.

Coase, R. H., "The Problem of Social Costs," *Journal of Law and Economics*, Vol. 3, October 1960, pp. 1–44.
Examines the separation of issues of efficiency and issues of equity in resolving common property problems.

Crocker, T. D., and Rogers, A. J., III, *Environmental Economics*, Hinsdale, Ill.: Dryden Press, 1971.
An engagingly written primer on pollution problems.

Dales, J. H., *Pollution, Property and Prices*, Toronto, Canada: University of Toronto Press, 1968.
Emphasizes the role of property rights in pollution problems.

Davis, O., and Whinston, A., "The Economics of Urban Renewal," *Law and Contemporary Problems*, Vol. 26, 1961.
Discusses the parallels between private renewal efforts and the Prisoner's Dilemma of game theory.

Dempsetz, H., "The Exchange and Enforcement of Property Rights," *Journal of Law and Economics*, Vol. 7, 1969, pp. 11–31.
Discusses role of transaction costs in market failure.

Gordon, H. S., "The Economic Theory of a Common-Property Resource: The Fishery," *Journal of Political Economy*, Vol. 62, April 1954, pp. 124–142.
Stresses the wastefulness of common property arrangements.

Knight, F. H., "Some Fallacies in the Interpretation of Social Cost," *Quarterly Journal of Economics*, Vol. 38, August 1924, pp. 582–606.
A classic analysis of the inefficiency of nonmarket rationing.

3
POLITICAL PROCESSES FROM AN ECONOMIC POINT OF VIEW

When one contemplates the circumstances portrayed in the concluding passages of Chapter 2, one cannot help but be convinced that we have not achieved an optimal mix of public and private consumption. But it is much easier to agree that we have too much pollution than to determine *how much less* we should have; to agree that roads are badly paved than to determine how much better they should be, or indeed if it would not be better to improve mass transit and reduce the need for better-paved streets. The problem in getting *quantitative* agreement is rooted in the difference in preferences, which people are likely to possess. Not everyone would be willing to sacrifice the same value of private goods in order to secure a given increase in some specific public good. Indeed, many would prefer a reshuffling of the mix of public goods to a reduction in private-good consumption. (For example, compare the attitudes of the Hawks and Doves with respect to the relative importance of military and nonmilitary public-goods production.)

In markets for private goods, differences in preferences are reconciled by allowing different individuals to purchase different quantities of the same good. Each individual can independently tailor his consumption pattern to suit his own tastes and income. But public goods do not allow the adjustment of quantity to individual taste. By their very nature, public goods require that all individuals receive the same quantity even if they place different values on that quantity. If the provision of public goods is to conform to consumer preferences, therefore, it must be by varying the amounts different individuals pay for the same public good.

The absence of a market in which each individual may bid for a public good makes it difficult to gather accurate information about how people value public goods relative to private goods. For example, the benefits from a reduction in pollution emission levels include such things as an improved sense of physical well-being and an esthetically more attractive environment. These benefits are not easily evaluated except by observing how much people would be willing to pay to secure them. For private goods, individuals reveal this information whenever they make a purchase. However, there are no formal markets in which these attributes of pollution reduction are sold. Economists may attempt to derive such information by analyzing purchases in which these factors may be relevant. For example, Ridker has attempted to identify the value individuals place on a cleaner environment by analyzing differences in the real estate values of properties that are subject to different levels of pollution.[1] But such indirect estimation is tenuous and not always possible. Consequently, one must often look outside the market for information on consumer preferences.

Various voting processes represent alternatives to the market in gathering information about consumer preferences and in guiding resource allocation according to those preferences. Such nonmarket devices are essential in handling public goods and externality problems. In this chapter, we shall explore several aspects of democratic decision procedures.

THE RULE OF UNANIMITY

● The *rule of unanimity* represents a natural extension of the principle of voluntary exchange from the marketplace to the political arena. In free markets, no exchange will take place unless both parties to the transaction believe that they will be better off as a result. By appealing to each individual's self-interest, free markets coordinate decisions without coercion. In a similar fashion, the rule of unanimity protects the interests of the individual. If a proposal is to carry unanimously, each voter must believe that his interests will not be harmed by the proposed action. Put differently, if a proposal is to carry unanimously, it must confer net benefits to each voter. For this reason, the rule of unanimity guarantees that any proposed reallocation that wins unanimous support will move the economy to a pareto superior position.

If a proposal is to be capable of producing net benefits for every individual, then the total benefits stemming from the proposal must exceed the total costs. While the rule of unanimity guarantees that any proposal that is accepted satisfies this social profitability criterion, it does not guarantee that proposals that are rejected are not capable of producing total benefits in excess of their costs. The reasons for this indefiniteness are as follows:

1. If the total benefits of a proposed measure would exceed the costs, then there must be many possible distributions of the burden of the costs that leave some (perhaps all) members of the community better off and none worse off than if the measure were not adopted.
2. The group cannot attain unanimous consent if any member is assigned a burden greater than the actual value he places on the measure.
3. But the only person who knows the true value an individual places on a measure is that individual himself. Therefore, it is in the interest of each individual to conceal his true valuation in order to increase his share of the joint profits should the measure carry. Consequently, failure of a measure to carry may simply be the result of strategic moves by some voters. By voting nay, an individual may encourage others to resubmit the proposal with a lower-cost assignment to him, even though he would actually be a net gainer under the proposal he has rejected.[2]

DEPARTURES FROM UNANIMITY

● Once one moves away from the rule of unanimity, there is no more assurance that measures adopted carry total benefits in excess of total costs. A program, which a large majority favored under one distribution of the costs (Soak the Rich), may lose by a large majority under some other cost distribution. In either case, the result of the vote will not indicate whether the sum of the benefits did or did not exceed the costs.

It might be argued that if the sum of the benefits of a given proposal passed by a majority did not actually exceed the costs, then the minority could have gotten together and bribed a sufficient number of those who were in the majority to vote against the proposal. In that event, the proposal would not have carried. Similarly, one might argue that if a measure turned down by a majority actually did possess total benefits in excess of the costs, then the minority could have gotten together and bribed a sufficient number of those who actually voted against the measure to vote for it. The problem with this "solution" to the proper provision of public goods is that the same strategic motives, which may prevent the formation of a coalition of the whole, are operative in interfering with a coalition of a part of the whole.

The strategic elements implicit in joint decisions pose a serious dilemma for those who wish to appeal to the set of preferences of a group of individuals when judging between alternative resource allocations. One can only be certain that an individual is revealing his true preferences when that individual knows that his vote will be decisive. But the only circumstances in which a single individual's vote is decisive are (1) when he is a dictator or (2) when there is no positive net benefit to the group. If he is a dictator, then there is no sense in judging alternative resource allocations in terms of other individuals. If there is a potential net benefit to the group as a whole, then it must be possible for him to offer to pay less than he would be willing to pay and still have the proposal win unanimous consent.

THE COSTS OF DECISION MAKING

● The strategic interplay of individuals, each of whom is attempting to increase his share of the potential joint profits, is itself a resource-using activity. All of the potential gains can be whittled away in the process of coming to a decision. (Every married man knows that when there is a choice between going to one theatre and another, it is always better to let his wife make the decision unilaterally than to arrive in time for the second act of the play she has finally convinced you to see.) Buchanan and Tullock have argued that when an individual takes these decision-making costs into consideration, he will find it rational to accept a departure from the rule of unanimity and its attendant protection of individual interest for a system over which he has less control, but which has a lower cost of producing decisions.[3] On the one hand, the smaller the percentage of voters needed for affirmative action on a particular class of proposals, the greater the chance that one will be in the adversely affected group on any given proposal. But on the other hand, they argue, the smaller the required decisive group, the more rapidly a decision may be reached. According to their thesis, therefore, the infrequency with which groups use the rule of unanimity (how many groups can you think of that make decisions by the rule of unanimity?) and the widespread use of *majority rule* can be accounted for by an attempt to strike the appropriate balance between the costs of coming to a decision and the costs imposed on individuals by that decision rule.

MAJORITY RULE AND DEMOCRATIC PARALYSIS

● Although it seems plausible that majority rule should entail lower decision-making costs than the rule of unanimity, this result will not necessarily obtain. As we noted in Chapter 1, certain combinations of

Table 3.1

	Individuals		
	1	2	3
Preference			
rank	A	B	C
highest	B	C	A
to	C	A	B
lowest	D	D	D

individual preferences generate so-called cyclic majorities in which proposal A wins a majority over proposal B; proposal B wins a majority over proposal C; but proposal C wins a majority over proposal A.

Suppose the community decision rule is to choose the alternative that can win a majority over each of the others and that each individual votes according to his preferences. If the preference rankings are like those in Table 3.1, there is no such alternative. Therefore, under the proposed decision rule, the community is deadlocked. Whenever no other alternative is chosen, then the status quo remains. Suppose that alternative D is the status quo. By assumption, D is the least-preferred alternative according to each individual's preferences. Nevertheless, if no motion can win over all others, D will, in fact, be chosen by default. Examples of this kind illustrate what is meant by the notion of a "democratic paralysis." The community does not change from the status quo simply because it cannot decide from among several better alternatives which to choose. This is precisely the kind of inaction produced under the rule of unanimity when each individual is attempting to change the distribution of income in his favor. Each possible distribution of the joint profits represents a possible alternative, all of which may be preferred unanimously to the status quo. This example illustrates, moreover, that deadlock cannot always be broken by getting people to reveal their true preferences. It is apparent that the principal obstacle to an improvement in the efficiency with which resources are used by using jointly made decisions is that it is generally impossible to separate distributional or equity considerations from efficiency considerations in matters of political choice. We shall return to this point later.

LOG ROLLING

● Majority rule creates the possibility that the majority coalition on every issue be composed of the same members. If this were actually the case, then majority rule would lose its appeal (at least to those in the minority). Madison argued that as long as preferences, talents, and interests differ among individuals, this possibility is not likely to arise.[4] Rather, the formation of coalitions is likely to take place by explicit or implicit vote swapping or log rolling, and these coalitions are likely to be different on every issue. Vote swapping is somewhat analogous to market exchanges by which individuals with differing preferences can secure that alternative about which each feels most strongly. Log rolling is often considered by observers to be sacrificing the common good to the special interests. Others would argue that the "common good" is a metaphysical notion and that, in any case, if log rolling were not practicable, then apathetic majorities could frustrate intensely interested minorities on specific issues. On the other hand, it may take much more effort and resources to put together a coalition than to keep it together. (Consider the relative stability of the two-party system in the United States.) Coalitions that have existed long enough to have become institutionalized seem to have a distinct advantage in the political game. There is always the possibility, therefore, that by letting coalitions form, one is allowing the formation of a majority which agrees to vote as a bloc on every issue.

ADDITIONAL ASPECTS OF MAJORITY-TYPE PROCESSES

● The typical voting procedure is one in which a previously defeated measure is not reintroduced. When preferences are such that there is no alternative that can carry a majority over all others, this voting procedure must favor those alternatives that are introduced latest in the voting process.[5] For example, suppose that three individuals are going to make a group choice between issues A, B, C, and D and that their individual preferences are listed in Table 3.1. If A is first paired against B and the majority choice then paired against C, C will be the eventual winner. If C were first paired against A, however, the eventual winner would be B. And finally, if B were first paired with C, the eventual winner would be A. There must always be a winner under this type of majority rule. However, the person or group that decides the order in which the alternatives are to be considered may have much more influence than the other members of the group. A second characteristic of this voting rule is that it allows a series of majority coalitions to be put together to pass each of several pieces of legislation which, if voted on as a single package, could not secure a majority vote. Restrictive trade laws, each of which is in the interest of some minority, get passed by vote-swapping techniques on individual laws even though all such laws taken together might not be capable of securing majority support since, in the form of a package, each voter would be able to assess the costs to him of all of the bills that work against his interest and weigh them against those few bills that favor his interests. It is a curious process, which leads you to take decisions that might ultimately be rejected. Of course, many see virtue in merely "playing the game."[6]

Unlike the rule of unanimity, majority rule allows the distribution of wealth to be an object of social choice. The rule of unanimity will frustrate attempts to use the political process to redistribute wealth, thereby elevating the prevailing wealth distribution to an ethically superior position. Many would argue that this represents an unwarranted arbitrariness in the social decision process. Even if a society were to start out with an ethically acceptable distribution of wealth, with the passage of time the uncertainties of commerce are likely to make some rich and others poor. But the lucky speculator can, after winning, refrain from further speculation and retain his wealth and pass it on to his heirs. Similarly, those specially gifted (or merely sufficiently different) will secure privileged positions if the market is allowed to work its way. The luck of genetic inheritance or mutation seems a weak reed upon which to elevate a particular distribution of wealth to an ethically superior position. The question of ethics aside, if a sufficiently large group feels itself disadvantaged and does not have access to peaceful means of changing the wealth distribution, violence is likely to result (war is the last tool of diplomacy).

As we noted above, majority rule is not without elements of arbitrariness, either. There is nothing particularly attractive about the possibility of an intransitive sequence of choices, which either leads to deadlock or grants unusual power to the rules committee which determines the order of presentation. Nevertheless, majority rule does embody other desirable features. First, the rule embodies a kind of "citizen's sovereignty." Choice from among alternatives is positively, or at least not negatively, related to individual preferences. If an individual changes his order of preference from xP_1y to yP_1x, this does not reduce the possibility of y becoming the social choice. There is no choice that is sacred; depending upon the composition of the individual preference orderings, any alternative could become the group's choice. No one individual's preferences always determine the social choice irrespective of the preferences of others. In addition, majority rule, conceived of as the selection of the alternative that can win a majority when paired against any other alternative, produces decisions which are independent of the addition or deletion of alternatives which would not themselves be chosen as the majority choice. This *independence of irrelevant alternatives* implies that there is no advantage to strategic misrepresentation of preferences under the rule. The method of majority voting, in which a proposal once defeated is not paired against any subsequent proposals, does not have this independence property. A motion, which becomes the community choice under one sequence of voting, may not be chosen if the sequence is altered. As noted earlier, this method favors proposals introduced latest in the sequence and, therefore, creates an incentive to vote against a proposal introduced early in the process simply to prevent it from being matched against a favored proposal which will be up for adoption later. By removing the incentive to misrepresentation, majority rule of the first kind is likely to reduce bargaining costs. It will assure that when the true individual preferences do not imply a cyclic majority, that the choice finally made is actually better, from the point of view of the majority, than any of the alternatives rejected.

THE ARROW POSSIBILITY THEOREM

● The question arises: Is it logically possible to construct a social decision rule that never leads to deadlock or an arbitrary choice and has the properties of "consumer sovereignty" and independence of irrelevant alternatives which are characteristic of majority rule? Arrow has shown that under "reasonable" specifications of what is meant by "consumer sovereignty," no such rule is generally possible. The Arrow theorem applies to Vickery's axioms defining "consumer sovereignty" and the range of individual orderings from which a social ordering must be produced.[7]

Axiom 1 If an alternative x is unanimously preferred to an alternative y, then x is socially preferred to y.

Axiom 2 There is no individual, k, such that if all other individuals prefer x to y and k prefers y to x, then the social ranking is yPx.

Axiom 3 The social ordering is transitive, asymmetric, and reflexive.

Axiom 4 The rule must provide a ranking for all possible combinations of individual rankings.

Axiom 5 The social ranking of any two alternatives, a and b, is independent of changes in the individual orderings between any other pairs of alternatives.

These "axioms" are not assertions of empirical reality, subject to refutation by an appeal to facts. Rather, they are assertions of the conditions that Arrow believes a good social decision rule *ought* to satisfy. The test of their propriety does not lie in an appeal to fact, but to their essential reasonableness. Axiom 1 is the pareto postulate. Axiom 2 rules out a dictator. Axiom 3 rules out deadlock. Axiom 4 when combined with Axiom 1 rules out any sacred alternatives. Axiom 5 is the independence of irrelevant alternatives axiom. It rules out not only possible gains through strategic misrepresentation, but also denies any relevance for social decisions of assessing the relative strength of preferences among individuals, since such judgments involve asking questions of the kind, "Do you prefer a to b by more or less than you prefer x to y?"

Arrow's possibility theorem: There is no decision rule that satisfies the five axioms listed above.

The proof of the theorem relies upon the notion of a decisive set. Definition: A set of individuals, D, is decisive with respect to a social choice between two alternatives if when that group prefers a to b (aDb) and all other individuals prefer b to a (bOa), social choice is a over b (aPb).

The proof is divided into two parts. First, it is shown that if a group is decisive with respect to one pair of alternatives, then it is decisive with respect to all pairs of alternatives. Next, it is shown that if a group is decisive, then there is a subset of that group that is decisive. But this means that if there is a decisive group, then there is a dictator. Finally, since the set of all individuals constitutes, by Axiom 1, a decisive group, Arrow's theorem is derived. An outline of the proof of the theorem is given in the appendix to this chapter.

Axiom 5, which plays a crucial role in the proof of the theorem, embodies an extension of the positivist philosophy to the field of ethical judgment. The positivists do not deny that individuals make interpersonal judgments, but they argue that at the present time, there is no empirical basis for adopting a common unit of measure of relative intensities. Without such a basis, there are no grounds for common agreement on how interpersonal comparisons are to be made. Therefore, they would argue that there is no room for interpersonal comparisons in an "acceptable" social decision rule.

Point Voting

Point voting is a voting rule which violates Axiom 5. In this system, each individual is given a fixed number of "points" which he may distribute over a set of alternatives in any manner he chooses. The rule is then to add the points of all the voters on each alternative and select the alternative that received the greatest total number of points. The

Table 3.2

Voter	A	B	C	D
		Alternative		
X	10	9	8	7
Y	10	9	8	7
Z	7	10	8	9
Total points	27	28	24	23

rationale behind the point system is to have a system which is responsive to expressed intensities of preferences. If one individual feels so strongly about alternative A that he gives all of his points to it and none to any others, while everyone else divides their points almost evenly over all of the alternatives, then A would win under point voting, but not necessarily under majority voting. Point voting might tend to protect minority interests against the "tyranny" of an apathetic majority. In point voting, the number of points assigned any alternative depends upon the number of alternatives. Dropping an alternative which would not win may, therefore, affect the choice of the eventual winner. But, as we noted earlier, whenever this is possible, then it is also possible to effect the outcome by distributing your points in a manner which does not truly reflect your own preferences. Consider the true set of preferences recorded in Table 3.2.

Under majority rule, A would win. Under point voting, if *individuals* assigned points according to their true preferences, B would win. But voter Y could affect the outcome by "falsely" assigning 7 points to B and 9 to D. The problem in interpreting the outcome of the vote is that no one other than the voter himself knows whether he is voting his true preferences. When the voting procedure is conducive to strategic misrepresentation, therefore, it is not at all clear that collective decisions lead "to a greater achievement of ends actually desired and pursued" than if the scope of collective action were severely circumscribed.

Single-Peaked Preferences

Axiom 4 asserts that the social decision rule should be capable of making an assignment of social rank that satisfies the other axioms whatever the individual ranks might be. Black has shown that if individual preferences are "single peaked," then majority rule satisfies Axiom 3.[8] As we noted earlier, majority rule also satisfies Axioms 1, 2, and 5. A preference ordering is said to be "single peaked" if the alternatives can be thought of as a single dimensional variable in which the ranking of an alternative relative to the most-preferred alternative is inversely related to its "distance" from the most-preferred alternative. One important class of problems for which individual preferences may be singled peaked is voting for public-goods expenditures when the proportion of those expenditures that each individual must finance is already determined. For example, the law may require that local school expenditures be financed by local property taxes. Each person knows his tax rate. The total tax he pays will depend on the community's decision with respect to public school expenditures.

In Figure 3.1, we have drawn the indifference curves of a typical individual between public educational expenditures and all other (private) goods. The line EE' represents the budget line for this individual. If no public expenditures are voted upon, he may consume OE of private goods. For each unit of public expenditures the group decides upon, this individual will be taxed at the rate of OE/OE'. Faced with this budget line, our individual's most-preferred combination of public and private goods is A. Furthermore, the further from A is any point on EE', the lower the preference rank it is given. Hence A is preferred

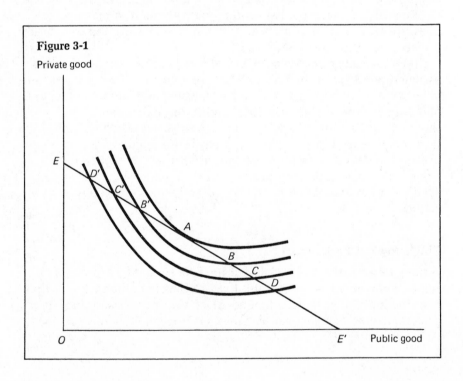

Figure 3-1

Private good

E

D'

C'

B'

A

B

C

D

O

E' Public good

to B, B to C, C to D. Similarly, in the other direction, A is preferred to B', B' to C', C' to D'.

Suppose now that we have three individuals, Mr. Rich, Mr. Average, and Mr. Poor. For simplicity, we assume they all have the same tastes represented by the indifference curves labeled I in Figure 3.2. The tax structure is such that the rich must pay more in taxes per unit of public goods than the poor. This is reflected in the slopes of the budget lines RR, MM, and PP for Mr. Rich, Mr. Average, and Mr. Poor, respectively. Given their budget lines, Mr. Rich's preferred bundle is z; Mr. Average's is y; and Mr. Poor's is x. Of course, they must decide jointly upon the actual quantity of public good to be produced. Looking at the public-good axis, Mr. Poor would rank the alternatives A, B, and C in descending order of preference. Mr. Average's rank would be B, A, and C, while Mr. Rich's rank would be C, B, and A. B is the median of the most-preferred choices and will be chosen by majority rule. This is simply an illustration of Black's theorem. When preferences are single peaked,

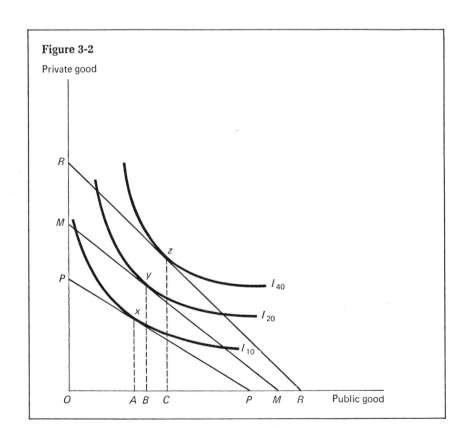

Figure 3-2

the median-preferred alternative will be the winner by majority rule. In a political context, this implies that when individuals' political views are distributed over a spectrum from far left to far right, the successful candidate's platform will appeal to the middle ground.

In a classic article, Bowen showed that if the cost of a public good is divided equally among all members of the group, majority rule will not only choose the median-preferred expenditure, but also that the level of expenditure may be pareto optimal.[9] In his model, each individual faces 1/N of the total cost of any expenditure agreed upon. Consequently, the most-preferred level of expenditure for each individual will be that level at which his marginal rate of substitution of the public for private goods is equal to 1/N the rate at which private goods can be transformed into public goods. If individual preferences are normally distributed, the mean and the median of the most-preferred expenditures will coincide. Since the median is the majority choice, the majority choice will be one at which the average of the individual rates of substitution is just equal to 1/N of the rate at which the private good can be transformed into the public good. This, in turn, implies that the sum of the individual rates of substitution just equals the rate of transformation.

It is the assumption that the tax share has been predetermined that creates a single-peaked preference structure among alternative expenditure levels. In effect, the introduction of a budget line reduces the alternatives to a set, which can be represented by a single-dimensional variable. Unfortunately, the choice of alternative tax shares must also be made. This and other choices involve a determination of the distribution of income. These choices involve alternatives which have as many dimensions as there are individuals. They do not, therefore, necessarily permit the existence of a measure of "distance" implicit in the single-peaked preference structure.

What Black's theorem shows is that if the preferences of individuals share a particular feature in common, then a well-functioning democratic political system is possible. But single peakedness does not seem possible when the choices involve the distribution of income. Nevertheless, Arrow's theorem seems to imply that a society can only have a reasonably well-functioning democratic political system if its members share a similarity of preferences. The processes of acculturation, education, religious, and ethical training, by which a society develops a core of commonly shared values, would therefore appear to be a prerequisite to the use of democratic procedures for social choices. A major unanswered problem is where to draw the line between inculcation of uniformity and of diversity of opinion and taste if a democratic form of government is to continue to be viable.

SUMMARY

● There are essentially two forms of social organization by which coordination of specialized activities may be achieved. The military represents one form — organization by command. The essence of such a system is the chain of command spelled out in the organization chart. This chart is itself a physical entity, the product of the leadership. The leadership "orders" both in the sense of issuing commands and in the sense of deciding what is and what is not to be done. Each individual is to suppress his own sense of order, his own sense of propriety, and to submit to the dictates of his superior. "There is the right way, the wrong way, and the army's way." Only by following the army's way can the military machine function smoothly.

In contrast to the command economy, a free-market system achieves coordination by letting each person seek his own purposes, subject only to the mutual voluntary cooperation of others. Democratic decision making shares with the market the common foundation of liberal philosophy that the importance of the consequences of actions should be defined by the individuals who undertake them.

The rule of unanimity embodies this principle most closely. Application of the unanimity rule will assure that any affirmative action moves the allocation of resources in a pareto superior direction. But there are two principal drawbacks to the rule. First, it provides wide latitude for the use of strategy to attempt to alter the distribution of profits. As such, it is likely to be too time- and resource-consuming a process to be considered practical. Secondly, it limits the scope of action that can be considered, since it cannot be used to change the distribution of income. Consequently, it is likely to encourage illegitimate activity to redress perceived inequities.

Under some conditions (the absence of a set of individual preferences which generate cyclic majorities), majority rule becomes a practical alternative to the rule of unanimity. But when individual preferences are such that cyclic majorities are generated, the alternative to deadlock is to increase the power of the rules committee, admit the use of strategy, and allow the possibility of the process actually leading everybody to a worse situation than the one from which they started.

The principal import of Arrow's theorem is that it is not possible to find a social decision rule that has all of the desirable and none of the undesirable features of majority rule that will be applicable over all possible varieties of individual preferences. An important problem for social research is, therefore, to characterize the sets of individual preferences which allow a decision rule to be developed that leads to transitive choices, prevents strategic misrepresentation, and is sensitive to the preferences of all individuals.

APPENDIX:
SKETCH OF A PROOF
OF THE ARROW THEOREM

● Suppose a social decision rule satisfies Axioms 1 to 5 on page 67. Suppose further that the group is divided into two sets, D and O, such that all members of D have the same preference orderings and that D is decisive with respect to a social choice between x and y. Let there be three alternatives: x, y, and z.

Theorem 1: If D is decisive between x and y, then D is decisive between x and z and between y and z.

Proof: Suppose $xDyDz$, while $zOyOx$. By Axiom 5, the social ranking of z relative to x is independent of any individual ranking of y relative to z. If all individuals in O changed their ranking of y relative to z, this would not, by Axiom 5, change the social ranking of x relative to z. Therefore, assume the ranking by O is changed to $yO'zO'x$. In this case,

xPy by assumption
yPz by Axiom 1
xPz by Axiom 3

therefore, by Axiom 5, when $xDyDz$ and $zOyOx$, xPz. That is, D is decisive between x and z. By Axiom 5, the social ranking of y relative to z is independent of the individual rankings of x relative to y or to z. Therefore, assume the individual rankings are changed to:

$yD'xD'z$

and

$xO'zO'y$

In this case,

yPx by assumption
xPz by Axiom 1
yPz by Axiom 3

therefore, by Axiom 5, when $yDxDz$ and $zOyOx$, yPz. That is, if D is decisive with respect to x and y, then it is decisive with respect to y and z.

The independence axiom, which allows a change in the individual orderings of all but two of the alternatives, allows the proof of Theorem 1 to be extended so as to show that if a group is decisive with respect to any two alternatives, then it is decisive with respect to all pairs of alternatives, irrespective of the number of alternatives considered. By the independence axiom, one can always arrange triples to utilize the transitivity axiom to prove D is decisive with respect to every pair within a triple if it is decisive with respect to any pair within that triple. The independence axiom also assures that you can always work with triples when extending the proof to any number of alternatives. Theorem 1 can, therefore, be extended to read as:

Theorem 1': If a group is decisive with respect to one pair of alternatives, then it is decisive with respect to every pair of alternatives.

The second component of the proof of Arrow's theorem is:

Theorem 2: If there is a decisive group, then there is a subset of the group that is decisive.

Proof: Let the decisive set D be subdivided into two sets D_1 and D_2. Assume the rankings to be:

xD_1yD_1z
yD_2zD_2x
$zOxOy$

then

1. yPz since both D_1 and D_2 prefer y to z;
2. if xPz, then D_1 is a decisive set, therefore, assume zPx;
3. if yPz and zPx, then by transitivity yPx. But if yPx, then D_2 is a decisive set. Therefore, if $D_1 \cup D_2 = D$ is a decisive set, then either D_1 or D_2 is a decisive set.

By Axiom 1 the entire community constitutes a decisive set with respect to a given pair of alternatives; by Theorem 1' the community is, therefore, decisive with respect to all alternatives; by Theorem 2 if the community is a decisive set, then there is a dictator. This establishes Arrow's theorem.

Notes

1. R. Ridker, *The Economic Costs of Air Pollution.* New York: Praeger, 1967.
2. In game theory, such dilemmas are described as resulting from a conflict between individual rationality and group rationality.
3. J. Buchanan and G. Tullock, *The Calculus of Consent.* Ann Arbor: University of Michigan Press, 1962.
4. See J. Madison, *The Federalist Papers.* No. 10.
5. Such situations are called *cyclic majorities.* because the voting process never terminates with a definite winner, but goes around in cycles.
6. Knight reminds us of this aspect of motivation by recalling a conversation as related by Plutarch between Cineas, "a man of sound sense," and Pyrrhus, a king bent on conquest. When Cineas asked Pyrrhus why he wished to

make war on one group, Pyrrhus's reply was that it was a necessary preliminary to invading another country. Cineas then asked, ". . . But when we have conquered all, what are we to do then?" "Why then, my friend," said Pyrrhus, laughing, "we will take our ease, and drink and be merry." Cineas, having brought him thus far, replied, "and what hinders us from drinking and taking our ease now, when we have already those things in our hands, at which we propose to arrive through seas of blood, through infinite toils and dangers, through innumerable calamities which we must both cause and suffer?" "This discourse of Cineas gave Pyrrhus pain, but produced no reformation . . ." (F. H. Knight, *The Ethics of Competition and Other Essays*. New York: Harper and Brothers, 1935, p. 33.)

7. W. Vickery, "Utility, Strategy, and Social Decision Rules," *Quarterly Journal of Economics*. Vol. 74, November 1960, pp. 507–535.

8. D. Black, *The Theory of Committees and Elections*. New York: Cambridge University Press, 1958.

9. H. R. Bowen, "The Interpretation of Voting in the Allocation of Resources," *Quarterly Journal of Economics*. Vol. 58, November 1943, pp. 27–48.

Questions for Discussion

1. Let there be three issues and three voters. Suppose each individual were to order a set of three alternatives (A, B, C) such that the most-preferred alternative were assigned the number 2, the next preferred the number 1, and the least preferred the number 0. The voting rule is that the alternative with the largest sum of points wins.

   a. Prove that under some individual orderings, there is no winner.
   b. Prove that if there is a winner, it is the alternative preferred by the majority.
   c. Suppose each individual ordering of (A, B, C) is such that the voter is indifferent between any two choices immediately adjacent to his most-preferred choice (for example, if B is the most preferred, both A and C are assigned the value 1), but prefers alternatives closer to his most-preferred choice over more distant alternatives (for example, if A is the most preferred, B is assigned 1 and C is assigned zero. Prove that under this restriction, there is always a winner.
   d. Is the restriction on individual orderings in Part c one that is reasonable no matter what the alternatives being ordered may be?

2. Suppose that each of three communities is currently disposing of their solid wastes using no facilities in common with one another. Assume there are economies of scale in solid-waste handling such that if any pair of communities shared a common facility, the pair would realize a saving of 2.5, which they could divide between the members of the pair. If all three communities shared common facilities, the triple would realize a savings of 3.0, which they might divide among themselves. Suppose each community will give its approval to a proposed consolidation scheme if and only if its share of the savings from that scheme is at least as large as it might possibly get

under any other scheme which might be accepted. No consolidation scheme will be adopted. Prove this statement. *Hint:* There is no way of dividing 3 units of gain among three communities such that each receives at least 1.25 units.

Suppose that any pair, excluding the third community, could receive only 1.5 joint savings, while the triple could still divide 3. Prove that in these circumstances, there are many proposed consolidation schemes that might possibly be accepted. What will determine which, if any, of the schemes are accepted? What light, if any, is shed by this example on the problems of metropolitan areas that do not have metropolitan government?

3. In Figure 3.3, the curves labeled AA' represent individual A's marginal

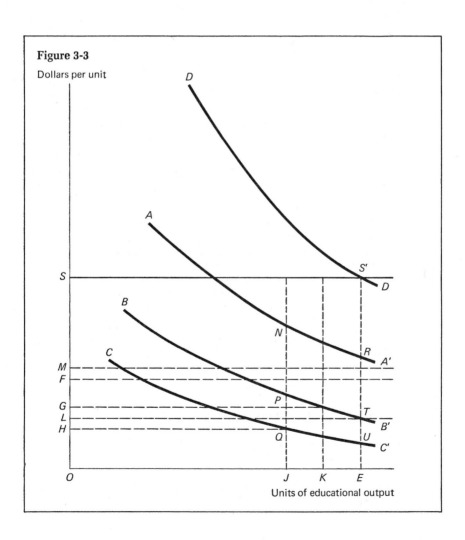

Figure 3-3

Dollars per unit

Units of educational output

valuation of various levels of educational output. (By the marginal value of J units, we mean the amount he would be willing to pay for one more unit given that he has J units.) Similarly, BB' and CC' represent the marginal valuation curves of individuals B and C, respectively. The marginal total cost of output is represented by SS'.

a. Prove that if the tax laws require A to pay a fraction OF/OS of the total bill for education, B to pay a fraction OG/OS, and C to pay a fraction OH/OS (OH + OG + OF = OS), that a majority will choose OK as the community's desired level of output.

b. Prove that this is not a pareto optimal choice.

c. Prove that the majority choice of level of output will not always be individual B's choice.

This problem is discussed by Robin Barlow, "Efficiency Aspects of Local School Finance," *Journal of Political Economy*. Vol. 78, No. 5, pp. 1028–1039.

4. *The political economy of a tax loophole.* Assume the population were composed of individuals with identical preferences and that all individuals have the same before income tax. Suppose that a bill is passed that allows every brown-eyed person to take a 10 percent deduction from his gross income before calculating his taxable income. Will brown-eyed people necessarily be made better off relative to nonbrown-eyed people as a result of the tax deduction?

In answering this question remember (1) that both groups benefit from the supply of public goods, (2) that the supply of public goods is limited by the volume of taxes collected, (3) that marginal cost of a public good to a particular group depends upon that group's marginal tax rate, and (4) that the lower a group's marginal tax rate the more public goods it will desire. In other words, remember that the supply of public goods cannot remain unchanged in the face of the tax deduction unless tax rates are raised. Also remember that the group that received the deduction also has, in consequence, an increased demand for public goods.

For a formal analysis of a tax deduction within a general equilibrium framework, see James Buchanan and Mark Pauly, "On the Incidence of Tax Deductibility," *National Tax Journal*. Vol. XXIII, No. 2, June 1970.

5. *The importance of the voting process when cyclic majorities are possible.* In this chapter we demonstrated that if the set of preferences were such that cyclic majorities would be produced, then the actual outcomes using a modified form of majority rule will depend upon the order in which issues are raised. As a further example of this principle, consider the following problem.

There are three issues which are to be settled: How much should the community spend on schools; how much should it spend on police; how much should it spend on both police and schools. Clearly, these issues are not independent, deciding any two of them decides the third. We have three possible methods for voting on these issues. For each method, the decision rule is to select that "alternative" which commands a majority when paired against other "alternatives." Our methods differ only with respect to a definition of the "alternatives" which are to be voted upon.

In Method 1, we first define the "alternatives" as the possible levels of school expenditure. After this amount has been determined, we then have a second voting sequence in which the "alternatives" are possible levels of police expenditures. The results of these two processes then determine total expenditures. In Method 2, the "alternatives" are defined as every possible school expenditure–police expenditure combination. A single voting sequence, therefore, simultaneously decides all three issues. In Method 3, we have two voting sequences. In the first sequence, the "alternatives" are defined as every possible level of total expenditure. After the total expenditure is determined, a second voting sequence takes place. In this second sequence, the alternatives are defined as possible divisions of this total between school and police expenditures.

Suppose that there are three individuals in the community, A, B, and C. Each individual's preferences are such that his ranking of various amounts of expenditure on schools is independent of the amount of police expenditures that may be made, and conversely. Suppose each individual's preference ranking of expenditures on schooling is single peaked and that his preference ranking of expenditures on police is also single peaked. It, therefore, follows that each individual's preferences are single peaked with respect to various school–police expenditure combinations. Points A, B, and C in Figure 3.4 represent their respective most-preferred bundles.

For simplicity, assume that the preference rank an individual assigns any point away from his most-preferred point depends only upon its "distance" from his most-preferred point. (This means that each individual's indifference curves are circles, centered upon his most-preferred point.)

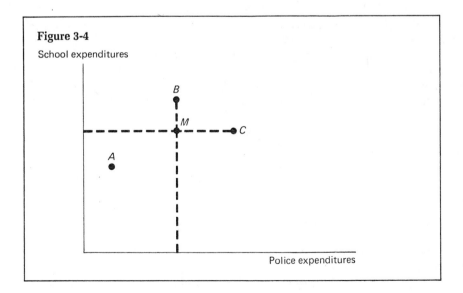

Figure 3-4

a. Prove that if Method 1 is followed, the community choice will be point M.
b. Prove that if Method 2 is followed, the community cannot make a choice. (This implies that Black's single-peaked preference theorem does not hold when the alternatives are multidimensional.)
c. Prove that if Method 3 is followed, the community choice may be other than point M.

Hints: For Part a, note that M corresponds to the median of the most-preferred school expenditures and also to the median of the most-preferred police expenditures.

For Part b, note that three circles cannot be tangent to one another at a common point.

For Part c, note that an individual's vote on total expenditures may be conditioned by the way he believes they will eventually be divided. That is, for any given total expenditure, he will be attempting to estimate its division. To solve the problem, therefore, find the majority choice division for every possible total expenditure. Once this locus of points is found, consider choosing a particular point on it by majority rule.

This problem is discussed in J. Buchanan, *The Public Finances: An Introductory Textbook.* 3rd ed., Homewood, Ill.: Irwin, 1970, ch. 13.

Suggested Readings

Arrow, K. J., *Social Choice and Individual Values,* 2nd ed., New York/London/ Sydney: Wiley, 1963, pp. 92–120.
Contains not only a proof of the theorem, but also general discussion of the nature of the problem of social choice and the ethical views upon which his formulation of the problem is based. Chapter 8 of the 2nd edition reviews much of the literature that his theorem generated.

Bergson, A., "On the Concept of Social Welfare," *Quarterly Journal of Economics,* May 1954, pp. 233–252.
Discusses a conception of the notion of social welfare which differs from Arrow's.

Boulding, K., *Economics as a Science,* New York: McGraw-Hill, 1970, ch. 4.
A wide-ranging essay on the relationship of economics to political and public policy decisions.

Bowen, H., "The Interpretation of Voting in the Allocation of Economic Resources," *Quarterly Journal of Economics,* Vol. 58, November 1943, pp. 27–48.
A classic article discussing the analogy between market and voting processes. Focuses on the problem of providing conditions under which voting will lead to an optimal provision of public goods.

Buchanan, J., and Tullock, G., *The Calculus of Consent,* Ann Arbor: University of Michigan Press, 1962.
Discusses the nature of the problem of devising a constitution from an economic point of view.

Galbraith, J., *The Affluent Society,* Boston: Houghton Mifflin, 1958, ch. 18.

Discusses the importance of, and the impediments to, an appropriate division of resources between private and public consumption.

Hicks, J. R., *A Theory of Economic History*, Oxford: Clarendon Press, 1969. A treatise on the evolution of different forms of socioeconomic organization.

Knight, F. H., *Freedom and Reform*, New York: Harper & Row, 1947.

Knight, F. H., *Economic Organization*, New York: Kelley, 1951.

Musgrave, R. A., *The Theory of Public Finance*, New York: McGraw-Hill, 1958, ch. 6.

Vickery, W., "Utility, Strategy and Social Decision Rules," *Quarterly Journal of Economics*, Vol. 74, No. 4, November 1960, pp. 507–535.

4

EFFICIENCY IN GOVERNMENT SPENDING

Someone once said that the character of a nation is written in its budget. A nation's aspirations for peace or conquest, for the elimination of poverty, for an improvement in its physical environment or cultural life are translated each year into the words and numbers that make up its budget. It is the inevitable necessity to provide the funds which force the issues and requires the choices that reveal a nation's sense of values. As such, the budget is a product of a process which establishes objectives, chooses among programs to achieve those objectives, and allocates resources among those programs. In this sense, it is a plan or a blueprint for guiding the activities of the public household.

A budget serves other functions as well. It serves as a set of contracts delegating authority and specifying responsibility. Without a budget, the various bureaus and agencies of government and others with whom they subcontract must come to a halt. For example, in 1970 many state-related colleges and universities in Pennsylvania were almost faced with the necessity of closing their doors because the state legislature was not able to agree on a state budget until after the end of the fiscal year. Schools found the cost of borrowing against future appropriations increasing rapidly and loans becoming more difficult to secure, for they were, in effect, spending money they were not certain they would be authorized to spend. It is the budget that specifies who can spend which amounts for what purposes and provides a basis for judging accountability.

Furthermore, the budget is also an instrument for managerial control. By displaying the proposed operations of different agencies in a single place, the budget facilitates comparison of the operating efficiencies of units in different agencies which perform the same task. The budget document, when proposed, must be supported with statements of objectives. Are the same objectives shared by more than one program? Then a decision must be made as to which program to accept. Is there reason to believe that the objectives stated can be accomplished with the resources requested? Check the performance of the agency with respect to its previous budgets. Efficiency in execution of tasks, resolution of interagency disputes, and coordination of efforts and assessing reliability of budget estimates are all managerial tasks, which the budget both requires in its making and facilitates by its existence.

When the range of governmental activity was narrow and governmental expenditures small, there was little need to develop budgetary techniques which embodied systematic analyses and formal coordination of departmental activities at the planning stage in the budgetary process. Of more concern were the specifications of administrative control, accountability, and efficiency in program execution that are characterized by such traditional budgetary principles as:

1. Authority should be commensurate with responsibility.
2. Estimates of resource requirements should come from those responsible for seeing the program executed.
3. Measures of work output should be developed to compare the relative operating efficiencies of different agencies and bureaus.

As the scope and magnitude of governmental activity have grown, so have the planning and programming aspects of the budgetary process. The growth of the government sector has created a vast bureaucracy. This has required organizational separation of responsibilities and a division of labor. As a result, the budgetary process has come to serve as the fundamental instrument of communication and coordination within the public household.

The extent to which the government serves the public interest, and is sensitive to changes in public preferences, depends on the nature of the budgetary process. The kinds of information which get channeled through this process, the way in which it is presented, and the people who have access to it will greatly determine the alternatives from which the legislators will finally choose the programs that are to be adopted. In this chapter, we shall discuss the budgeting process and the role economic analysis may play in improving the outcomes of the process.

CHARACTERISTICS OF THE BUDGETARY PROCESS

● Aaron Wildavsky, a perceptive observer of the federal budgetary process, claims that "the largest determining factor of the size and content of this year's budget is last year's budget."[1] The reasons for this are several. First, the variety and complexity of programs are such that it is impossible for any one group to systematically sift through and choose among them, given the constraint of producing a budget each year. To a significant extent, this is true at the departmental level as well as at higher levels. Once a particular program has been budgeted, it is likely to become an accepted part of the budgets in following years. The complexity and size of the budget force those responsible for its review and ultimate form to concentrate on an evaluation of newly proposed programs. Secondly, many old programs carry explicit commitments into the future. Furthermore, once a program is under way, it develops a clientele outside government as well as vested interest groups within the bureaucracy who can muster strong political pressure for its retention. It is politically easier to reject a new program than to drop an old one. In the marketplace, the various actors whose decisions lead to the demise of some products or firms and the rise of others retain their anonymity and are relatively immune from retribution. But budget making is out in the open. This openness encourages attempts to reach a consensus. One way of minimizing political conflicts is to agree to accept "sacred cows." For this reason, last year's budget forms the "base," and the conflict is then narrowed down to each agency trying to get a "fair share" of the increment.

An illuminating documentation of the base-share mode of budget determination is provided by a statistical analysis done by O. Davis, M. Dempster, and A. Wildavsky ("On the Process of Budgeting: An Empirical Study of Congressional Appropriations," *Papers on Nonmarket Decision Making*, Vol. 1, 1966, pp. 63–132). They attempted to account for the actual appropriations made to federal civilian agencies over a period of years as the result of the interaction of simple decision rules for agency budget submittal and legislative committee review. The most simple pair of decision rules they postulated were:

1. Each agency's total budget request was to be chosen in such a way that over time it would simply try to maintain a constant percentage increase in its actual appropriations.

2. The legislative committee saw its role as a watchdog of the purse and applied a simple rule of allowing, on average, only a constant fraction of the request.

Formally, they characterized the agency decision rule as

$$X_t = \beta_0 Y_{t-1} + \xi_t \tag{1}$$

and the committee rule as

$$Y_t = \alpha_1 X_t + \epsilon_t \qquad (2)$$

where X is the requested appropriation; Y is the actual appropriation, β_0 is a constant greater than 1; α_0 is a constant less than 1; and ϵ and ξ are randomly distributed variables with mean values of zero. Substituting Equation (1) into Equation (2), we find that these simple decision rules imply a characterization of the budget process by the equation

$$Y_t = AY_{t-1} + M_t$$

where

$$A = \alpha_1 \beta_0 \quad \text{and} \quad M_t = \xi_t + \epsilon_t$$

That is, these decision rules imply that, except for random variations, this year's agency budget is predicted to be some constant multiple of last year's budget. Such a model would seem to be much too simple to characterize what, on the face of it, seems so complex a process. However, not only did they find that such a model gave a reasonably good account of the actual outcomes, but they also found that for 36 of the 58 agency budget sequences analyzed, this simple model gives a better statistical account of the actual appropriations than one based on more complex decision rules.

A second implication of the complexity of the budget and the political environment within which it takes shape is that its final form is not truly the creation of any single entity. Although the President presents "his budget" to Congress, there is relatively little in it that is truly his. The President is as constrained by the weight of the past and the political alliances which past programs have created as anyone else in the budgeting process. An interesting, typical example was the attempt of President Eisenhower to carry out his 1952 campaign pledge to get government out of businesses which private enterprise could effectively perform. He came into office along with a Republican-controlled Congress also bent on bringing economy into government and shifting activities back to the private sector and/or state and local governments. The Harden Subcommittee of the House Committee on Government Operations, among others, held hearings to provide a forum at which business firms and trade associations could testify as to their ability to handle various tasks better than government-owned operations. Considerable public support was generated. Secretary of Defense Charles Wilson issued several directives calling for the termination of business operations of the Defense Department that could not be justified on grounds of cost savings. At that time, the Defense Department had over $15 billion invested in shipyards, clothing factories, auto repair shops, and some 2500 other business-type facilities.

While the principle of moving government out of businesses was widely endorsed, actual cutbacks generated substantial resistance in Congress as key congressmen felt the potential impact of such cutbacks in their own districts. Accordingly, Congress passed a rider to the 1955 defense appropriations bill, which required the Defense Department to seek the approval of the Appropriations Committees of the House and Senate before the disposal or transfer by contract of any civilian type work now performed by the Defense Department. This rider struck at the heart of the Eisenhower economy drive and was vigorously opposed by the administration. Of course, this piece of legislation was drawn as a rider rather than as a separate bill in order to circumvent the likelihood of a Presidential veto. Eisenhower could not veto the appropriations bill, but did threaten to ignore the rider on the grounds that it represented an unconstitutional interference of the legislature with the prerogatives of the executive branch of government.

Nevertheless, the administration complied with the "letter" of the rider. Prior to the passage of the rider, 171 projects were discontinued. In the first year after its enactment, only 103 facilities, none of significant size, were closed. This was partly a result of Defense Department strategy. As the House Appropriations Committee noted,

> In ten of the cases submitted employment was on a part-time basis. . . . In one case the request indicated that the item was so inconsequential that the Department could not determine the extent of the work. It would appear that this is stretching the intent of the Congress to unreasonable lengths and that in the future similar inconsequential activities need not be submitted.

This strategy led Representative Gerald Ford to remark that his work on the committee reviewing these proposals "was the greatest and most complete waste of time I have ever experienced on that subcommittee." In the end, Congress repealed the rider in 1956. But the principle of congressional overview had been established, and the Defense Department was forewarned of the pressures it would face if it attacked facilities in strategic districts in the name of economy.[2]

The budgetary aims of the President may be subverted within his own administration as well as overridden from without. In the budgetary process, the agencies are supposed to advocate their respective programs to the departments and the Bureau of the Budget. Since the summed total of their requests is likely to exceed what the President wishes to seek and will not necessarily reflect the President's priorities with respect to that portion of the total that represents new or increased expenditures, the Bureau of the Budget has the task of attempting to reconcile, however roughly, the requests submitted by the agencies with the preferences and priorities of the President. Once the executive budget is drawn up and presented to Congress, members of the executive branch are not to challenge it. But, in the conduct of congressional hearings on the budget, the alliances of the various agency personnel with members of Congress inevitably come into play. For example, the frequent hassles that Secretary of Defense McNamara had with congressional committees over such programs as the F111 Navy–Air Force fighter were in part exacerbated by alliances between various groups within the Defense Department and members of Congress.

A third important characteristic of the budgetary process is that congressional committees charged with reviewing budgets tend to focus on particular items of expenditure rather than the programs in which they are imbedded; this is, to a large extent, a consequence of the practice of accepting past budgets as a base. If an agency is asking for increased funds, for, say, more lab technicians, the Appropriations Committee will want to know why *more* technicians are needed, but are not likely to ask if *any* are really needed, if the entire program should be scrapped and resources transferred elsewhere. As a consequence of ignoring the nature of the program in which expenditures are imbedded, the process encourages agencies to hide the possible future commitments implied by a current request. When challenged on a request, the agency can then reply that if this request is not satisfied, then all of the previous expenditures will have been for nought.

PROGRAM BUDGETING

● Historically, the major criticism of the federal budgetary process has focused on the three characteristics described above: It is fragmented, ill designed to focus on the problems of choosing between alternative programs; it is historical and incremental, accepting the past as gospel, discouraging new approaches; it is fundamentally nonprogrammatic, does not force a consideration of future consequences on current choices. As such, it is fundamentally a decision structure for reducing conflict and promoting consensus. Critics of the process believe that, given the magnitudes of government expenditures, the cost of securing political agreement in this way is too high, that it allows too many important decisions to be made in ignorance of their consequences and too many programs to continue to exist when better alternatives for them might be available.

Most governments present their budget in what is known as a line-item or object-accounts format. A comprehensive line-item budget will list the amount in each expenditure category such as salaries, equipment, supplies, and their subclassifications which have been allocated to each administrative unit. As such, it represents a statement of the inputs under the control of each administrator for which he may be held accountable and subject to financial audit. Line-item budgets are essential in this regard. But a line-item budget conceals as much as it reveals, since it does not classify inputs according to specific purposes or activities into which they enter. As a result, individuals higher up the hierarchy have difficulty discovering upon what programs funds were spent in past years and how the various operating agencies and bureaus will spend their funds this year. The line-item budget focuses attention on aggregates rather than programs in the budget review process. As a result, salaries, total expenditures, and other aggregates become objects of higher echelon scrutiny in the budget process, rather than performance which requires a knowledge of outputs as well as inputs. This does not mean that performance is not reviewed, but rather that such review at upper echelons is not an integral part of the budgeting process when the budget is presented only in line-item format.

The principal recommendation for budgetary reform to improve the selection from among the possible alternatives has been the advocacy of the program budget.[3] In one sense, a program budget is simply a document which describes an expenditure program in terms of both its resource requirements and its outputs as they relate to specified objectives. The format of a program budget represents a disaggregation of budget categories from organization units such as Public Health Service and general program categories such as housing, which, in fact, encompass many different programs and objectives. But the intent of introducing program budgets is not simply to have information presented in a different format. Rather, the program budget is conceived as an integral part of *program budgeting.* That is, proponents of the program budget believe that by requiring the budget to be processed in a program format, participants in the budgeting process will be given a different perspective. Looking at the budget differently, participants will, according to the reformers, tend to act differently.

In particular, the aim of the program budget is to facilitate the application of systematic analysis to program decisions. The program budget asks for a well-defined statement of ends as well as means for each proposed project. It asks for an operational specification of the output of projects, for specific criteria by which the success or failure of a program can be judged. In so doing, the program-budgeting format facilitates judgments as to whether or not a program has been successful and tends to supplement judgment based on political feedback. Moreover, by requiring that outputs of similar programs be measured in common terms, it facilitates comparison among proposals. In addition to imposing a format upon the planning process by which the relative merits of similar competing projects are easily compared, program budgeting requires planners to determine just what kinds of programs are similar. For example, if the objective of flood-control projects is specified as controlling floods by building dams, then the only choice to make is from the set of dam sites and designs. In effect, building dams becomes an end in itself. However, if the objective is to reduce flood damage, then dam building is only one of several means by which this objective may be obtained. Systems of dikes, zoning regulations, and relocation of activities are other projects with similar outcomes in that they can also reduce flood damage. Whether or not a dam should be built will then depend upon how well the best dam project compares with other means of flood-damage control. An agency which is familiar with construction projects will have a tendency to opt for a construction solution to flood-damage problems, but a well-designed program-budgeting system should force the consideration of other methods, such as flood zone planning, as well. Program budgeting, therefore, does not constrict judgment to individual agencies, but rather encourages an examination of the competing and complementary character of programs of various agencies.

Program budgeting also encourages multiyear planning. Few major programs are fully implemented in a single year or have impacts that are concentrated in a single year. A full description of a proposed program will, therefore, include the presentation of costs and target dates of attaining objectives for several years ahead. It, therefore, lets decision makers know what they are letting themselves in for with those initial year appropriations.

ECONOMIC ANALYSIS IN THE BUDGETING PROCESS

● The program budget calls for a statement of ends as well as means. In so doing, it implicitly recognizes that budgeting is an allocation process, that in choosing one program or set of programs, it is rejecting another. The program-budgeting format is well adapted to the use of analytical tools in the decision-making process, for it focuses upon the specification of the links between means and ends and seeks a comparison of means to the same ends.

The Translation Problem

There are several strategic decisions that must be made in the translation of a budgeting problem into a framework capable of systematic analysis. The first step is to translate announced policy objectives into specific performance criteria. Consider, for example, the development of plans for utilizing the nation's water resources. The basic objectives of federal water resource policy were agreed upon by several agencies of government involved with water resource activities and stated in Senate Document 97, 87th Congress, 2nd Session entitled, "Policies, Standards and Procedures in the Evaluation of Water Resources." In this document, they stated that water resource projects were to be judged by three criteria. An acceptable project must contribute to the well-being of all of the people; it must contribute to national and regional development; and it must insure the conservation of water resources to be available for best use when needed. As they are stated in the policy document, the criteria by which projects are to be judged are too ambiguous to be incorporated into an evaluation format appropriate for program budgeting. The program budget requires agreement between policy makers and planners as to the appropriate variables to be used in measuring such things as the "development" of a region and the "well-being" of all the people. Is one region more developed if it has a larger population than another, or if its per capita income is higher? Is the "well-being" of all of the people increased if per capita income is increased, or if the distribution of income is made less unequal? Should the present population of a region serve as the basis for measurement or some extrapolation of migration trends? Without operational specification of the output variables, it is not possible to compare different water resource programs in such a way as to make a rational choice among them.

The Simplification Problem

Secondly, in looking at a specific program, the analyst must determine the scope of the program, the kinds of benefits and costs that are to be included in the analysis. In principle, the effects of a program such as the construction of a dam might be spread throughout the entire economy. In practice, it is impossible to assess all of the potential consequences of a proposed program. An important skill of the analyst, therefore, is to simplify his problem by separating out on a priori grounds the important from the inconsequential effects of a proposed program. An investment in water resources for industrial and recreational development in area A will tend to attract additional resources to A from other areas. If A is a relatively depressed area for which the government has a regional development goal, then this secondary impact of the investment program may be an important component, and this type of output should be measured so that the water resource program can be compared with other development proposals. In other cases, these secondary impacts, which raise property values and employment in one area while reducing them in others, are considered on a priori grounds as offsetting one another in social significance so that no estimation of these secondary effects is attempted.

The Valuation Problem

Once the scope of the program has been determined and agreement reached upon the quantitative measures of output and input, one must decide how to value these outputs and inputs. For example, the output of a water-quality improvement program may be measured in terms of increases in the dissolved oxygen level, which has an important bearing upon the varieties of life a body of water may support. Similarly, the output of an educational enrichment program may be measured in terms of improved reading scores on a standardized test. Since society's resources are limited, one is forced to choose between the water-quality improvement program, the educational enrichment program, or other uses to which resources may be put. If the water-quality or education or any other program is to be justified, then its outputs must be worth more to society than the outputs of alternative uses to which the proposed program's inputs might be put. In other words, the analyst must estimate both the value society places on the opportunities which *will be sacrificed* by undertaking a project and the value of the opportunities which society would be *willing to sacrifice* in order to have the project if he is to do a cost-benefit analysis.

The market value of the inputs of a project provides a basis for estimating its cost. The market value of an input is related to its marginal value in the production of all those goods in which it might enter as an input. Consequently, if undertaking of this project requires marginal reductions in the production of other goods, the value of this foregone production will be reflected in the market value of the inputs that are drawn away from these opportunities. If the market value of inputs is to exactly reflect the value of the output that would be lost if those inputs were taken out of their current uses, two conditions must be satisfied. First, the marginal value of a given kind of input must be the same in all uses for the input. Otherwise, the value of lost production caused by diverting an input to public use will depend upon the particular outputs from which the resource is diverted. Secondly, there must be no difference between the value of the input to the producer, who acts as the consumer's agent in bidding for resources, and the value the consumer would place on having that resource enter into production. Otherwise, the market price of the input will not be fully reflective of consumer preferences.

Many circumstances arise that prevent the market prices of inputs from accurately reflecting the social cost of diverting those inputs from their current uses. For example, when there is substantial unemployment, men are not able to get work at the prevailing wage. Therefore, if some who would be otherwise unemployed are used on a government project, the total wage bill will overstate the social cost of the labor utilized. On the other hand, if resources are diverted from the production of monopolized goods, the market value of the resources will understate the value of the lost production. This is because the value of the lost production must exceed the market value of the resources by the amount of the monopoly profits. In a similar way, the presence of excise taxes and subsidies in product markets also implies that the cost to consumers of resources diverted from the private sector is different from the price the government must pay to secure those services in open competition with producers. The reason that taxes create a divergence between market value and social value is that when the government levies an excise tax on a product, the marginal value of the product to consumers will be greater than the marginal value of the product to producers by the amount of the tax. Since the producers purchase the inputs, the market value of the inputs will reflect the value of the output to the producer. But this understates their value to the consumers, who ultimately make the sacrifice. The converse holds true when resources are diverted from a subsidized product. As an extreme case, consider the diversion to public use of agricultural land for which the farmer has been paid to leave untilled. Because the farmer is deriving income from the "land bank" subsidy, the land has a positive market value, which may represent no more than the capitalized value of the stream of subsidy payments the farmer could expect by keeping the land in the "land bank." What private production does society lose if this land is diverted to a public project? Obviously, none. Therefore, although the land may have a market value, the social cost of using it would be zero. Even if the land can be secured for public use only by paying its private owner its market value, this payment should not be counted as a cost to be set against the public project, for it is, in fact, no more than a lump sum payment of the subsidies which the government would have paid if the project were not undertaken.

The existence of varying degrees of monopoly, nonprice rationing, involuntary unemployment, and other manifestations of incomplete market price adjustments, commodity taxes and subsidies, tariffs and differential treatment of various classes of activities guarantees that input prices will not precisely reflect the value of the opportunities which will be sacrificed if inputs are diverted from their current use to some public project. When the source of the distortion is known and its magnitude considered significant for the project under consideration, the analyst may attempt to measure it and substitute a "shadow" price for the market price of the inputs into his project. In practice, however, it is often practically impossible to trace the impact of a given resource withdrawal upon the subsequent composition of output so as to substitute directly calculated values for the market values of the inputs which are used.

The cost of a program represents only one-half of the ledger sheet. Against these costs the analyst must determine what people would be willing to pay for the outputs of the program, that is, the value of the benefits of the program. If an output of a program, such as electricity, is sold on an open market, the market price can be used to measure the benefits. It is, however, the nature of most public projects that their outputs are not marketed. People do not individually purchase the services of a defense system or medical research or improved highways. Indeed, the principal reasons for government purchasing these and other services are either that it is difficult and costly to market the services or that the establishment of such markets in private hands would involve social loss. For this reason, evaluation of the benefits of government programs is often much less straightforward than evaluation of the costs. In some cases, the analyst can utilize market data on related activity to infer what people might be willing to pay for the services of a project or program. For example, in evaluating the benefits of a rural highway-improvement program, one might attempt to estimate their value by calculating the savings in shipping costs on the original volume of traffic plus the value of the increase in farm output net of the expense of increasing the output which could be expected to occur as a result of improved access to markets. (Question: Suppose after making these calculations on the basis of a knowledge of shipping costs and the demand for agricultural products, you also observe that when previous improvements in rural roads had been made, the market value of rural real estate rose. Why should you not add the expected increase in real estate values to the other benefits you have calculated?)

Not all of the benefits of improvements in the rural road will be captured in the impact of the road on costs of marketing agricultural products. The improvements may reduce road hazards and the frequency of injury and death per vehicle mile of use. In part, this benefit may be reflected in reduced insurance costs. But when an individual purchases insurance, he is not purchasing a service which reduces *physical* hazards and their physical consequences. Rather, his insurance purchase represents a purchase of a reduction in the personal *financial* hazards he might face in the event of a physical misfortune. It is, therefore, difficult to judge from market transactions what people might pay for an increase in life expectancy or a decrease in accident rates.[4]

Another component of a road program is represented by its contribution to national defense. The defense capability of a nation depends in part upon its ability to move goods and services without interruption even in the face of bombing attacks. From this point of view, the larger the number of possible routes from one place to another, the better the defensive posture of the nation. How is the analyst to attach a value to these defense services? Here the market gives no clue at all. He must leave this judgment directly to the political process.

The Discount Rate Problem

Many government projects have the character of investments. They produce net benefits (benefits minus costs) over a long period of time. Net benefit streams from different projects or project designs may have very different shapes. The net benefits of one project may exceed the net benefits of another over some intervals and be exceeded by the other over other intervals of time. For example, it is possible to design a highway so as to need only minor repairs for the next 25 years or to design it with a much lower initial cost, but with programmed major resurfacing every 6 to 8 years. Each time resurfacing work is required, traffic flow is interrupted and diverted.

Suppose the more durable roadbed costs $25 million and the less durable roadbed costs $15 million. The less durable road needs to be resurfaced twice at intervals of 8 years. Each time it is resurfaced, the construction plus inconvenience costs are $7 million. What project design should be selected, the more or less durable design? At first glance, it would appear that the more durable design was less expensive ($25 million versus $29 million), but this is not necessarily true. Suppose that one started out with $25 million and built the more durable road. At the end of 25 years, you would have neither money nor usable road left. Suppose, instead, that starting with $25 million you spent $15 million to construct the less durable road and invested the balance ($10 million) at interest. If the interest rate were 10 percent, then at the end of seven and a half years your balance would have grown to $20 million if you had left the interest in to also earn interest.

At the beginning of the eighth year, you draw out $7 million to pay the resurfacing and associated costs, leaving you a balance of $13 million. By the end of the fifteenth year, that $13 million will have grown to $26 million. You again withdraw $7 million for resurfacing costs and are left with $19 million, which by the end of the twenty-fifth year would have grown to almost $38 million. Consequently, at a 10 percent rate of interest, the less durable road is a better investment than a more durable road. On the other hand, if you could not earn any interest on the $10 million difference in initial costs, the more durable design would represent the more profitable investment. At the rate of interest of 4 percent the two designs would be almost equally profitable. Below 3 percent the more durable design is preferable; above 4 percent the less durable design is preferable. The choice of interest rate to represent the rate of return on alternative uses of resources (alternative to the project under consideration) is, therefore, an important element in the decision process. Small changes in the interest rate can radically change the profitability rankings of alternative projects and project designs.

Making a choice from among alternative net benefit streams requires reducing each stream to a single number by some formula for adding benefits produced in different intervals in time. In the example above, we converted the streams to terminal-value equivalents. At 10 percent, the more durable project has zero terminal value, the less durable, approximately $38 million. An analogous method for converting a flow over time to a single number is to express the flow over each interval in terms of its *present-value equivalent.* The present-value equivalent of x dollars available k intervals from the present is defined as that quantity which, if invested in alternative ways, would be worth x dollars at the end of period k. The present value of a whole stream of benefits is then simply the sum over all of the intervals of the present value of net benefits produced in each interval. If the present value of the stream of net benefits producible by a project is negative when discounted by the rate of return on alternative uses of the resources, then the project is not justified since, by devoting the resources to those alternative uses, a net benefit stream can be produced which yields more net benefits in each of the intervals than the project under consideration.

The higher the discount rate, the smaller the present value of a project. Choice of a discount rate, therefore, represents a third important component of program analyses. If the discount rate is appropriately chosen, it will be equal to the rate of return necessary to compensate individuals for not having resources available for immediate consumption or investment. Unfortunately, it is much easier to state this criterion than to decide how to estimate the opportunity cost of diverting capital from private to public uses. The economist's usual technique for measuring costs is to refer to the marketplace. But when he turns to the capital market, he observes not just one rate of interest, but a whole spectrum of interest rates. The question, therefore, arises as to how to use the capital market information to estimate the social opportunity cost of capital.

Krutilla and Eckstein argue that since different individuals face different interest rates, the opportunity cost of the marginal tax dollar depends upon whom the tax is levied.[5] This point of view leads them to compute the opportunity cost of the marginal tax dollar as a weighted average of market rates. The weights are determined by the distribution of the burden of the tax.

Hirshleifer has criticized this procedure on the basis that it includes an unknown risk premium, which will not necessarily bear any resemblance to the risk premium appropriate to any given public project.[6] This results from the fact that a contract to lend also implicitly includes some sharing of the risk. Therefore, the price that private borrowers pay for capital is composed of two elements. First, it incorporates a charge for foregone current consumption on the part of the lender—this is a pure interest premium. Secondly, it incorporates a charge for subjecting the lender's assets to risk—this is a pure risk premium. If the capital market is competitive, the pure interest premium can be expected to be the same for each borrower, while the risk premium will vary according to the risk class of the borrower. Since the expected yield on a private investment must cover both the pure interest and "insurance premium" charge to cover the risk the lender faces, the Krutilla–Eckstein measure would equal the sum of a pure rate of interest plus a weighted average risk premium. But, if there is no correspondence between the social cost of insuring against the risk entailed in a given public project and a weighted average of risk premiums charged for private projects, then there is no logical relationship between a weighted average of market rates of interest and the opportunity cost of public investment.

Instead of the Krutilla–Eckstein approach, Hirshleifer recommends measuring the cost of capital for a particular government project by the marginal expected rate of return on private investments, which are similar to the government project in terms of riskiness. Hirshleifer's criterion may be useful for projects in the water resource field in which he was writing, but does not seem generally operational. How do the risks associated with different configurations of nuclear defense and attack compare with private projects? Moreover, it ignores the fact that the risk premium required to finance a given private project depends upon who is going to undertake the project. The larger the number of people sharing in the risk of a given project, the smaller the risk held by any one person and the smaller the summed total of risk premiums that will be demanded. When government finances a project, it inevitably spreads the risks among all taxpayers, since they are all liable for the government debt. Since the government has superior risk-spreading ability, it is not clear that government-financed projects should be subject to the same risk premium as privately financed projects with the same objective risks of variation in total payoff.[7]

In estimating the pure interest component of the opportunity cost of public investment, one can utilize the rate of return government bonds yield to their purchasers. If individuals are willing to lend the government resources at the going rate on government bonds, then this must be a sufficient rate to compensate them for their *foregone current consumption*. However, because of the corporate income tax, the government bond yield is *not* an appropriate measure of the social cost of diverting funds from *private investment opportunities*. The existence of the corporate income tax forces private investors to seek investments whose yield *after tax* is at least equal to the government bond rate; otherwise everyone would buy government bonds, and no one would lend to private borrowers. Diverting resources from private to public investment not only reduces the flow of returns to stockholders, but also reduces the tax flow to the government.

If those tax receipts do not come from the corporate income tax, then they must come from some other private source. Use of the government bond rate will, therefore, lead to an underestimate of the value of private opportunities foregone to the extent that resources are diverted from private investment uses. Because the corporate income tax impedes the transfer of resources from private consumption to private investment opportunities and prevents the marginal rate of return from every activity from being brought into equality with one another, the actual cost of deferred private resource use will depend upon the extent to which different kinds of private activities will be affected by the diversion of resources into the government sector.

There are at least two schools of thought which argue that current market rates *ought not* to be used as sources of information about the social opportunity cost of increased public investment. One school (the Conservationists) argue that when individuals make decisions regarding the future, they discount future benefits simply because they are in the future (that is, independently of and in addition to discounting by the rate of interest that prevails). In other words, they assume people are myopic. Such moral axioms as "Never put off until tomorrow what you can do today" are presumably reflections of the fact that people erroneously assume that an onerous task will be less onerous if done tomorrow rather than today. But if people are myopic, then they will tend to undersave or overconsume. Future generations will be left with a smaller stock of resources than if people did not discount the future simply because it was future. In effect, the desires of future generations receive less weight in the present allocation of resources between consumption and investment than do the desires of the present generation. According to the conservationists' view, this is unethical. It is, therefore, their recommendation that the government act as the representative of all of the people, including the generations yet unborn, and adopt as a measure of the opportunity cost of capital a measure which is free from the pure time preference discount embedded in the market rate.

The second school of thought (the Compassionists) rests its argument for ignoring the market on a very different political philosophy. The Compassionists assume that in a democracy, government should be responsive only to those who actually *vote*. The Compassionists assert that each individual's level of satisfaction is dependent upon the level of consumption of the other people, both currently living and in the future. However, the market does not reflect this interdependency. Therefore, if the aggregate level of savings were determined by a political process in which this interdependence could be expressed, it might be very different from the simple sum of individually determined savings which governs the market rate.

Since it is not possible to estimate the degree of pure time preference discounting embedded in the market rate, the practical import of both of these views is to make the choice of discount rate a political rather than a market-determined decision.[8]

Do Market Prices Provide the Appropriate Information?

The foregoing discussion of the uses to which market information may be put in evaluating the costs and benefits of public programs implicitly assumed that what people reveal they are willing to pay in the market for goods and services should have social and political significance. This assumption may be challenged on two grounds. First, market prices reflect the existing distribution of income. Since the government's programs are financed out of taxes rather than by sales to program consumers, the distribution of the benefits may be quite different from the distribution of the costs. The benefits may accrue disproportionately to the rich, and the cost fall disproportionately on the poor. The use of market prices masks these distributional aspects of a program and implicitly represents a judgment that they are not socially significant.[9] But this amounts to asserting that for the purposes of one's analysis, the existing distribution of income is to be considered socially acceptable. Those persons who look to government to change the distribution of income consider this position ethically untenable.

A second criticism of using market prices to evaluate benefits and costs is a more pragmatic one. The legislators for whom the program analysis is being prepared do not calculate costs and benefits in terms of dollars, but in terms of votes. What they seek is a politically attractive set of programs. In putting together a legislative package which is passable, it may be necessary to include programs that could not be "justified" if evaluated at market prices, but have distributional consequences which are poltically favorable. An analysis that fails to highlight these distributional aspects may not be very useful to the legislators who must reach some consensus; an analysis which casts a program that legislators want desperately in a bad light because of its low benefit-cost ratio may be viewed as a positively disruptive force in the process of legislation.

In reply to such criticism, the analyst may respond that the impact of any one program on the distribution of wealth is likely to be small. Furthermore, the legislators need not assess a program's worth solely on the basis of a benefit-cost ratio. They are entitled to consider distributional consequences and accept programs which would fail a benefit-cost test when evaluated at market prices. But they are entitled to know what it would cost to use a particular program for redistributive purposes.

PROGRAM BUDGETING AND THE BUREAUCRACY

● If program budgeting and systems analysis are to be done effectively, the bureaucrats in the lower echelons of government who have day-to-day responsibility for the operation of specific programs must have some self-interest in the application of these techniques. Higher echelons must look to the line officers or heads of bureaus for detailed cost information and must rely upon line officers' practical knowledge for the formulation of alternative programs of action. Without the cooperation of heads of bureaus, program budgeting will have little or no impact upon the shape of the budget.

A bureaucrat, like the rest of us, may be motivated by many things such as salary, public reputation, power, and the support of his subordinates. The most obvious and direct way for him to secure increases in these rewards from work is to win increases in the size of his bureau's budget. Increasing budgets not only increases power, but also makes the tasks of management easier. A growing bureau provides opportunities for advancement. It attracts and retains able and imaginative personnel. It affords room to maneuver and experiment. On the other hand, a bureaucrat can continue to get budget increases only if he demonstrates a sense of responsibility. He must offer programs that are acceptable to his bureau's sponsor and must demonstrate that he can deliver what he promises. We may, therefore, characterize the bureaucrat as an individual who wishes to maximize the size of his bureau's budget subject to the constraint that his budget be large enough to finance the cost of the programs to which his sponsor has agreed.

We may expect cost-benefit analyses and program budgeting to be enthusiastically welcomed by a bureaucrat if, and only if, its introduction increases the size of his budget. Since it is unlikely that all bureaus would find their budgets increased as the result of budgetary reform, we should expect at least some bureaus to be quite uncooperative. Of course, some bureaus will find that the size of their budgets is effectively constrained by the cost of producing the outputs that they have promised. Sponsors would be willing to expand their allotments if the bureau could deliver additional output. But the bureau finds that, using its current methods of production, the increment that the sponsor would grant would be insufficient to cover the cost of the additional output. Such bureaus will be interested in cost-effectiveness studies, since they can only increase the size of their budgets by reducing the marginal cost of their activities. Other bureaus may perceive an unwillingness of their sponsors to push for a larger budget even if they effectively reduce costs on existing programs. It is doubtful, for example, that a peacetime army could get larger budget appropriations simply by lowering costs through better organization of existing activities. We should expect its major program emphasis, therefore, to be on divising new military strategems using different, more expensive techniques rather than emphasizing a more cost-effective method of executing its current strategies. Until recently, one suspects that educational bureaucrats perceived their budget opportunities in the same way. The size of the budget was not constrained by the cost of producing their product. Cost reductions brought no increase in budgets; therefore, there was no incentive to seek out more cost-effective techniques and every incentive to expand the scope of services offered. Since bureaus that do not find the size of their budget constrained by cost considerations are likely to have considerable "fat" padded in their cost estimates, we can expect them to resist efforts to bring their programs under closer scrutiny and more thorough review.

Even many bureaus whose budgets are effectively cost-constrained may oppose program budgeting. For while cost-effectiveness studies may reduce their costs, an analysis of their program benefits may reduce the budget amounts their sponsors can successfully get the legislature to approve.

In the absence of an analysis of the benefits of a program, the bureaucrat need only convince the bureau's sponsors in the executive and legislative branches of government that the bureau's programs are valuable to the sponsors' constituencies. The sponsor may place a higher value on the output of the bureau than the median value placed upon it by the population as a whole. (Consider the membership of the Armed Services Committee and the location of military installations.) Therefore, a program which would fail a cost-benefit test when all costs and benefits were weighed might appear quite attractive to the sponsor. For this reason, a bureau would attempt to avoid measuring both costs and benefits, or, if forced to make such measurements, would produce misleading information.[10]

PROGRAM BUDGETING IN A POLITICAL CONTEXT

● The budget is the product of a political process. Changing the way budgets are conceived must inevitably impinge upon the distribution of political power among the various participants in the budgeting process. The implementation of a program-budgeting system may call into question the current administrative structure of government, because the system invites a comparison of programs with similar objectives. There may be pressures to reorganize activities, regrouping them according to functional purposes as defined by their statements of objectives. Secondly, program budgeting seems conducive to centralization of decision making, to shifting effective decision-making power from operating units to department heads and other staff personnel. The principal gain from this move is to achieve greater coordination of effort, less duplication, and a greater sensitivity to the interrelatedness of efforts. For example, a centralized defense decision apparatus would recognize that the worth of additional sea-based aircraft depended upon the number of land-based aircraft in the budget. Operating separately, and without a well-articulated statement of objectives, the budget proposals and the ultimate budgets of the air force and the navy might never reflect this interdependence. Such gains are not necessarily achieved costlessly, however. When decision-making power is shifted from lower to higher echelons, some incentives to the operating units to search for new alternatives may be diminished as they may not be able to capitalize on their efforts. Centralization reduces competition and the incentives to innovate and diversify that competition entails. Centralization may also further shift political power from the Congress to the President as the budget will more nearly become the "President's budget." There is a danger here of a reduced responsiveness of the budget to questions of equity and to a change in priorities. A nation may not wish to give too much power to any one man or element of government. Because of these political aspects to program budgeting, the debate over its introduction into the budgeting process has been, and is likely to continue to be, a most interesting one.

APPENDIX:
PROGRAM BUDGETING

● In this chapter we have dealt with budgeting at a rather abstract level. One may get a greater appreciation for the intent and content of program budgeting by listening to or reading testimony of witnesses at budget hearings. For this reason, we have appended to this chapter a statement given in behalf of a concerned citizen's group at a school budget hearing in Pittsburgh, Pennsylvania.

EAST END EDUCATION COMMITTEE – TESTIMONY
1970 Budget Hearing
November 13, 1969

I appear as a representative of the East End Education Committee, a group which favors the expenditure of tax dollars for public education. We also share your concern about the difficulty of obtaining sufficient dollars to do this well in a large city where educational needs are great at the same time that other municipal expenditures are rising and the tax base is shrinking. We know that long-range solutions lie in political changes which you and I have no immediate power to effect.

Recognizing all of this, we would like to make a number of comments about the budget and ask some questions.

We would like to point out that State Code 664 has been violated. Citizens received the budget on Tuesday. The State Code requires five days prior to the hearing, and even that is not sufficient time.

1. We appreciate the detailed line items presented but feel no sense of direction. From where have we come and where are we going? Is this a holding action until more federal and state funds are available or is it part of a five-year plan for improving this school system? What were last year's budgetary goals? Were they achieved?

Obviously you cannot meet all of the needs, not even all of the most pressing ones at this time. Which programs are receiving priority? Which programs have been so successful that you are expanding them? Or would if you had the money? Which programs are of dubious success? What is happening in the schools where children are achieving poorly? What is happening in schools where classes are too large? What about team teaching and ungraded schools and the Oakleaf experiment?

We want the Budget to answer these kinds of questions for us so that we can see where we're going, what our money is being spent for, where the biggest gaps and gains are, and so on.

Could you not introduce the budget with some text which might say, for example: These are our five most pressing problems; last year we were able to allocate funds to begin to tackle Problems 1 and 2 with the following results (or it's too early to see results); this year we can continue on Problems 1 and 2 and begin to tackle Problems 3 and 4 with the following programs; there is no money to even begin to handle Problem 5 this year, and so forth. You see our point.

2. We have a question to ask about the surplus of nearly $3 million which was desperately needed in many of the city's schools last year. Why was there no contingency plan for a surplus? Do you have contingency plans to use such a surplus if it develops in 1970?

3. And on the other hand, you are counting on $2½ million from passage of HB 717. What are the items that will be cut if this Democratic bill does not pass the Republican Senate? They should be itemized now.

4. We know that this Board is concerned with basic changes in the revenue structure that will offer significant increases of money to Pittsburgh's public schools. The budget should indicate at least the directions for longer-range solutions to Pittsburgh's fiscal problems in education. What are your plans for obtaining increases and different kinds of federal and state aid?

5. Frank Hawkins in the *Post Gazette* last summer quoted some figures for expenditures per pupil in different schools, for example, $813 in Fifth Avenue High School as compared with $510 at Taylor Alderdice. He got the figures from the *School News*. If I were a new member of the School Board, I would want to know how these figures correlate with achievement levels at the respective schools! I would want to know how much of the difference in expenditure is not bringing results. I would want to know whether the resources allocated with the additional money are relevant to the problems. Are the funds for security guards when psychologists and counselors are needed? Are they for reducing class size from perhaps 32 to 28 when a combination of larger class sizes and individual instruction might be preferable?

6. Like the new members of the Board, we received this budget just a few days ago and were, therefore, not able to study it as thoroughly as we would have liked to. We would like to have totaled the number of instructional staff and compare that figure to the number of supportive positions such as 21 employees in purchasing, 24 in

accounting, 17 on the staff of the Associate Superintendent for Personnel. These may be very reasonable numbers, but the new School Board members would want to know more about allocation and priorities, and we do want to know as citizens. Why are there 10 employees and expenditures of $½ million in physical education at the administrative or nonteaching level as compared to 4 employees and expenditures of $115,000 in art, for example (you could select music or math)? Does this tell us anything about priorities in the Pittsburgh Public Schools?

7. In order to have a complete picture, we would like to know how much in federal funds was received and how it was spent. If that cannot be incorporated into this budget because of state accounting regulations, it should certainly be appended to it. Do federal and state poverty funds go into the General Budget? How much was received? Where and how were they spent?

8. We see a 50 percent increase in expenditure for employment of security police since 1969 (more than 1000 percent since 1968), a short-range and possibly necessary measure to control the crisis in the high schools. The text of the budget does not tell me how much is being spent or what programs are being initiated toward long-range solution of this problem and phasing out of the police. At this rate we'll be spending $1,000,000 for police shortly.

Again we repeat none of these remarks indicate opposition to the size of the budget, but a desire to have the budget give vital information about goals, long- and short-range emphasis or direction, evaluation of programs, and possibilities of solving the fiscal crisis. Overall, without feeling sufficiently well informed because of the time restraints and the nature of the budget, we get the impression of insufficient allocation for curriculum changes, program development, and special student needs such as learning disabilities, physical, mental, and psychological handicaps. This perhaps points to a top-heavy administrative structure.

Notes

1. A. Wildavsky, *The Politics of the Budgetary Process*, Boston: Little, Brown, 1964, p. 13.
2. A full account of the history of the defense appropriations rider can be found in Edith T. Carper, *The Defense Appropriations Rider*, The Inter-University Case Program #59, Indianapolis: Bobbs-Merrill Company, 1960.
3. The call for program budgeting at the federal level goes back as far as the 1911 Taft Commission on Economy and Efficiency.
4. Markets do provide some clues in some cases. Different occupations are subject to different accident rates, and individuals living in different areas experience different mortality rates. But many factors influence the occupational and geographical distributions of the population so that the extent

of income differences that could be attributed to differences in physical hazards is most difficult to determine. Similarly, insurance companies which offer liability policies must estimate what the typical jury will award for "pain and suffering" in liability claims. Hence, liability insurance rates must reflect some social (that is, jury estimates) value attached to pain and suffering. H. Klarman ("Syphilis Control Programs," in R. Dorfman, ed., *Measuring Benefits of Government Investments*, Washington, D.C.: Brookings Institution, 1965, pp. 367–410) uses expenditures made on terminal cancer patients with no chance of recovery as an estimate of what people are willing to pay to avoid pain and suffering. A difficulty with this method is that such expenditures are most often paid through insurance for which the premiums are not based solely upon the incidence of such expenditures. For a further discussion of the problems in evaluating the benefits from reduced morbidity and mortality rates, see E. J. Mishan, *Cost-Benefit Analysis: An Introduction*, New York: Praeger, 1971, chs. 22–24.

5. O. Eckstein and J. Krutilla, *Multiple Purpose River Development*, Baltimore: Johns Hopkins Press, 1958.

6. J. Hirshleifer, J. De Haven, and J. Milliman, *Water Supply: Economics, Technology and Policy*, Chicago: University of Chicago Press, 1960, ch. 6.

7. For a further discussion of this point, see K. Arrow and R. Lind, "Uncertainty and the Evaluation of Public Investment Decisions," *American Economic Review*, June 1970, pp. 364–378.

8. The Conservationists' view is represented by Pigou. See A. C. Pigou, *Economics of Welfare*, London: Macmillan, 1920. The interdependence argument is well stated by Marglin. See S. Marglin, "The Social Rate of Discount and the Optimal Rate of Investment," *Quarterly Journal of Economics*, February 1963, pp. 95–112. Baumol provides a useful discussion of many issues raised in the preceding pages. See W. Baumol, "On the Social Rate of Discount," *American Economic Review*, September 1968, pp. 788–802.

9. The rule of accepting a project whenever the market value of its benefits exceed the market value of its costs is known as the *compensation principle*. We discuss this principle more fully in Chapter 10.

10. For an elaboration of the view of bureaucratic behavior presented in this section, see W. Niskanen, Jr., *Bureaucracy and Representative Government*, Chicago: Aldine, 1971.

11. This problem is discussed in Stephen Enke, "Using Costs to Select Weapons," *American Economic Review, Papers and Proceedings* (LV), May 1965, pp. 416–426.

Questions for Discussion

1. Suppose that you were manager of a city water supply system which, until you took office, supplied water free of charge. Faced with a growing popu-

lation, you find that the demand for water at a zero price will outstrip the supply from existent facilities within three years. It will take three years to build new facilities. On the other hand, experience in other cities of similar size indicates that a 5 cent a gallon charge on water use reduces water demand by 5 million gallons per year. What other information would you require, and how would you use it to determine if it would be better to build a new facility or to cut down demand by charging a price for using the water?

2. Suppose that as director of the budget, you had decided to install a program-budgeting system into your organization and had therefore asked each of the department heads to "specify their objectives" when submitting new budget proposals.

    a. Would you feel that your directions had been followed if each department submitted a statement of definite targets to be achieved (for example, "build 150,000 low-income dwelling units next year) or a list of the kinds of desirable outcomes they hope their programs might have (for example, the objective of this program is to reduce unemployment)?

    b. What information might you supply each department head for his use in designing his budget proposal in order to make better decisions about allocating funds among the various departments?

3. Suppose that the total volume of government spending were determined prior to any decisions about which projects the government would finance. In this case, of what relevance, if any, would the social rate of return on private investments be in determining the projects to be undertaken by the government?

4. a. Suppose you were an employee of the Atomic Energy Commission, an agency charged with managing the nation's stockpile of fissionable materials. You are asked to design a bomb for use on strategic missions. What criterion or criteria would you use in choosing the fissionable materials content of each bomb?

    b. Suppose you were an employee of the air force. You are asked to design a system to deliver bombs to some strategic target. What criterion or criteria would you use to choose among alternative delivery systems?

    c. Suppose you were in charge of both designing the bombs and the delivery systems. How might this alter your perspective as to the choice of criteria and subsequent analysis of the problem of choice?[11]

5. *The role of financing in a cost-benefit analysis.* The benefits produced by a facility depend upon how extensively it is used. One factor determining use is the method by which the facility is financed. As a concrete illustration, consider the benefits to be derived from opening an improved road into the interior of an agricultural region (see Figure 4.1).

All produce is delivered to a port at point P in the above figure and is sold in the international market at $\$K$ per ton. The world market is so large relative to the potential output of the agricultural region to the east of the seacoast that any increase in tonnage shipped through P will have no impact on the world price. For simplicity, we assume that traffic can only

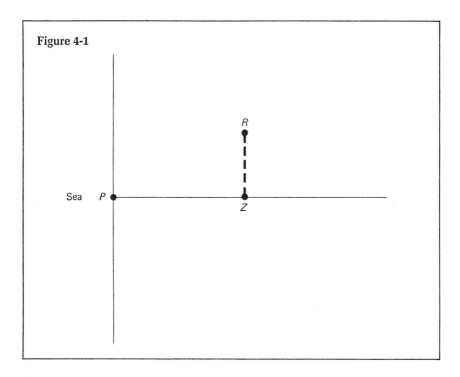

Figure 4-1

move in the vertical and horizontal directions. For example, to get to P from R produce must first move from R to Z and then from Z to P. Prior to any road improvement, it cost farmers $A per ton mile to move their produce to market.

Suppose an improved road is built due east of the port, P. In the absence of any charge for using the road, it will cost farmers $B per ton mile to move goods along the road $(B > A)$. Assume that one ton of produce can be produced per square mile of cultivated land. What is the maximum benefits that can be derived from the road improvement?

Two possible means of financing the road are being considered: a gasoline tax and a port tax. A gasoline tax is equivalent to a tax per ton mile. A port tax is equivalent to a tax per ton shipped into port. In raising a given amount of revenue, which tax will induce the least reduction in potential benefits from use of the road?

Hint: The benefits from the road are derived from extending the area under cultivation. The area under cultivation is bounded by the set of points at which the cost per ton of produce produced is just equal to the market price less taxes and the cost of delivery to port.

This problem is extensively discussed by A. A. Walters, The Economics of Road User Charges, World Bank Staff Occasional Papers #5, 1968, ch. 5.

Suggested Readings

Braybrocke, D., and Lindblom, C. E., *A Strategy of Decision Policy Evaluation as a Social Process*, New York: Macmillan, 1963, rev. ed., New York: Free Press, 1970.

Burkhead, J., *Government Budgeting*, New York: Wiley, 1956.

Dorfman, R., ed., *Measuring Benefits of Government Investments*, Washington, D.C.: Brookings Institution, 1965.
Applications of cost-benefit analysis in several areas.

Hinrichs, H., and Taylor, G., eds., *Program Budgeting and Cost-Benefit Analysis*, Pacific Palisades, Calif.: Goodyear, 1969.
A case study text on program budgeting.

McKean, Roland, *Efficiency in Government Through Systems Analysis*, New York: Wiley, 1958.

McKean, Roland, *Public Spending*, New York: McGraw-Hill, 1968, chs. 2, 6, 7, 8.

Novick, D., ed., *Program Budgeting: Program Analysis and the Federal Budget*, Washington, D.C.: U.S. Government Printing Office, 1965.
A series of Rand studies on the applicability of program budgeting in civilian agencies.

Prest, A., and Turvey, R., "Cost-Benefit Analysis: A Survey," *Economic Journal*, Vol. 75, No. 306, December 1965, pp. 683–735.

Schultze, C. L., *The Politics and Economics of Public Spending*, Washington, D.C.: Brookings Institution, 1968.
A former director of the Bureau of the Budget discusses the problems and virtues of bringing analysis to bear on budgetary decisions.

Smithies, A., *The Budgetary Process in the United States*, New York: McGraw-Hill, 1955.

Subcommittee on Economy in Government, Joint Economic Committee, Congress of the United States, *Analysis and Evaluation of Public Expenditures: The PPB System*, a compendium of papers, 3 vols. Washington, D.C.: U.S. Government Printing Office, 1969.
The most comprehensive collection of papers on the theoretical and practical aspects of program-budgeting extant.

Wildavsky, A., *The Politics of the Budgetary Process*, Boston: Little, Brown, 1964.

5

PRINCIPLES OF TAXATION

In Chapter 1 we identified four roles that government can play in the economy. It can act as society's agent in securing resources for use as public goods. It can act as magistrate, determining who has claims to the output of the economy. It can control individual behavior, and it can act to regulate aggregate demand. Taxes are the principal instruments which governments use in performing these functions. Taxes represent the principal source of revenue to finance the purchase of public goods and services. The tax structure, combined with transfer payments such as public assistance, and the kinds of goods and services that are publicly provided constitute a principal means of redistributing wealth. Taxes and subsidies can be used to induce individuals to change the pattern of their activities. Taxes on alcoholic beverages tend to reduce their consumption; subsidies to the merchant marine tend to insure a larger domestic fleet, and so on. Changes in taxes, by changing private disposable incomes, tend to change total private expenditure.

Since taxation is so central to government activity, whether or not that activity improves the general welfare will depend upon whether or not the government has a "good" tax system. Much of the nineteenth-century writings on public finance centered upon proposing maxims to which a "good" tax system should conform. These writers also sought ways by which a tax system might be designed to conform to such maxims. For the most part, their maxims or principles can be classified into three groups: principles of equity, the principle of voluntary contract, and the principle of maximum aggregate utility. Because they have played an important role in the evolution of public finance, in this chapter we shall discuss each of these principles and the problems of evaluating tax systems in terms of them.

EQUITY IN FINANCING PUBLIC EXPENDITURES

● It is universally agreed that each individual ought to contribute his "fair share" toward the purchase of public goods, whose benefits are commonly shared. But what does fairness require? Pigou sets as a criterion of equity that "different persons should be treated similarly unless they are dissimilar in some relevant respect." This is sometimes translated as "equals should be treated equally" (horizontal equity) and "unequals, unequally" (vertical equity). As ethical statements, these seem unexceptional. But they provide little guidance in deciding how to finance public expenditures fairly, since they do not indicate how one can tell whether two individuals are equal or unequal. For this reason, the basic area of disagreement among various writers on tax equity is in defining the basis upon which one could decide if two persons were or were not similar in all relevant respects.

For example, Adam Smith's first maxim on taxation states:

> The subjects of every state ought to contribute toward the support of the government, as nearly as possible, in proportion to their respective abilities; that is, in proportion to the revenue which they respectively enjoy under the protection of the state. . . . In the observation or neglect of this maxim consists what is called the equality or inequality of taxation.[1]

This maxim seems to imply that taxes to pay for public goods ought to be assessed upon an individual in proportion to the benefits that individual derives from those commonly provided goods. This *benefit principle* remains a widely held principle of fairness, which arises in many contemporary popular discussions of taxation. This is especially true in discussions of metropolitan finance in areas that do not have a metropolitan government. Central cities complain of the burden placed on them by suburbanites who use city facilities in their work and recreational activities, but allegedly do not pay taxes to support these facilities. We use the word "allegedly" because the value of commercial property in the central city depends, in part, upon the attractiveness of such locations to shoppers and workers from the suburbs. Since such properties form a significant part of any city's tax base, it is not clear that central city governments do not collect in increased real estate taxes at least as much as the value of services they provide to suburbanites to induce them to shop and work in the city. In fact, an important argument for taxes on land at the local level is that much of the value of land is derived from the value of local public services provided in the area.

The benefit principle has rarely been accepted as the sole criterion of fairness, however. For example, John Stuart Mill argued that application of the benefit principle to the support of government, in general, would imply that the poor ought to pay more than the rich since, in the absence of government, the poor would need infinitely more protection. But asking the poor to pay more than the rich seems patently unfair. In Mill's view,

> Government must be regarded as so preeminently a concern of all, that to determine who are most interested in it is of no real importance. If a person or class of persons receive so small a share of the benefit as makes it necessary to raise the question, there is something else than taxation which is amiss, and the thing to be done is to remedy the defect instead of recognizing it and making it a grounds for demanding less taxes. As, in a case of voluntary subscription for a purpose in which all are interested, all are thought to have done their part fairly *when each has contributed according to his means, that is, has made an equal sacrifice for the common object, . . .* it is superfluous to look for a more ingenious or recondite ground to rest the principle upon.[2]

Mill conceived of the ability to pay in terms of its psychological dimensions. According to this view, a rich man should pay more taxes than a poor man not simply because his objective ability was greater but, more fundamentally, because a given absolute loss in income would represent a smaller psychological loss to the rich than to the poor man. From this utilitarian point of view, equity demanded equality of sacrifice in its psychological dimensions.

The Meaning of Equal Sacrifice in Terms of Tax Rates

The notions (1) that equity requires equal sacrifice from all individuals for the common good and (2) that equality of sacrifice requires taking more tax dollars from a rich man than from a poor man are logically separable. Statement (1) is an ethical judgment, while statement (2) is an assertion of fact. Statement (2) rests upon the assumption that income is subject to diminishing marginal utility and that utility is commensurable among individuals. As we noted in Chapter 1, this is a widely held belief, but no one has yet provided conclusive evidence that it is true. Nevertheless, in popular discussions of tax reform, it is often asserted not only that equality of sacrifice requires taking more tax dollars from a rich man than from a poor man, but also that equality of sacrifice requires taking a *greater proportion* of the rich man's income in taxes than of the poor man's income. In other words, it is often asserted that a progressive tax rate structure is fair, while a regressive structure is unfair. In spite of this widespread belief, it is easy to demonstrate that equality of sacrifice does not necessarily require a progressive tax rate structure. (See Figures 5.1 and 5.2.) Suppose, for

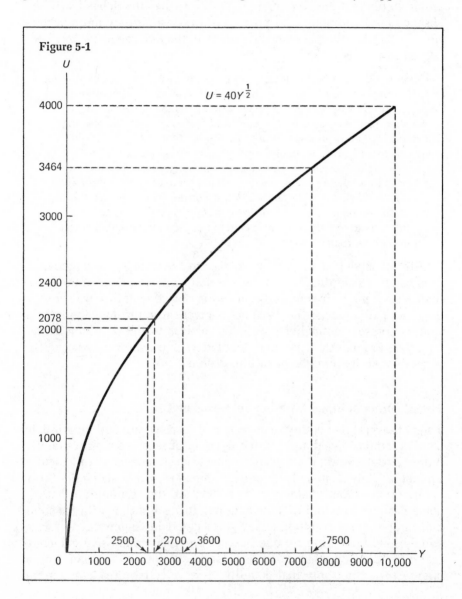

Figure 5-1

$U = 40Y^{\frac{1}{2}}$

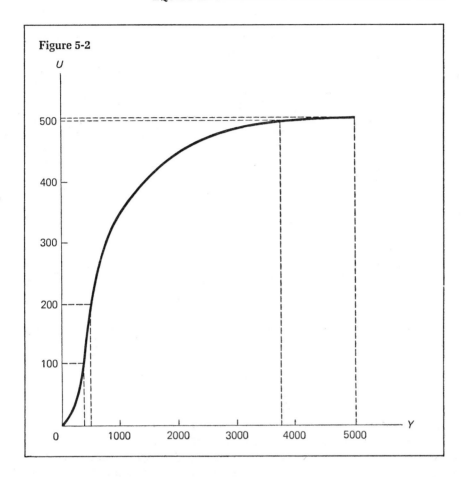

Figure 5-2

example, that utility were related to income by the relation $U(Y) = 40Y^{1/2}$. Since utility increases with the square root of income, doubling income will raise utility by a factor of only $2^{1/2}$. Therefore, the relation assumes diminishing marginal utility of income. Suppose now that we compare the utility sacrifices of a 25 percent tax on incomes of $3,600 and $10,000, respectively. The utility of $3,600 is 2,400 "utils," while the utility of $2,700 (75 percent of $3,600) is only 2,078 "utils." The 25 percent tax, therefore, takes 322 "utils" away from the man whose pretax income is $3,600. On the other hand, the utility of $10,000 is 4,000 "utils," while the utility of $7,500 (75 percent of $10,000) is approximately 3,464 "utils." The rich man, therefore, sacrifices about 214 more "utils" than the poor man when taxed at the same 25 percent rate. Therefore, if by equal sacrifice we mean sacrificing the same number of "utils," we would in this case have to impose a regressive tax rate structure, imposing a lower rate of tax on the rich than on the poor. Suppose, however, that the marginal utility of income diminished much more rapidly, as in the relation graphed in Figure 5.2. Then, as Figure 5.2 shows, a 25 percent tax on $500 would produce a greater loss in utility than a 25 percent tax on $5,000. Evidently, justifying a progressive tax rate structure on grounds that equality of sacrifice requires it assumes a much more detailed knowledge of the way individuals' satisfactions vary with income than we, in fact, possess. Therefore, assertions of the fairness of progressive tax rate structures seem to be more firmly rooted in a preference for an equal *distribution of income* than in equality of sacrifice in payment for public goods.

The Implementation of the Ability to Pay Principle

There are several problems that arise when one attempts to determine whether two individuals have the same ability to pay taxes. One problem arises out of the distinction between income and wealth. We illustrate the problem by the following example.

Suppose two men each own annuities, which will pay them $10,000 per year until death. Suppose further that one man has an expected remaining life of 20 years and the other of 30 years. As long as they are both living, they will have the same income, but the second expects to receive that income for a longer period of time so that he is definitely wealthier than the first. Does he, on that account, have a greater ability to pay taxes? The answer depends upon whether you use income or wealth as an index of ability. In making a choice between income and wealth as the tax basis, one is implicitly deciding whether difference in expected remaining life is an ethically relevant or irrelevant difference between two people. This is because the individual who has the longer life expectancy could sell his annuity and with the proceeds buy a 20-year annuity which would give him an annual income in excess of $10,000 for 20 years.[3] Of course, at the end of 20 years, he would receive no further income.

A second problem is the definition of the tax-paying unit. Suppose one man's income is one-half another's. But the first man is a bachelor living in moderate luxury, while the second has a family so large that he can barely provide them food and shelter. Is the difference in family size relevant or not? In most countries, the income tax structure allows exemptions depending on the size of family. But such exemptions are not administratively feasible for most taxes.

A third problem lies in the definition of income itself. As Hicks puts it:

> The purpose of income calculations in practical affairs is to give
> people an indication of the amount they can consume without

impoverishing themselves. Following out this idea, it would seem that we ought to define a man's income as the maximum value he can consume during a week, and still expect to be as well-off at the end of the week as he was at the beginning.[4]

Suppose now that two men have the same annual receipts of money from the sale of their services, but that one is paid every week and the other is paid once a year. Do they have the same income? Clearly not, on the basis of Hicks's definition. For the second individual must borrow throughout the year against his year-end payment in order to maintain a constant weekly rate of consumption. But since he must pay interest on the borrowed amount, his sustainable weekly consumption rate must be less than the individual who receives payment every week. If taxes are levied on annual receipts (as they usually are), then these two individuals will pay the same tax although they have different incomes. Of course, it is unusual for the payment periods to vary as much as in our example. But it is not at all unusual for individuals with the same payment periods to have the same *average* receipts over a number of periods, but very different receipts each period. When this occurs, the same problem arises. Consider the construction worker who is paid weekly when he is working, but works only when the weather permits and when work is available. He may earn $100,000 over a period of 10 years. Yet his income (in Hicks's sense) is much smaller than the individual who earns $200 a week each week for 10 years.

Another problem that occurs when receipts are used as a proxy for income arises when services are rendered without payment. If one woman does work in her own home that another woman does in somebody else's, the second woman's income is taxable, but not the first. Similarly, if one individual invests in a home which he rents out to someone else, while a second individual purchases a home which he occupies himself, the first person pays tax on the rental income, but the second person does not.

The reason receipts are used as a proxy for income, of course, is that it is administratively much easier to base a tax system on transactions that are recorded than on those that are not. Fairness is not the only criterion by which tax systems are judged. Administrative feasibility and the impact of taxes on the efficiency of resource allocation are also relevant. We shall discuss aspects of the latter criterion later in this chapter and in Chapter 6.

THE PRINCIPLE OF VOLUNTARY CONTRACT

● Principles of taxation must ultimately be imbedded in legislation if they are to be more than topics of idle discourse. As such, they carry with them, at least implicitly, a political philosophy of how they might be implemented. It is on this ground that Wicksell attacked the ability-to-pay and equal-sacrifice theories and defended the benefit principle.[5]

As Wicksell saw it, the ability-to-pay doctrine represented advice to a benevolent despot who

> . . . would make every effort—especially when new direct taxes become necessary—to adjust the burden in accordance with the citizen's varying ability to pay and he would try thereby to diminish rather than increase the existing inequalities of wealth. On the other hand, our ruler would probably not worry overmuch about the thorny question whether the activities of the State adequately compensate his subjects for their sacrifice. . . . But since taxes so levied from above are almost bound to seem burdensome to the taxpayer, our ruler would try to avoid the appearance of burdensomeness . . . he would give preference to indirect taxation . . . user fees and dues rather than tax revenues . . . (and) if the ruler thereby succeeded in increasing public revenue and expenditure "on the quiet," that is, if the imposts, dues and fees were not considered as taxes by the people, he would probably congratulate himself on having combined such prosperous finances with so slight a (visible) tax pressure.

The reason that the ability-to-pay doctrine seems well suited to a monarchical and ill suited to a democratic form of government is that it leaves the determination of the absolute level of taxation completely aside. In a monarchy, the level of expenditures may be the king's prerogative, but a legislative representative must consider whether the benefits to his constituents exceed their tax sacrifice if he hopes to have their continued support. Furthermore, the ability-to-pay doctrine assumes that there is one way of distributing the burden of taxation which is appropriate for financing each and every public expenditure proposal. However, when one becomes concerned with the expenditures likely to be approved by a legislature, the adoption of a predetermined distribution of tax burden appears quite unattractive, for it will prejudice the legislative outcome against many proposals that might carry unanimously under some alternative tax distribution. Not to adopt a tax-expenditure combination proposal, which makes everyone better off, simply because the distribution of the tax burden did not conform to the ability-to-pay principle, is to let one's principles override good sense.

As an illustration of the way a predetermined tax-sharing arrangement can lead to inefficient public expenditure choices, let us carry out a further analysis of the problem described in Question 3 of Chapter 3. Figure 5.3 reproduces Figure 3.2, with the addition of the two curves labeled Σ MRS and TT'. The slope of the Σ MRS curve at each point is

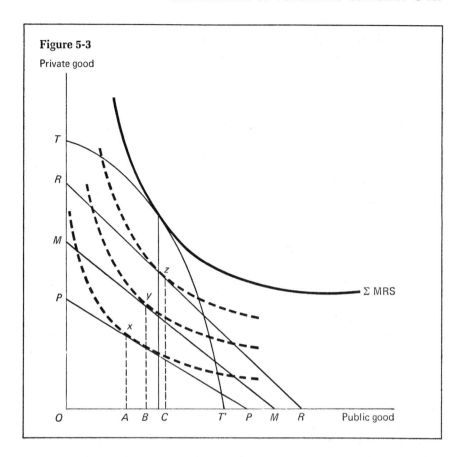

Figure 5-3

Private good

Public good

simply the vertical summation of the slopes of the three indifference curves immediately below it. Each point on this curve represents the sum of the individuals' rates of substitution of public schooling for private goods at the associated level of schooling. The curve TT' represents the various bundles of public schooling and private goods that society can produce with its resources. The pareto optimal level of schooling is determined by the point of tangency of TT' and Σ MRS. (Why?) However, given the predetermined tax shares represented by the three budget lines, the majority choice is not the pareto optimal point.

Therefore, society makes a nonpareto optimal choice by adopting a predetermined method of sharing the cost of public education. (Question: How would the tax burden have to be divided in this case if the majority choice were to be pareto optimal?)

Wicksell advocated the rule of unanimity as a legislative device to assure that the benefits of a proposed expenditure exceeded the costs. He felt that the unanimity rule would not prejudice legislative action with regard to any expenditure that yielded benefits in excess of its costs, since any such expenditure could be covered by some tax distribution which could win unanimous approval. At the same time, it would prevent passage of any proposal whose benefits did not exceed its costs. Of course, as we noted in Chapter 3, the unanimity rule would prevent use of the powers of taxation to be used to consciously redistribute wealth. In advocating the benefit principle, therefore, Wicksell was committing himself to a position that public expenditures be judged solely by an efficiency criterion. He was not insensitive to issues of equity. Rather, he believed that equity extended to questions of command over private goods as well as to the payment for public goods. But a change in the distribution of income would require a change in general social policy concerning property rights. According to Wicksell, "A revision of property rights would, by its nature, be independent of financing state needs." Whether or not it is logically possible to judge public expenditures solely on an efficiency criterion, without regard to questions of wealth distribution, is a question to which we shall return after considering some additional aspects of the benefit principle.

Taxes Versus Fees

The benefit principle is sometimes interpreted as meaning that individuals who receive no particular benefit from a given public service ought not to be made to support the upkeep of that service. Each man's relation with the state would then take on the character of a voluntary contract, which bound only those parties who freely gave their consent because they felt they would individually profit from the bargain. This interpretation suggests that those government services that can be financed by fees ought to be so financed. For example, it is perfectly possible to charge admission fees to the public zoo. Anyone who thinks the fee too high may decline to use the facility. If the zoo is entirely financed by fees, the benefit principle would seem to be followed.

However, this fee principle need not correspond to the spirit of the benefit principle as an efficiency criterion. Efficiency does not simply require that the benefits exceed the costs of providing a public good. If, for example, one takes the view that civilized life is impossible without government, then individuals might be willing to pay almost anything rather than see all government activity cease. However, the typical choice is not between government activity or chaos, but rather between more or less such activity. If the benefits from transferring *some* resources from government to the private sector would outweigh the lost value of government activity, then the present level of activity is inefficient. In other words, efficiency requires a balancing of *marginal* benefits with *marginal* costs. To continue with the example of the public zoo, if a zoo is to be of any interest to many people, it must contain a variety of animals and exhibits. These will cost a considerable sum to collect and build, but their upkeep is essentially independent of the number of visitors to the zoo. In cost terms, the average cost per visitor may be substantial, but the cost of allowing one more visitor, the marginal cost, may be almost zero. If the zoo is financed entirely by fees, the admission price must be high enough to cover the average cost. Since average cost will exceed marginal cost, many individuals who place a positive value on a visit to the zoo, and would be willing to make some tax contribution in excess of the additional cost their visits would generate, may, nevertheless, be deterred by the necessity of paying a fee for making such visits. By financing the zoo by taxes rather than by admission fees and allowing everyone to visit without additional charge, it would be possible to find a distribution of the tax bill which could win unanimous approval and which would make everyone better off than under the fee-financing arrangement.[6,7] (Prove this statement.)

The Impossibility of Treating Efficiency and Equity Separately

Every analyst tries to break down his problem into separate subproblems in order to increase its manageability. In so doing, he runs the risk of neglecting important interrelationships between those aspects of the problem that he is treating separately. Wicksell was interested in establishing a method of legislative organization which would control the legislative process in such a way that it would tend to produce the appropriate composition and levels of expenditure programs. To do so, he attempted to separate the (equity) issue of affecting the distribution of wealth from the (efficiency) issue of providing the optimal levels of public goods. Whatever the merit of separating questions of finance from a revision of property rights in Wicksell's time, today the importance of government services relative to gross national product is so large that the distribution of the benefits and costs of those services represents a very significant determinant of the distribution of property. As a pragmatic matter, therefore, it does not seem appropriate to judge government expenditures on an efficiency criterion alone. There are also logical grounds for rejecting the separation of equity from efficiency considerations in judging whether or not an appropriate level of public expenditures has been made. Since the demand for public goods depends upon the distribution of wealth, while the quantity and kinds of public goods provided are themselves an important determination of the distribution of wealth, it is logically impossible to know whether the appropriate quantity of public goods has been provided until one has determined what the distribution of wealth, including the public goods, ought to be. We can demonstrate this argument by means of an example illustrated in Figure 5.4.

Suppose our economy consists of two persons, whose preferences

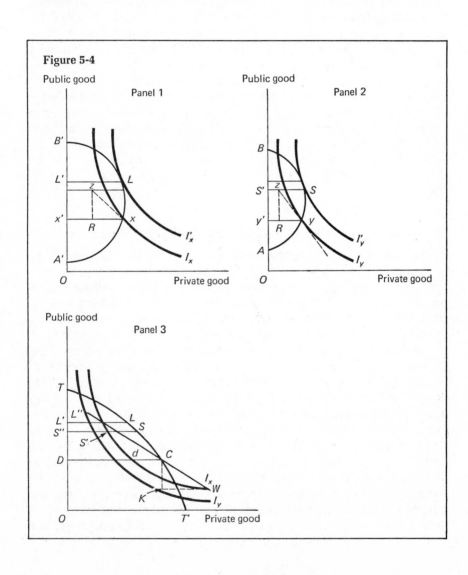

Figure 5-4

between a public good and private goods are represented in Panels 1 and 2, respectively. Suppose that the possibilities of production allow this economy to produce any combination of public and private goods along the transformation curve TT' in Panel 3. Further suppose that the economy is currently producing bundle C consisting of OD units of the public good and DC units of the private good. The first person owns Dd of the private good, and the second owns the rest, dC. Each can enjoy the public good without diminishing the quantity available to the other, so that each effectively "owns" OD units of the public good. These initial shares are represented by points x and y in Panels 1 and 2, respectively. Recall from Chapter 1 that if resources are allocated efficiently between the public good and private good, then the sum over both individuals of rates of substitution between those goods must equal the rate at which society can transform private into public goods. If we add the rates of substitution of x and y $(RX/ZR + RY/ZR = KW/CK)$, we find that their sum exceeds the rate at which the private good can be transformed into the public good. Consequently, both individuals could be made better off if they gave up some private goods (paid taxes) and secured more public goods. The question that Wicksell wished to answer was how much additional public goods should be produced. However, as our analysis will presently show, this cannot be answered before some agreement is reached as to how the "profits" are to be shared. We shall consider only two extreme cases. First, suppose that it is determined that the reallocation is to leave the person whose preferences are represented in the first panel no better off (and by the benefit principle, no worse off) than in his initial position. This can be accomplished by varying his tax contribution and the output of public goods so that the new allocation yields, for him, any bundle along the indifference curve I_x through x. We have transposed I_x of Panel 1 into Panel 3. The curve AB in Panel 2 is related to the curves I_x and TT' in Panel 3 in the following manner. The perpendicular from any point on AB to the vertical axis is equal to the horizontal difference between TT' and I_x for the point on I_x, which is of the same height as its associated point on AB. For example, the point d on I_x is of the same height as point y on AB. The distance between I_x and TT' at d is dC. This is equal to yy' in Panel 2. By construction, therefore, the curve AB represents the choices of public and private goods open to the second person subject to the community production-possibility constraint TT' and the condition that the first individual's share in total output lie along his indifference curve I_x. If the second individual were to choose OA of public goods, then all private-good production would go to the first person in order to keep him as well-off as before. If OB of public goods were chosen, then again the first person must be given all of the private goods produced. Faced with the constraint curve *AB*, the best choice the second person could make is allocation *S*, giving him *SS′* of private goods and *OS′* of public goods. The first individual would also have *OS′* (= *OS″*) of public goods, while he would receive *S″ S′* of private goods. (Prove that this is a pareto optimal allocation.)

If we now switch the roles of these two persons, holding the second person's utility constant at the level I_u and letting the first person determine the community output, we would have the choice set bounded by *A′B′* in Panel 1. Given this set of choices, the first person would be best off choosing allocation *L*, giving him *L′L* of private goods and *OL′* of public goods. This choice would imply for the second person *OL′* of public goods and *LL″* of private goods.

Since *OS′* ≷ *OL′*, it is clear that the optimum provision of public goods cannot be determined independently of a determination of the division of the gains from a change in government activity. In Wicksell's legislature, the division of the gains from providing public goods would be determined by the bargaining power of the respective representatives. But when public-goods production represents a significant portion of total activity, and when the current division of property rights seems inequitable, it does not appear morally appropriate to allow the financing of public goods to be determined by such a process. Indeed, since access to publicly provided goods is a valuable right, financing these goods by an ability-to-pay criterion may represent the most practical way of redistributing wealth.

MAXIMUM AGGREGATE UTILITY

● The principle of maximum aggregate utility represents an attempt to treat the problems of establishing criteria for an efficient allocation of resources and an equitable distribution of wealth in an integrated fashion. This integration is accomplished by the construction of a *social welfare function*. The social welfare function represents a set of rules by which an index number is assigned to every possible state of the world. The ratio of the index numbers assigned to any pair of possible states represents the judgment of the community (or more realistically, of the author who designs the particular function used) of the relative social value of the pair of possibilities being compared.

Most people who suggest the rules by which such index numbers are to be assigned assume that the preferences of the individuals who compose society are to "count" in establishing the social rankings of possible states of the world. One way of making individual preferences "count" is to specify that the ordering of social states produced by a social welfare function obey the pareto postulate. But as our discussion of the pareto postulate in Chapter 1 indicated, this requirement is not, in and of itself, sufficient to construct a complete social ordering. It is, therefore, necessary to specify additional requirements concerning the way individual preferences are to "count" in making social choices in order to completely specify a social welfare function that can rank all possible social states.

The practical significance of the need to supplement the pareto postulate with additional decision rules is clearly revealed by the problem of determining the optimum provision of public goods. As the example illustrated in Figure 5.4 showed, the "correct" quantity of public goods to provide depends upon the presumed division of the gains. Although we only illustrated the outcomes for two extreme distributions, it should be clear that as we change the minimum-utility requirement constraint for one individual, we change both the optimum level of public-goods provision and the maximum attainable utility level for the other. By continuously varying the minimum-utility constraint, therefore, we would trace out a utility-possibility frontier such as that shown in Figure 5.5. By construction, each point on this utility-possibility frontier is associated with a pareto optimal combination of a level of public-goods output and distribution of private goods among the two individuals. But if each point is a pareto optimal point, then we need a further specification of the social welfare function to choose the "best" point on the utility-possibility frontier. Since the utility levels of the two individuals vary inversely to one another along the frontier, these further specifications will represent the *degree* of significance to be given each individual's preferences in determining the social optimum.

The nineteenth-century approach to this specification problem was to assume commensurability of utility and then to make the judgment that the social utility index was to be simply the sum of the utilities attached by each individual in the community. This specification implies that the pareto postulate will be satisfied, since if one individual's utility is larger in state A than in state B and no one else's is smaller, then the sum of the utilities is also larger. Unlike the pareto postulate, however, the sum of utilities rule imposes a requirement on the assignment of the social index rank between every possible pair of social states. That is, it allows for a complete ordering.

Given this social welfare function, the principle of maximum aggregate utility asserts that the social choice among alternative possible

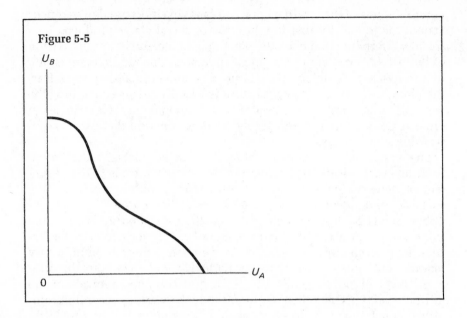

Figure 5-5

of financing any given amount of expenditure should be distributed in such a way as to represent the smallest aggregate sacrifice. To achieve this result requires taxation according to the principle of equal marginal sacrifice. For suppose the payment of an additional tax dollar would cause individual A to sacrifice an additional 10 utils, while the marginal utility of a tax dollar to B was 20 utils. In this case, increasing A's tax by $1 and decreasing B's by $1 would increase aggregate utility by 10. Such reshuffling of the tax burden would always increase aggregate utility if the marginal utility of tax dollars were different for different individuals.

Of course, the entire formulation of the problem in terms of measurable utility rests upon an assumption of fact which has not, so far, been supported. We have currently no method for measuring the utilities of different individuals. In the absence of such a method, the aggregation of individual preferences must depend upon some kind of voting procedure. It is at this point that Arrow's theorem, which was discussed in Chapter 3, becomes significant, and we are forced to admit that we do not yet have any clear standard for determining what the optimal level of public spending ought to be (or, indeed, when it would be an improvement to spend more or less).

THE INFLUENCE OF TAXES ON PRIVATE DECISIONS

● One important contribution that writers on the principle of maximum aggregate utility have made to the problem of evaluating tax programs is to have called attention to the indirect effects of various taxes which may cause the sacrifice embodied in a given tax program to exceed the value of the taxes collected. These indirect effects reflect an important difference between public and private finance. In a sale between private individuals, the terms of the sale are usually not contingent upon how the purchaser organizes his economic affairs. The cost of a Chevrolet is not different for a carpenter than for a doctor. In contrast, an individual's total tax bill will, in general, depend upon the occupation he chooses, the goods he buys, the investments he makes, and so on.

Because his tax payments are a function of his economic choices, an individual has an incentive to make a different set of choices than he would make if his tax "bill" were independent of his subsequent choices. To illustrate this point, consider the effect of an excise tax on the way a consumer allocates his budget as illustrated in Figure 5.6. In this figure, the line MM' is the pretax budget line facing a typical consumer. The imposition of an excise tax on good x means that every dollar expended on x yields fewer units of x than before, so that the after-tax budget constraint is represented by a line with steeper slope, MT. The best the consumer can do, given the constraint MT, is to choose point a. His tax bill is aa', which is equal to MN, and his purchase of x is OC units. If instead of an excise tax, his wealth had been reduced by a lump sum tax of MN dollars, and he had been able to trade at the original prices, his budget constraint after tax would have been NN'. Faced with that budget constraint, he would have purchased OB units of x. The excise tax, by raising the *relative price* of x, induced the individual to choose a different bundle than he would have chosen if the method of taxation did not affect relative prices. Furthermore, from the individual's point of view, a lump sum tax is preferable to a tax of equal yield based on some kind(s) of exchange(s). If the lump sum tax were substituted for the excise tax in Figure 5.6, the individual could increase his level of satisfaction. The difference in obtainable level of satisfaction between the budget constraint associated with a lump sum tax and the budget constraint with an excise tax of equal yield is termed the *excess burden of the (excise) tax*. [As an exercise, you should verify that a lump sum subsidy (a negative tax) will increase the beneficiary's level of satisfaction by more than a subsidy per unit of some particular commodity, which would involve an equal transfer of funds. This exercise will point out a potential conflict between bene-

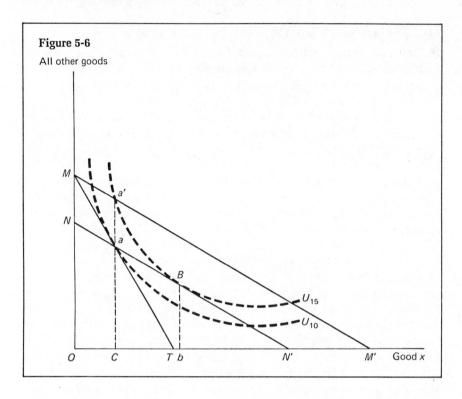

Figure 5-6

All other goods

ficiaries and donors. Donors may be interested in increasing only certain kinds of consumption by the beneficiaries, while the beneficiaries may be better off with unconditional grants (from the beneficiaries' point of view).] The principle of maximum aggregate utility requires that the tax program be chosen that minimizes the sum of the direct plus excess burden.

Shifting our point of view from the reaction of a given individual to the imposition of taxes that are based upon the volume of particular kinds of exchange to that of the economic system as a whole, we observe that the effect of such taxes is to make buyers and sellers of the taxed commodities use separate price systems in calculating the profitability of exchanges. The buyer is interested in the price per unit *including tax*, while the seller is interested in the price per unit *net of tax*. Recall that in equilibrium, the revenue a seller would receive from selling an additional unit must equal the amount he must pay out in order to secure the resources with which to produce that unit. On the buyers' side, equilibrium requires that the value to any buyer of an additional unit of a product be equal to the value of other products which he must give up in order to secure that additional unit. If the first of these conditions is not met, the seller will have an incentive to change the amount he offers for sale; while if the second condition is not met, the buyer will have an incentive to change the amount he orders.

Because of the imposition of a tax on certain classes of exchanges, the posttax equilibrium relationship between the rate at which consumers would be willing to substitute taxed for untaxed goods and the rate at which producers would be willing to transform untaxed into taxed goods will be different from the pretax equilibrium relationship. Recalling from the analysis of Chapter 1 that a necessary condition for pareto optimality is that the rate of substitution of x for y in consumption must equal the rate at which society can transform y into x, it follows that if the pretax equilibrium were pareto optimal, then the posttax system could not be pareto optimal. On the other hand, if the pretax equilibrium *were not pareto optimal*, then an appropriately chosen set of taxes might lead the economy to a posttax equilibrium that is pareto optimal.[8] The last point indicates that in a world of monopolies and externalities, a government may wish to use taxes not only as a source of revenue or means of income distribution, but also to increase the efficiency with which the nation's resources are used. More generally, the last point illustrates that whether a particular policy change leads to an improvement or makes matters worse depends upon the conditions that prevail prior to the policy change.

Direct Versus Indirect Taxes

Taxes are often classified into two groups, indirect and direct, according to whether they are assessed on the volume and/or value of exchange in particular markets or are assessed on income or wealth. This distinction was once thought to be of importance, since direct taxes from which there were no exemptions (such as a head tax) might have the same income effect as any set of indirect taxes with the same tax yield, but would not have any substitution effects. Since the substitution effects are effects induced by the changes in relative prices holding income constant, in the absence of substitution effects, a tax system would not change the relationship between the price system as buyers see it and the price system as sellers view it. If prior to the head tax, buyers and sellers were using the same set of prices to calculate their gains, then after the tax they would again be viewing a single (although different from the pretax) price system. In other words, *if* the pretax equilibrium were pareto optimal, the posttax equilibrium would be pareto optimal in the case of a head tax, but not in the case of an equal-yield indirect tax. However, there is no reason why the pretax equilibrium *should be* pareto optimal. If it is not, then the post-head-tax equilibrium will not be pareto optimal, but as was pointed out above, the post-indirect-tax equilibrium *may* be. Without knowing the actual pretax situation, nothing definite can be said about the relative efficiency of the two taxes.

Whatever a priori case might be made for the relative efficiency of direct taxes is further vitiated by the realization that most direct taxes are subject to exemption so that the amount of direct tax paid by an individual is determined by the way in which he uses the resources he has at his disposal. But in such cases, direct taxes also generate substitution effects, and the distinction between direct and indirect taxes is lost.

SUMMARY

● The structure of a tax system is one of the most important determinants of the individual citizen's relation to his government and his fellow citizens. As such, both theoretical and popular discussions of taxes are necessarily embedded in problems of political philosophy and of ethics.

Everyone agrees that taxes should be fair, but many opinions exist as to what fairness requires of actual practice. Does it require equal absolute, or equal marginal sacrifice? Taxation by ability to pay or by benefits received? How is sacrifice to be determined, psychologically or objectively? If psychologically, how is it to be translated to an objective basis? How is it to be determined if two individuals have the same "income" in a precise sense of that word? In the final analysis, income and wealth are themselves subjective, since a change in relative prices with no change in the general price level will affect the satisfaction of all but the mythical representative man.

For what purposes should the taxing power of the state be used? If the government were conceived as having been formed by a group of individuals for the sole purpose of achieving an optimum provision of public goods, then the requirement that the cost of governmental activity to a particular individual be related to the benefits he receives would appear to be an appropriate restriction on government financial policy. Not to adopt such a principle would contradict the intent of those who formed the social compact.

In general, the rule of unanimity, which is required to implement the benefit principle, is not a workable political rule, and tax systems are not otherwise readily controlled by the notion of quid pro quo. An exception may be in the area of local finance. If change of residence were a costless procedure and there were no impediments to the movement of people, then local communities would take on the aspects of the social contract conceived above. If an individual did not like the bundle of public services and tax bill he faced in one locality, he would seek out another that better suited his tastes. In effect, people would vote with their feet. In this way, the population would be formed into groups for each of which the bundle of public services and the distribution of the tax burden was satisfactory to most, if not all, of its members. Although people do not generally have the degree of mobility required to achieve this result, it seems clear that some of the movement to the suburbs can be explained in these terms.

Migrations have made our cities concentrations of poverty, as the poor move from rural to urban areas in search of better economic opportunities, and the upper middle class moves from the cities to the suburbs in an attempt to maintain for themselves high-quality public services without having to bear a burden of the poor in their provision. The public concern with the deterioration of public services in areas whose per capita income has fallen reflects a conception of government which extends beyond the benefit principle to the ethics of income distribution itself.

While the ethic embodied in the social contract theory would justify only those redistributions of income that could win unanimous support regardless of the degree of inequality of wealth which might remain, a different conception of the basis of democracy in which all men are equal views income equality a prerequisite for political equality. From this perspective, an important function of the tax system is to compensate for the unequal distribution of wealth, which is generated by historical and biologic circumstance. A second historical argument for income redistribution as a principle of government rather than a contingency of a social contract stems from the Benthamite doctrine of minimum-aggregate sacrifice. Attempts to redistribute wealth through the fiscal operations of government require that an individual's tax bill not be directly related to the value of public services that he receives. In such circumstances, predetermined tax shares, or separating tax legislation from expenditure legislation, might prevent society from using its resources as efficiently as it might if the benefit principle of taxation were followed. This means that in choosing a fiscal system, a nation must weigh the gains of "dividing the pie" more fairly against the costs of having a smaller pie to divide.

In recent years, there has developed an increased appreciation of the impact of changes in government receipts and expenditures on aggregate economic activity. Pursuit of a stabilization policy further divorces an individual's tax bill from the value of public services he receives. The exigencies of stabilization policy may call for reducing (increasing) current taxes at the same time that government expenditures are maintained.

As a consequence of the multiple functions of government, the practical constraints within which policy must operate, and the difficulty of agreeing on what constitutes fairness, we have no well-articulated, commonly accepted normative theory of taxation. In its stead, we have attempted to discuss in this chapter some of the ideas and doctrines that have played a significant role in the search for a theory of taxation.

Notes

1. Adam Smith, *An Inquiry into the Nature and Causes of the Wealth of Nations,* Book 5, ch. 2, Part 2, "Of Taxes."
2. John Stuart Mill, *Principles of Political Economy,* Book 5, ch. 2, "The General Principles of Taxation."
   If a progressive tax is "fair" and a regressive tax is "unfair," is a proportional tax "fair" or "unfair"?
3. Suppose the current rate of interest were 5 percent. Then the present value of an annuity yielding $10,000 for 30 years

   $$PV = \sum_{i=1}^{30} \frac{10,000}{(1 + 10)^i}$$

   is $153,725. With $153,725 one could, given the same interest rate, buy an annuity paying $12,298 for 20 years. The annuity formula is

   $$\text{Annuity} = 153,725 \left[\frac{0.05}{1 - (1.05)^{-20}} \right]$$

4. J. R. Hicks, *Value and Capital,* 2nd ed. New York: Oxford University Press, p. 172.
5. Knut Wicksell, "A New Principle of Just Taxation," reprinted in R. Musgrave and A. Peacock, *Classics in the Theory of Public Finance.*
6. The possibility of levying taxes on all users presumes that the only users of the facility live within the same legal district. Many cities find suburbanites over whom they have no legal jurisdiction using their facilities and are, therefore, tempted to use admission fees in order to prevent suburban free riders. Of course, this raises the dilemma of squeezing out local residents who find the fees too high.
7. Public utilities also display this decreasing average cost characteristic. The problem of finding an appropriate method of financing such activities is a major topic of Chapter 10.
8. To illustrate, suppose industry *M* were monopolized, while all other in-

dustries were competitive. Price theory tells us that in industry M the equilibrium price P_M will exceed the marginal cost of producing M, while in a competitive industry the equilibrium price P_C will just equal marginal cost. This means that P_M/P_C will exceed the ratio of the marginal cost of M to the marginal cost of the competitive industry's output. Recall from Chapter 1 that the ratio of the marginal costs is equal to the rate at which the competitive good can be transformed into the monopolized good, while the ratio of the output prices equals the rate at which individuals would be willing to substitute the competitive good for the monopoly good. Since these two rates are unequal, reducing the output of the competitive good by a small amount will release enough resources to increase the monopoly output by more than the amount necessary to compensate consumers for the lost competitive output. In other words, the pretax equilibrium is not pareto optimal.

The nonoptimality of the pretax equilibrium results from the fact that resource owners allocate their resources according to an input price system while purchasers allocate their purchases according to the effective output price system. The presence of the monopoly makes these two systems different, since the monopolist is able to set output price in excess of marginal input cost. These two price systems can be brought into equality by the imposition of an excise tax on competitive markets, which will raise their effective output price relative to the monopoly good. This will induce a reallocation of resources from the competitive to the monopoly market, which will tend to raise the input cost of the monopoly good relative to the competitive goods. Consequently, on both sides of the initial inequality $P_M/P_C > MC_M/MC_C$, the excise tax will work to move the two price systems into equality with each other. When equality is reached, the pareto optimality condition $RCS_{C \text{ for } M}$ equals $RPT_{C \text{ into } M}$ is satisfied.

9. This problem is discussed in K. Arrow, "A Utilitarian Approach to the Concept of Equality in Public Expenditures," *Quarterly Journal of Economics*, Vol. LXXXV, August 1971, pp. 403–415.

Questions for Discussion

1. *The military draft as a tax.*
   a. Some people have argued that replacing the military draft by a voluntary army would require an increase in taxes so that the switch to a voluntary army should be made when, for purposes of stabilization policy, the government wished to raise taxes anyway. Do you agree that if the size and composition of the army were to remain unchanged that a switch to a volunteer army would require an increase in the general tax level?
   b. One way of creating an all volunteer army is to allow conscriptees to "buy their way out" by paying someone else whom the army certified as a suitable replacement to take his place. This practice was utilized by some European governments. Would such a scheme affect the real cost of raising an army?

    c. Does a military draft, which allows occupational exemptions and deferments, correspond to a direct or to an indirect tax?

2. *Equality.* In debates over the way public expenditures for education ought to be divided among various classes of individuals, the point is often raised that equality of expenditures on different groups does not produce equality of benefit, since (for whatever reasons) different groups differ in the ability to transform these expenditures into personal gains. Suppose you had responsibility for distributing a fixed number of dollars for education so as to maximize the sum of the utilities derivable from that amount of total expenditure. Under what conditions would you distribute a larger share of the dollars to individuals with high ability than to individuals of low ability (merit scholarships)? Under what conditions would you give a larger share to individuals with low ability (compensatory education)?"

3. *Income redistribution as a public good.* Are there any "economic" reasons why all members of a society might unanimously agree to progressive income taxation? *Hint:* Consider the private risks attendant with specialization of labor and machinery in a capitalist society.

4. *Pollution taxes.* Suppose the same level of pollution abatement could be achieved by taxing emitters at a given rate per unit of pollution they emit or by subsidizing them at a rate dependent upon the reduction in emission levels they achieve. Why might the tax scheme be more *efficient* than the subsidy scheme? Is the tax scheme necessarily more efficient?

Suggested Readings

Blum, W. J., and Kalven, H., *The Uneasy Case for Progressive Taxation,* Chicago: The University of Chicago Press, 1953.

Hicks, J. R., *Value and Capital,* 2nd ed., Oxford: Oxford University Press, 1946, ch. 14.

Little, I. M. D., "Direct vs. Indirect Taxes," *Economic Journal,* Vol. 61, No. 243, September 1951, pp. 577–584.

Mill, J. S., *Principles of Political Economy,* London/New York: Longmans, Green, 1929; New York: Kelley, 1961.

Musgrave, R. A., *Theory of Public Finance,* New York: McGraw-Hill, 1959. Chapters 4 and 5 contain an extensive discussion of the benefit principle and the various notions of ability to pay.

Pigou, A. C., *A Study in Public Finance,* 3rd ed., New York: Macmillan, 1947, Part II, chs. 1–4.

Samuelson, P. A., "Diagrammatic Exposition of a Theory of Public Expenditures," *Review of Economics and Statistics,* Vol. 37, No. 4, November 1955, pp. 350–356. An exposition of the general equilibrium formulation of the problem of optimal public-goods production. Figure 5.4 in text is adapted from this article.

Smith, Adam, *An Inquiry into the Nature and Causes of the Wealth of Nations,*

London: Oxford University Press, 1904; New York: Dutton, 1910, Book V, Part II, "Of Taxes."

Wicksell, K., "A New Principle of Just Taxation," reprinted in R. Musgrave and A. Peacock, *Classics in the Theory of Public Finance,* New York: Macmillan, 1958.
The classic exposition of the principle of voluntary contract.

6
TAXES

As we noted in Chapter 5, taxes can have three effects: they make resources available for public use; they can alter the distribution of wealth; and they can affect the efficiency with which the resources of the community are used. In designing a tax system, it is desirable to know how a particular set of taxes will operate in terms of each of these effects. The task of this chapter is to analyze the economic effects of several types of taxes which are commonly used to finance government expenditures.

AN ILLUSTRATIVE PROBLEM

● Because resources can be shifted among uses in response to changes in the tax system, several difficulties arise in estimating the revenue, distribution, and efficiency effects of any proposed change. To illustrate these difficulties, suppose a particular state legislature is considering introducing a state income tax in order to raise an additional $500 million in revenue. It asks the state treasurer to estimate the tax rate required to produce the desired revenue. Suppose, for convenience, that the treasurer is advised by the head of the Department of Commerce that, in the absence of any change in the tax structure, they have estimated next year's taxable income to equal $50 billion. Since $500 million is 1/100 of $50 billion, the tax rate must be equal to at least 1 percent. But this estimate is almost certain to be too low, for it does not reflect the impact of the tax on the allocation of resources. Because the tax would reduce the return after tax from working, it can be expected to produce three kinds of effects in the state labor market. First, the tax, by changing the after-tax differential in wage rates among states, is likely to induce emigration of labor out of the state. Secondly, for those who find the new differential insufficient to induce them to leave the state, the tax will have reduced the relative price of leisure, thereby inducing people to increase the proportion of time not devoted to work. Third, a potential offset to this substitution effect is the response of the remaining labor to a reduction in income. Through this income effect, they may work longer in order to acquire the same money income as before. Unless the emigration, substitution, and income effects just sum up to zero, total income subject to income tax in the state will change as a result of the change in the tax rate.

In addition to these changes in the labor market, which may reduce the income subject to tax, the imposition of the income tax may adversely affect tax revenues from other sources. For example, if the state also has a general sales tax or various excise taxes, a fall in disposable income will reduce private expenditures on taxed goods, thereby reducing the revenues generated by these levies.

The state tax may also adversely affect the tax bases of local communities, who may then bring pressure on the state for additional grants. Local communities rely heavily on property taxes. To the extent that the income tax provides an incentive to people to leave the state, the demand for real estate will be less than before. There will be pressure for rents to fall and, as a consequence, for the market value of property to fall. The fall in property values, which are the base upon which property taxes are levied, implies smaller tax revenues for the local communities.

An interesting consequence of the impact of the income tax on the demand for use of property is that to the extent rents fall, it is the landlord who ends up paying the tax which was imposed on his tenants' income. Therefore, if the legislature is interested not only in the volume of tax receipts, but also on the distribution of the burden, it would be naive to believe that the burden of the tax cannot be shifted. It is important to remember that the distribution of the burden of a particular tax depends upon the impacts of the tax as they are felt in all markets. Therefore, after these adjustments in prices are made, the ultimate burden of the tax may be distributed very differently than before.

The perceptive reader will have noticed that the above analysis has not taken into account the purposes for which the revenue is used. When this is done, some, but not all, of the above analysis may have to be modified. The expenditures may improve the living conditions in the state sufficiently to overcome the migration incentive of the tax.

But the incentives to substitute leisure activities for money income-producing activities will not be offset (and may even be enhanced if the expenditures are for recreational improvements). Nor is it likely that the impact on disposable money incomes on tax revenues from other sources will be offset.

If our state treasurer is going to be able to estimate the tax rate needed to produce the required revenue and how the burden will be distributed, he is going to need much more information than the taxable income estimate supplied by the Department of Commerce. To make his forecast, he will have to estimate the parameters of a complete model of the economy.

THE COMPARATIVE ANALYSIS OF TAXES

● While quantitative forecasting of the effects of a tax change can be done most satisfactorily within the context of a model that allows its repercussions to be traced simultaneously throughout the economy, much insight into the properties of various taxes can be gained by a series of partial analyses of the direction of the direct effect of a given tax in different markets neglecting some aspects of the feedbacks among markets.

All taxes can be expected to effect changes in the allocation of resources, since changes in the level and/or distribution of disposable income will affect the pattern of consumer demands. But in addition to a direct effect on the pattern of demand via changes in disposable income, most taxes also induce changes in the pattern of resource allocation by directly changing the set of relative prices that consumers, producers, and resource suppliers confront. These changes in relative prices generate substitution effects, which would lead to a change in the pattern of economic activity even if there were no change in disposable income.

When one wishes to analyze the comparative effects of taxes, it is convenient to assume that different taxes directly affect disposable income in the same way (that is, that they produce the same tax yield) and to focus upon the differences in their substitution effects alone. This will be the method followed here.

INCOME TAXES

● There are two reasons why income taxes may generate substitution effects. First, there are both conceptual and administrative problems of defining the tax base—what constitutes taxable income—which lead to some forms of income left untaxed. Individuals are thereby given the incentive to organize their affairs to receive a larger portion of their income in untaxed forms than they would choose in the absence of the tax.

Secondly, the rate structure may be such that the after-tax rewards from engaging in one activity relative to another are changed. This will induce people to switch activities toward those activities that have become relatively more attractive.

The Tax Base

The basic conceptual problem in defining the base of an income tax is to give an operational definition of income. The theoretical definition proposed in Chapter 5 — *a man's income is the maximum value he can consume during a period of time and still expect to be as well-off at the end of the period as he was at the beginning*—raises several operational questions.

Income, Leisure, and the Labor Supply

First, one of the things a man can "consume" over a given period of time is leisure or time off from work. Few would deny that leisure has a positive value, that it is possible to substitute additional leisure for a little less goods which can be bought with earnings from labor and be as well-off as before. Suppose that a labor union, instead of asking for a higher annual salary for its workers, bargains for an additional two weeks' paid vacation. Clearly, the income (according to our theoretical definition) of its workers will go up since each worker will command the same money income, but will also have more leisure time. Should the value of this increased leisure time be counted as taxable income? Theoretically, one may argue, yes. But administratively, it is much easier to keep track of individuals' receipts of payments for services rendered than it is of the division of their time between work and leisure. Who "keeps book" on the hours worked by lawyers or professors, or indeed of the hours worked by anyone who is not paid on an hourly wage basis? Treating the value of changes in leisure as income changes is administratively unfeasible. Consequently, leisure is a source of value not counted as income for tax purposes.

It was once thought that the exclusion of leisure from the tax base would seriously impair the possibility of using the income tax as a means of generating substantial revenue. The basis of the argument was that an income tax reduced the price of leisure in terms of other goods. By reducing the renumeration for giving up leisure and going to work, the tax makes leisure activities more attractive than they would be in the absence of the tax. Furthermore, the higher the tax rate, the more attractive leisure becomes relative to other goods. Consequently, it was argued, a progressive tax structure would have the greatest work disincentives on that segment of the population whose labor was most valuable.

It is, of course, not only income taxes that reduce the relative price of leisure. Any tax that reduces the after-tax purchasing power of an extra hour's work will do so. The above argument would, therefore, appear to be an argument against high rates of taxation in general, since it raises the distinct possibility that an increase in the level of taxation may induce so large a fall in the supply of labor as to reduce total tax revenues collected. The probability of this occurring is mitigated by consideration of the effect on work incentives of having one's income reduced independently of any change in the price of leisure relative to other goods. Such a reduction may put considerable pressure on individuals to increase the number of hours they work in order to attempt to maintain their former standard of living. We illustrate the nature of these two effects (the substitution and income effects) on the supply of labor in Figure 6.1.

In Figure 6.1, the line MN represents the possible combinations of goods and leisure open to an individual before a change in taxes. Suppose that as the result of the imposition of an income tax, his opportunities are reduced to the set bounded by MN'. This new set recognizes that if he does not work, he can still have OM hours of leisure a day, but for each hour of leisure he gives up, he will receive less goods than before. In virtue of his new opportunities, the best he can do is work $B'M$ hours which is greater than the $A'M$ hours he would have chosen to work in the absence of the change in tax. The total change in his working hours can be decomposed into two steps — (1) an income step and (2) a substitution step. The income step can be found by assuming his opportunities for leisure and other goods had been uniformly reduced by shifting his budget constraint down parallel to MN to the position ZZ'. Given ZZ', he would have chosen to work $C'M$ hours and purchased CC' units of goods with the income he earned. This bundle of leisure and goods (denoted C) is, by construction, at least as good as bundle B, the bundle actually chosen as a result of the income tax, which changed his opportunities in a nonuniform way. The difference between $C'M$ and $B'M$, therefore, represents the effect of the change in relative price of leisure on the amount of work supplied, holding utility unchanged. In our example, the income effect outweighs the substitution effect, so that total hours worked increased as a result

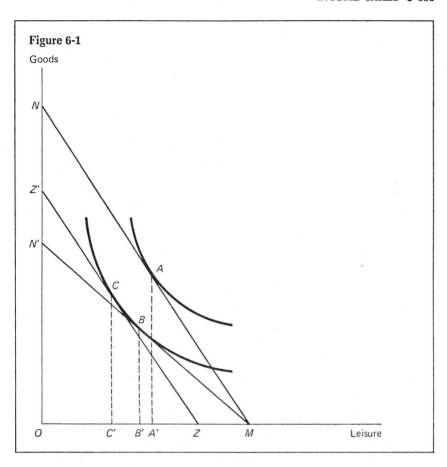

Figure 6-1

Goods

N

Z'

N'

A

C

B

O   C'   B' A'   Z   M   Leisure

of the tax increase. But it could clearly happen that the substitution effect outweighs the income effect as in Figure 6.2.

Whether the disincentive effect on work of a fall in the relative price of leisure outweighs, or is outweighed by, the incentive effect of a reduction in income is an empirical question. In summarizing the results of a survey designed to test whether, on balance, high taxes led to a reduction in labor supply, George Break concluded, "On the whole, . . . there is no escaping the fact that, thus far at least, disincentives, like the weather, are much talked about, but relatively few people do anything about them."[1] Other studies by Sanders and by the Michigan Survey Research Center of the response of high-wage earners to high marginal tax rates appear consistent with Break's observations that the total disincentive effect of high tax rates seems weak.[2] These studies were not designed to estimate the magnitude of the income and sub-

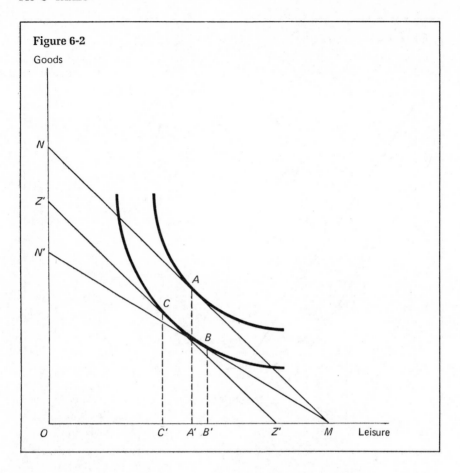

Figure 6-2

stitution effects separately. Therefore, their results are merely indicative that they tend to cancel out in the income brackets studied.

The Negative Income Tax

Discussions about the so-called negative income tax plan for subsidizing low-income families have renewed interest in acquiring estimates of both the substitution and income effects on labor supply of a change in tax rates among low-income groups. The basic arguments for adoption of a negative income tax are threefold.

1. Under traditional welfare programs, many working poor receive no assistance. An individual must demonstrate he has no means of self-support in order to qualify for welfare. Advocates of a negative tax program believe it desirable to *guarantee* all individuals a basic minimum income without qualification.

2. The traditional welfare program provides many services in kind and places restrictions on the use of monies given to the recipients. Proponents of a negative tax program argue that payment in the form of unrestricted cash grants would be preferable from both (a) the recipients' and from (b) a social point of view. Point (a) is simply an application of the excess burden of excise taxation applied to a subsidy or negative tax. The argument in support of (b) is that payments in kind reduce an individual's sense of responsibility for his own welfare, whereas cash grants force the individual to participate in decisions which will affect his welfare. This latter type of experience, it is alleged, is necessary to develop skills in judgment and self-esteem and to break the "welfare mentality" of complete reliance on the welfare system.

3. The traditional welfare programs, with their means tests and close supervision of the lives of recipients, require a large bureaucracy to administer. By eliminating these characteristics, a negative tax program should be much less costly to administer. On the other hand, by giving subsidies to those who are capable of working, a negative income tax program may generate a reduction in labor supply and hence total output. This reduction must be set against the savings in administrative costs in assessing the net benefits of such a program. It is for this reason that it is important to get estimates of the work disincentive effects of a negative tax program.

A negative income tax plan consists of two elements: (1) a guaranteed minimum income and (2) a rate schedule by which the payments by the government are reduced as earned income increases. A typical plan may be a minimum total income guarantee of $1500 whether or not the individual earns anything at all, and a reduction in subsidy of 50 percent of the value of any earnings made. Thus, if an individual earns nothing, the government pays him $1500, while if he earns $1500, the government pays him an additional $750 = $1500 − ½ (earnings). If he earns $3000, he receives no subsidy, and if his earnings exceed $3000, he starts paying taxes. The interesting feature of this kind of tax scheme is that it reduces the relative cost of leisure just as in the positive income tax case, while it increases disposable income. Hence *both* the substitution and income effects are likely to reduce total work supply. We illustrate this possibility in Figure 6.3.

In Figure 6.3, point E represents the bundle of income, work, and leisure an individual would choose in the absence of the negative income tax. LZ represents the guaranteed minimum income, and the ratio of the slope of WZ to the slope of WL represents the rate at which the subsidy is reduced as earned income increases above 0. In terms of our example, LZ = $1500, and the slope of WZ is one-half of the slope of WL.

Prior to introduction of the negative tax plan, the individual's opportunities are bounded by the line KL. The negative tax plan increases the alternatives open to the individual by the area WZL. From the

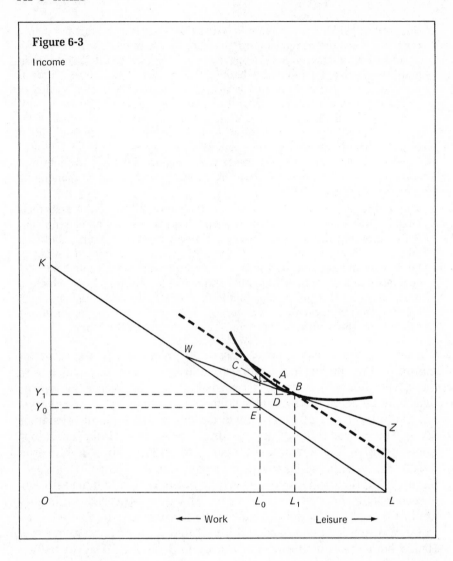

Figure 6-3

enlarged opportunity set, *KWZL*, the individual can choose both more income and more leisure than he chose before the negative tax plan was put into effect. We denote his original choice as *E* and his choice after the adoption of the tax scheme as *B*. We can decompose the movement from *E* to *B* into a movement caused by a change in his income via the subsidy and a movement caused by a change in his effective (after-tax) wage as a result of the provision that the subsidy be reduced (increased) by 50 percent of any increase (decrease) in his earned income. The income effect is calculated as the change in work which the individual would have chosen if his income had gone up enough for him to have chosen bundle B at the original, pretax effective wage rate. This is represented by CA in Figure 6.3. The effect of the change in after-tax wage rate (that is, the substitution effect) is then measured by the distance DB. As drawn, the effect of an increase in income is to reduce work supplied, and the effect of reducing the after-tax wage rate is also to reduce the supply of work.

Christopher Green and Alfred Tella attempt to estimate the substitution effect of a negative tax plan by analyzing a cross-section sample of families in the same total income bracket, but with differing quantities of nonemployment-related income.[3] They computed the average hourly wage for persons with and without nonemployment income for persons in the $2000 to $3000 total income bracket. Their calculations indicate that the average hourly wage for those without nonemployment income was 24 percent higher than for those with the same total income, some part of which was nonemployment related. They also observed approximately 11 percent higher average annual hours of work for those with no nonemployment income than for those with nonemployment income, total income constant. They, therefore, estimate that a 25 percent reduction in the effective wage rate would, income constant, lead to about a 11 percent fall in labor supply. They also estimated the effect of raising income from $2500 to $3500 would have a negative effect resulting in about a 0.5 percent decrease in labor supply. Consequently, they estimate that a negative tax plan, which raises income of full-time full-year workers in the $2000 to $3000 bracket by $600 to $1000, while incorporating a marginal tax rate of 25 percent would reduce the supply of labor from people in that bracket by about 11.5 percent. Making similar calculations for other groups and translating their estimates into losses of GNP, Green and Tella estimate the loss of GNP as a result of a negative tax scheme described above to be in the neighborhood of $1 billion per year.

While one might ask whether the average cross-sectional differences in labor supply are biased and not fully reflective of the response that might be expected as people adjusted over time to higher incomes produced by a negative tax plan, the Green and Tella estimates do seem to indicate that the effect on labor supply of a negative tax program with, say, a $1500 guaranteed minimum and a 25 to 50 percent marginal tax rate would not be an insignificant fraction of the total cost of such a program.

Expenditures: Maintenance Expense or Consumption

A second problem encountered in translating our theoretical notion of income into operational terms is posed by the following question:

What kinds of expenditures are "consumption" and what kinds are necessary to maintain one's net worth from the beginning of the period to the end? That is, the definition of income implies that deduction from gross receipts of all costs of obtaining those receipts should be made in order to calculate income; but to do so requires designating which expenditures are costs of obtaining income and, hence, deductible expenses and which are not. An illustration of the problem is the treatment of expenses of general education. Are such expenses necessary costs of obtaining future income or are they consumption? Everyone realizes there is a positive market value to possessing an education. Yet, if one has been truly educated, then one appreciates the intrinsic value of education itself. These two kinds of values are not separable in any nonarbitrary way so that the tax treatment of such expenditures will always appear discriminatory in some cases. Other examples of expenditures that contain some element of consumption and business expense are commuting expenses, clothing expenses, food and entertainment expenses. The magnitude of each of these kinds of expenditures depends partly on consumer preference and partly on business necessity. One must certainly travel to work, but how far one travels and in what style depend on one's preferences. Similarly, one's standard of work attire is partly a matter of business custom and partly a matter of individual taste. It may be standard business practice to carry out business over the noon hour, but there is no particular, standard business lunch. (Perhaps two martinis are standard.) If businesses are allowed to deduct such expenditures, then they will be in the position to give employees some portion of their compensation in the form of expense accounts, which represent an element of nontaxable personal income. "Unreasonable" expense accounts are, of course, in violation of the tax law, but what constitutes "ordinary and necessary" expenditures is a matter of debate that makes administrative checks against expense-account abuse fairly ineffective. As a consequence of the difficulty of separating consumption expenditures from the expenses necessary to obtain and maintain income, the imposition of an income tax creates some forms of nonmonetary renumeration that are not taxed and induces people to take some portion of their income in nonmonetary forms. From our discussion in Chapter 5 of the excess burden of taxation and subsidies in kind, it should be clear that this substitution of means of payment entails an excess burden of the income tax.[4]

Income and Capital Gains

A third operational question raised by the definition of income is specification of the period over which there is to be no change in a man's net worth. Suppose an individual buys an asset, which is guaranteed to yield him $100 per year for the next 10 years and to be worthless at the end of the tenth year. At a 8 percent rate of interest, that asset has a current value of

$$\$671.00 = \sum_{i=1}^{10} \frac{100}{(1 + 0.08)^i}$$

At the end of 10 years, it will be worth nothing. If the relevant period for calculating taxable income is 10 years, then over the 10-year period the income subject to tax will equal the total receipts minus the change in capital value, which is $1000 − $671 = $329. Suppose that immediately after the purchase of the asset, the rate of interest falls to 7 percent. As a consequence, the present value increases to

$$\$702.35 = \sum_{i=1}^{10} \frac{100}{(1 + 0.07)^i}$$

Nevertheless, if the relevant period for calculating taxable income is 10 years, the taxable income remains $329, since the interest-rate change does not change the total cash flow or the terminal value of the asset. Suppose, instead, that the tax is levied on income received each year rather than over the life of the asset. Then, given the interest-rate change, the yearly taxable income would be:

Year	Receipts	+	Change in Net Worth	=	Taxable Income
1	100		702.35 − 671 + [−(702.35 − 651.52)]		80.52
2	100		−(651.52 − 597.12)		49.17
3	100		−(597.12 − 538.92)		45.60
4	100		−(538.97 − 476.65)		41.80
5	100		−(476.65 − 410.02)		37.73
6	100		−(410.02 − 338.72)		33.37
7	100		−(338.72 − 267.43)		28.70
8	100		−(262.43 − 180.80)		23.71
9	100		−(180.80 − 93.45)		13.65
10	100		−93.45		6.55
				Total	360.80

As our example illustrates, if taxable income per period is defined as receipts plus change in net worth over the period, and if the interest rate changes, then taxable income depends upon the length of the period. In our example, if the period for tax calculation is one year, then total taxable income over 10 one-year periods is $360.80. But if the income period is 10 years, then the taxable income is only $329. Since the taxable income produced by an asset over its economic life depends on the income period for tax calculations, any period chosen to define taxable income will treat income from assets with economic lives that exceed that period as producing a different income per period than assets with economic lives shorter than that period if the interest rate changes. To avoid this arbitrariness, changes in capital values due to interest-rate changes are not treated as ordinary taxable income.

Distinguishing between ordinary income and changes in capital values in defining the base of the income tax does create an important opportunity for individuals to reduce their ordinary taxable income by taking it in the form of capital gains. The most widespread method by which this is accomplished in the United States is through the purchase of shares in a company, which currently pays only a small fraction of its income out in the form of dividends and reinvests the remainder. The shareholder must treat the dividends he receives as ordinary income. But as a consequence of the expanded investment of the company financed through earnings not paid out in dividends, he can expect the value of his shares to increase. The increase in stock value is a capital gain not subject to ordinary income tax under United States law. Any attempt to prevent this method of tax avoidance must lead to treating capital gains not dependent on interest-rate changes the same as ordinary income. The difficulty in implementing such a rule would be in determining what portion of the increase in the value of a stock was attributable to an increase in its potential earning flow (the numerator of the present-value formula) and what portion was attributable to the change in the rate of discount people were applying to that potential flow (the denominator of the present-value formula). With respect to stock prices, the implicit discount factor reflects such things as attitudes toward risk, while the numerator refers to people's estimates of an uncertain future stream of earnings of the company. Therefore, two individuals may agree on what the price of the stock should be, but disagree as to why. For this reason, treating any portion of capital gains as ordinary income will appear arbitrary and unfair.

Savings and Interest

A fourth problem that arises in the application of the theoretical definition of income to concrete cases is the treatment of receipts from savings. The amount of possible current consumption an individual will choose to defer until the future depends upon the additional future consumption he can secure as a result of his act of saving currently.

That is, savings depend upon the effective rate of interest. An individual will, for any given rate of interest r, find it in his interest to reduce current consumption and increase current savings until the present utility value of $(1 + r)$ dollar's consumption one period from now is equal to the utility value of one dollar's present consumption. Therefore, if an individual is choosing the best division of his current money receipts between present consumption and savings, his present income measured in terms of the utility value of his consumption opportunities will be reduced by the same amount if one dollar's worth of present consumption or $(1 + r)$ dollar's worth of future consumption is taken away from him. However, if the income tax is based upon his current *money income including interest income*, then the utility loss will be higher if some of his money was saved than if all of his money income went for current consumption. The reason is that current savings will produce money interest income next period, which will be subject to tax. But this tax on interest must reduce the effective rate of interest below that just necessary to make the present utility value of one dollar's worth of current savings equal to the utility of one dollar's worth of current consumption. Consequently, the income tax, by changing the effective rate of interest, induces a substitution of present consumption for current savings out of a given money income. We illustrate this in Figure 6.4.

In Figure 6.4, AB represents the boundary of possibilities when interest income from savings is not subject to tax. AC represents the boundary when interest income is subject to tax. The tax on interest income has no effect if one was saving nothing. Otherwise, the tax on interest reduces the value of after-tax money income (which is equal to after-tax savings plus after-tax consumption) in Period 2. Suppose the initial savings rate in Period 1 was $S'A/OA$ and that after the tax on interest income the savings rate in Period 1 was $F'A/OA$. The bundle F could have been secured if Period 1 money income were reduced by EA and interest income received in Period 2 left untaxed. Such a change would have left ED as the boundary of the possibility set. If ED were the boundary, bundle G would be chosen. Therefore, the tax on interest income generated an income effect of $S'G'$ on current saving. After allowing for this pure income effect, the substitution effect of the tax on interest income is to reduce savings by the amount $G'F'$.

There are three kinds of objections to taxing interest as income. The first objection rests on ethical grounds. Suppose two individuals have money incomes which give them equal present value of consumption possibilities if they divide their money incomes between current consumption and savings in identical fashions. If interest income is subject to tax, then they will have different present values of consumptions

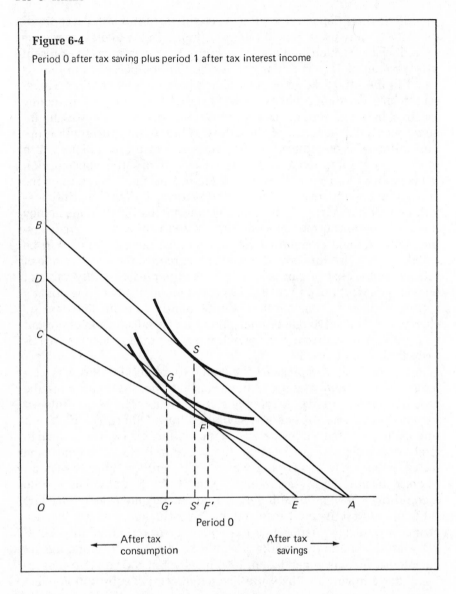

Figure 6-4

Period 0 after tax saving plus period 1 after tax interest income

Period 0

← After tax consumption

After tax savings →

if their savings decisions differ. This is because the tax, by reducing interest income, reduces the present value of future consumption made possible by saving. Opponents to taxes on interest income believe this results in the double taxation of the same income, once when it is earned, and again in the future when it is converted into actual consumption. They believe this is an unwarranted discrimination against people who prefer to defer their acts of consumption for some time after the receipt of income.

The second argument is an excess burden argument, which asserts that a lump sum tax on persons who save is preferable to a tax on interest income which yields the same tax revenue. Referring back to Figure 6.4, EA represents the tax revenue generated by the tax on interest income. If EA has been taken in such a way that the after-tax rate of interest were left unchanged, then ED would be the boundary of the possibility set, and the individual could have obtained a bundle of higher utility value than bundle F. Since F is the best he could obtain when the same tax revenue is collected by a tax on interest income, a lump sum tax would impose a smaller utility loss than the tax on interest income, given the same tax revenues. The difference in utility level achievable under the respective tax schemes is the excess burden.

The third objection to treating interest income as taxable income is that by reducing the effective after-tax interest rate, the tax induces a substitution of current consumption for savings. But the ability of an economy to increase per capita income depends upon its growth in equipment per worker. New equipment can only be purchased if some of the current output is withheld from current consumption, that is, only if there are current savings. Reducing the savings rate, therefore, reduces the possible rate of growth in per capita income. This is thought by some to be an objectionable consequence.

It is the unfortunate nature of the problem that understanding these objections provides little guidance as to how the interest income from savings should be treated. The most direct method would be to identify that portion of an individual's current receipts, which are a return of monies invested plus the interest income on those savings and exclude such receipts from current taxable income. But as was pointed out earlier, when those investments are in equities with no fixed yield, it is impossible to identify the implicit interest income. An alternative method is to substitute current expenditures for current income as the definition of the tax base. An expenditure tax does not involve double taxation of income saved. However, in an economy where aggregate saving is positive, the switch to the expenditure base would require a higher rate of tax (because of the smaller base) in order to produce an equivalent volume of tax receipts. This higher rate of tax would lead to a further substitution of leisure for work, thereby reducing current output so that total savings may be reduced even though the expenditure tax reduces the tax on savings. For this and other reasons, the desirability of an expenditure tax relative to an income tax, which includes interest income as part of the tax base, remains a highly debated topic.[5]

Nonmarket Sources of Income

A fifth problem in defining taxable income is the problem of treating nonmarket activity. If a tax system and the government that uses it are to be well received, the tax collector must not appear to have the capacity to act arbitrarily, calling this taxable and that not as his fancy moves him. At the same time, it would be folly to allow each man to judge what his taxable income is. It is, therefore, necessary that the tax be based on recorded evidence which, insofar as possible, is not subject to manipulation by either taxee or taxor. Such evidence of a person's income may be contained within the financial records of others with whom he deals. In principle, it is possible to obtain such information either by looking at receipts of others of payments made by you or payments by others to you. The latter course is easier, since the typical individual receives income from a smaller set of people than the set from whom he buys. Interesting examples of reconstructing income by the former method, however, are involved in attempts to get gangsters — whose income receipts are not recorded as payments for services rendered — on charges of tax evasion by examining their expenditures. When financial records are not kept, the income tax system breaks down.[6]

Reliance on financial records for tracing taxable income creates incentives for individuals to substitute nonmarket for market activity. One important substitution is of home ownership for other forms of investment. A home yields its owner an income equal to its rental value minus maintenance and other expenses. If the owner lives in his own home, that income is not subject to tax, while if he rents to others, it is. Suppose that a particular home has a rental value of $3,000 per year and could produce income before taxes of $1,000 per year. An individual is contemplating whether to purchase this home for $20,000 or to rent it for $3,000 per year. A $20,000 investment in the home will, if he occupies it himself, yield him a 5 percent (1,000/20,000) return on his investment, both before and after taxes. If he is in the 50 percent tax bracket, then he will place his $20,000 in an alternative investment from which the income is taxable only if that alternative will yield him more than 10 percent before taxes. The exclusion of income from owner-occupied housing from the tax base, therefore, indices a substitution of relatively low-yielding investments for relatively high-yielding ones.

A second important effect of excluding income generated by nonmarket activity is to discourage individuals from specializing on tasks in which their productivity is greatest. Women with special training and skills remain in the home even though the pretax difference in income they might earn outside the home relative to the payments that would be made for a full-time housekeeper would be sufficient to compensate them for leaving their home in the care of someone else (for the "liberated woman" this required compensation may be negative!) because the after-tax difference is insufficient.

Summary of Tax Base Effects

At this point, it may be useful to summarize the ways in which the operational specification of the income tax base generates substitution effects and thereby imposes excess burdens on the community. First, leisure is valuable but left untaxed. Consequently, the income tax reduces the price of leisure inducing people to work less than they would have chosen to work if required to pay the same sum to the government in a lump sum as they pay under the income tax. Second, income paid in kind can be camouflaged as business expenses and hence avoid taxation. The income tax, therefore, induces persons to take a larger portion of their income in kind than they would choose faced with an equal yield lump sum tax. Third, in order for the base to be equitable, capital gains must be treated differently than ordinary income. This provides an incentive to "convert" ordinary income into capital gains. Fourth, it is not operationally feasible to distinguish interest income from other kinds of income. But taxing interest income provides an incentive for people to save a smaller portion of their income than they would under an equal yield lump sum tax. Fifth, it is not operationally feasible to tax nonmarket income. This tends to discourage the movement of resources and talents from nonmarket to market activities, even though those resources may have a higher productivity in the market than out of it.

The Rate Structure

The substitution effects generated by an income tax depend not only upon its base, but also upon its rate structure. In the following paragraphs, we shall outline the comparative effects of a proportional, progressive, and regressive rate structure on the pattern of occupational choices and investment.

Apart from barriers to entry such as unions, incomplete information, inability to finance training, and so on, there are two reasons why one should expect different occupations to pay different wage rates. First, different jobs may differ in their inherent attractiveness. Workers in coke-making facilities are exposed to extreme heat and dangerous pollution levels. One would expect to receive a higher wage for such work than work that required similar skills in a more pleasant environment. The difference in wage rates represents the rate of compensation for accepting a relatively unpleasant environment as part of the job. The second source of wage differences rests on differences in the investment required to acquire the skills necessary to perform a task proficiently. The wage difference in this case represents the difference in the return necessary to compensate for the difference in investment. The imposition of an income tax may change the after-tax difference in earnings between different occupations and therefore induce a change in the distribution of a given number of workers among different jobs.

Choice of Work Conditions

Consider first the effect of a proportional income tax on the distribution of labor among jobs requiring similar skills, but taking place in environments of different degrees of pleasantness. Suppose that before the tax is imposed, job A pays twice as much as job B and that the absolute difference in wage rates is just sufficient to compensate the marginal A workers to remain in A. After the tax is imposed, job A will, because the tax is proportional, continue to yield an after-tax income that is twice that of B. However, the *absolute* difference in after-tax wage rates will be smaller than the absolute difference in wage rates before the tax.[7]

Because the proportional tax reduces the absolute difference in after-tax compensation, some workers will find this difference insufficient to compensate them for the difference in working conditions and will therefore attempt to switch from the higher-paying (but less pleasant) to the lower-paying (but otherwise more attractive) jobs. A progressive rate structure will, of course, reduce the after-tax difference in wage rate even more than a proportional tax which generates the same tax revenue. A progressive rate structure, therefore, also induces a substitution of more for less attractive jobs. On the other hand, if the rate structure is sufficiently regressive, the absolute *difference* in after-tax rates may increase (even though both after-tax wage rates fall). Therefore, a regressive rate structure may generate substitution effects in direction opposite of those generated by a progressive rate structure.

Choice of Skill Acquisition

The structure of the rates may also make a difference in the pattern of skill acquisition. Suppose that a particular skill can be acquired by foregoing earning opportunities and incurring other costs, the total value of which is $10,000. Once a worker secures the skill, he can use it for 20 years. Suppose further that as an alternative to using the $10,000 to improve his skills, he can lend it out at 5 percent interest. This second alternative will, therefore, yield him $500 per year for 20 years and return to him $10,000 at the end of the twentieth year. The investment in skills will return him nothing at the end of 20 years. Therefore, if it is to be profitable for him to invest in developing his skill, his income with the skill must be *more than* $500 per year greater than his wage income without the skill would be for the next 20 years. He will, in fact, have to earn at least $800 per year more with the skill than without it to make it worthwhile to invest in the skill.[8]

Suppose that the annual wage difference x is just large enough to make it profitable to acquire the skill.

In our example, this would be about $800. If a proportional tax at a rate t is imposed, then the present value of the alternative investment will fall to

$$\frac{10,000}{(1+r)^{20}} + \sum_{i=1}^{20} \frac{500(1-t)}{(1+0.05)^i} = \frac{10,000}{(1+r)^{20}} + \sum_{i=1}^{20} \frac{500}{(1+0.05)^i} - \sum_{i=1}^{20} \frac{500t}{(1+0.05)^i}$$

The tax will reduce the present value of the investment in skills to

$$\sum_{i=1}^{20} \frac{800(1-t)}{(1+0.05)^i} = \sum_{i=1}^{20} \frac{800}{(1+0.05)^i} - \sum_{i=1}^{20} \frac{800t}{(1+0.05)^i}$$

The reduction in the value of the first alternative is

$$\sum_{i=1}^{20} \frac{500t}{(1+r)^i}$$

which is less than the reduction in the value of acquiring the skill,

$$\sum_{i=1}^{20} \frac{800t}{(1+r)^i}$$

Therefore, the imposition of the tax will induce people to reduce the proportion of investment in skills and increase it in nonhuman capital. Furthermore, as indicated earlier, total investment (which equals savings) is likely to fall so that the skill level of the work force will fall.

Once again, a sufficiently regressive rate structure may reverse the direction of the substitution. Let t_1 be the tax rate on $W_0 + 800$ and t_2 be the tax rate on $W_0 + 500$, where W_0 is the value of labor income in the absence of skill acquisition. Set $t_2 > t_1$ such that

$$\sum_{i=1}^{20} \frac{500t_2}{(1+0.05)^i} > \sum_{i=1}^{20} \frac{800t_1}{(1+0.05)^i}$$

and it will now be relatively more profitable than before the tax to invest in skills. Of course, many different skills require different volumes of investment and consequent compensation so that finding a rate schedule that would induce an increase in all skills is likely to be an insurmountable task.

The Rate Structure and Risk Taking

We live in a world of uncertainty. When evaluating an investment, the typical investor is interested not only in what the return on similar investments has been on average, but also in the entire pattern of actual returns. Suppose, for example, that investments of type A yield no revenue 90 percent of the time and $10,000 10 percent of the time. Suppose that investments of type B yield $900 50 percent of the time and $1,100 50 percent of the time. On average, both type A and type B investments yield $1,000. But most investors would probably prefer B to A because of the smaller range and dispersion of the possible returns. The risk of an investment is related to various properties of the dispersion of possibilities around its mean or average. The higher the risk, the less attractive the investment, while the higher its average return, the more attractive. Therefore, if an individual is to find two investments with different risks equally attractive, it must be that the investment with higher risk has the higher average return.

The investor will choose a portfolio of investments such that any change he makes to secure a greater average return requires an unacceptable increase in risk, while any change that would reduce his risk would entail, for him, an unacceptable reduction in average return. Suppose that before the imposition of an income tax, an individual has $1400, which he is contemplating investing. Suppose further that he finds two assets, each selling for $1400, which appear to him to be equally attractive. Asset A has a 50 percent chance of being worth $1000 next year and a 50 percent chance of being worth $2000 next year. Asset B has 50 to 50 chance of being worth either $900 or $2105 next year. There is, therefore, a 50 to 50 chance of his income from asset A being either −$400 or +$600; and there is a 50 to 50 chance of his income from B being either −$500 or +$705. If we now impose a proportional income tax of t percent on positive incomes alone, the possible after-tax incomes from A will be $[-400, +600(1 - t)]$; and from B $[-500, +705(1 - t)]$. Since $-t(705 - 600) < 0$, the proportional tax reduces the difference in the possible positive after-tax incomes from investments A and B. But the pretax difference in possible income $(705 - 600)$ was just sufficient to compensate for the pretax difference in possible loss $(500 - 400)$. Since the tax does not affect the difference in possible loss, but does reduce the difference in possible gain, the tax will make A (the less risky asset) relatively more attractive than B (the asset with both greater risk and greater average return).

The Possibility of Loss Offset. Let us now modify our example by giving our individual income from a second source of, say, $1000 per year. He will now possess income against which he can offset losses from his investment if they occur. If he chooses A, he has a 50 to 50 chance of a posttax income of either $t(1000 - 400)$ or $t(1000 + 600)$; if he chooses B, he has a 50 to 50 chance of $t(1000 + 705)$ or $t(1000 - 500)$. In this case, the tax reduces the magnitude of the difference in possible loss in the same proportion as it reduces the difference in magnitude of possible gains. The government becomes a partner not only in the investor's "winnings," but also in his losses. If a $105 difference in possible gain was just sufficient to compensate for a $100 difference in possible loss, then $t(105)$ possible gain ($t < 1$) should more than compensate for $t(100)$ possible loss, so that the proportional tax with provision for full loss offset will make the risky investment relatively more attractive than the less risky investment.[9]

Under a progressive rate structure, the government becomes a larger partner in the possible gains than in the possible losses, so that if the rates are sufficiently progressive, the gain in security from sharing the risk will be more than offset by the reduction in average yield, and A will become more attractive than B. On the other hand, under a regressive structure, the government bears a larger share of the possible losses than it takes of the possible gains. Therefore, a regressive tax structure would make the individual favor the riskier investment, B.

In concluding this discussion of the impact of the rate structure on risk taking, we must remember that any tax reduces the average yield of investments and may, therefore, reduce the total volume of investment. Nevertheless, in spite of a likely reduction in total investment, a proportional or regressive rate structure with provisions for full loss offset will increase the proportion of relatively risky investments undertaken, and may even increase the total amount of risk to which persons will subject their assets.

TAXATION OF PROPERTY

● While taxation on the basis of income is predominant at the federal level, taxation on the basis of the value of physical property, or real wealth, accounts for the lion's share of local tax revenues. An asset has value currently only if that asset will yield an income (either dollar or in kind) over some period of time. The value of an asset is derived from its prospective income flow by taking a weighted sum of the incomes expected in all future periods. The income in any future period is "weighted" by a discount factor, which represents the cost per dollar of investment opportunities foregone while waiting for that income to materialize. Because the capital value of an asset is derived from the value of the income stream that asset can produce, there is no logical difference between a tax on the value of a particular class of physical property and a proportional tax on income produced by that class of property. For example, suppose that an asset will yield $x per year income in perpetuity. The present capital value, $PV(x)$, of that income stream is x/r, where r is the rate of discount. But then $\lambda PV(x) = \lambda(x/r)$, so that an annual capital tax of λ percent is equivalent to an annual income tax of λ/r percent. Consequently, we should expect the same allocative effects from a tax on the capital value of a particular class of property as a proportional tax on the income generated by that class of property.

Distribution of the Burden

One of the important questions about an annual property tax is who ends up paying the tax. The answer to this question depends upon two factors: (1) how savings respond to a reduced yield on all assets and (2) whether all assets are subject to the same rate of tax.

Savings and the Burden of Property Taxes

We first consider the role of the savings response, assuming all assets are subject to the same rate of tax. The annual pretax rental income from a particular asset depends upon the demand for and the supply of the services generated by assets of that type. The supply of services over a given period depends upon the stock of assets existing over that period. The larger the stock, the larger the supply of services; so that the flow of services supplied can only change as the stock of assets that generates that flow changes. Over any period of time, two processes are at work to change the stock of assets: (1) depletion of the stock via physical deterioration and (2) additions to the stock via the investment of savings. The imposition of the tax reduces the after-tax return to savings and will, therefore, tend to reduce the rate at which additions to the stock of assets are made. With an unchanged rate of physical deterioration, this implies that the stock of capital will grow at a smaller rate than before. The magnitude of the reduction depends upon the reduction in the rate of savings occasioned by the tax increase. In the long run, therefore, there will be a reduction in the stock of assets and the supply flow of services generated. This reduction in supply will cause higher rents to be paid, thus tending to offset a portion of the impact of the tax on the worth of assets. In other words, in the long run, the reduction in the stock of capital shifts the burden of the tax from the owners of the assets to the users (or rentees) of the assets' services.

The rate at which the rental price increases depends upon the rate at which the flow of services is reduced, that is, upon the rate of physical depreciation of the assets and the reduction in the rate of replacement. Since this process of change takes time, the burden of tax will be shifted only gradually from the owners of the assets to the users. During this process of stock adjustment, the owners of the assets will find their after-tax yields reduced. In the short run, therefore, the yield per dollar invested in the existing assets will be reduced from their pretax levels. The extent of the reduction will be inversely related to the duration of time that has passed since the imposition of the tax and to the tax-induced change in the rate of growth in the stock of assets. Recalling that the change in the rate of growth in the stock of assets depends upon the change in the savings rate, we can say that the smaller the reduction in the savings rate as a consequence of a reduced yield, the longer the period of adjustment and the greater at any moment during the process is the portion of the burden of the tax borne by the owner of the asset. In the limit, if the change in savings rate is zero, the owner of the asset absorbs the burden of all tax payments, while the users bear no burden of the tax.

Tax Capitalization

Note that under this extreme assumption of no change in the savings rate, anyone who was willing to buy assets at their pretax prices before the imposition of the tax will still be willing to offer the same prices after the tax has reduced its yield. An implication of a zero change in savings, therefore, is that the original owner of an asset turns over the tax burden to a new owner when he sells the asset. However, except in this case, the reduction in savings rate implies that after the tax is imposed, the demand price for any given asset will fall to reflect the unwillingness of potential owners to accept the tax burden. Hence, the burden for future taxes will be at least partially borne by the original owner in the form of a capital loss if he sells the asset. This concentration of the burden of the tax on a given owner at a single point in time is referred to as the *capitalization of the tax.*

Effects of Differential Property Tax Rates

In the preceding sections, we assumed that all property was subject to the same rate of tax. In fact, there are very significant variations in the rate of tax from community to community and from asset to asset. These variations arise for many reasons, principal among them being

1. an unequal distribution of property among communities;
2. the difficulty of assessing the value of personal property without invading the privacy of individuals, and the consequent ease of avoiding personal property taxation; and
3. the desire of communities to discriminate among assets in such a way as to minimize erosion of their tax bases.

The first two sources of variation are obvious. The third is a reflection of the fact that communities compete with one another for the attraction of investment in plant and equipment. By taxing such assets at a differentially lower rate than they tax land sites (which can neither be moved nor depleted), a community hopes to attract more industry. If successful, the higher levels of activity will increase the value of the community's taxable land and allow it to recoup, via a higher tax yield on a nonmovable asset—land—the lower tax payments to be gotten from taxes levied on plant and equipment whose location may easily shift in response to small changes in taxes imposed upon them.

A consequence of the variation in tax rates among assets is that a much larger portion of any tax increase is capitalized than would be the case if potential investors faced reduced yields from all assets. For in the face of a differential change in tax rates, any potential buyer of assets can reduce his tax burden not only by not investing at all, but also by choosing to invest in those assets with the smallest increase in taxes and the fastest rates of depreciation. Since land usually carries the highest tax rate and has the slowest rate of depreciation among all assets, it is usually assumed that a tax on land is capitalized to a higher degree than any other asset.

THE CORPORATE INCOME TAX

● In the United States, the third most important source of revenue for the federal government is the corporate income tax. The corporate income tax differs from the personal income tax in that it is a tax on income from a specific source, rather than on income in general. The tax is assessed on the gross profits of the corporation prior to any payments to stockholders. On corporate income in excess of $25,000, all income is taxed at the same rate. Therefore, for all intents and purposes, it is a proportional income tax on the income produced by corporate-owned property.

We can utilize the equivalence between a proportional tax on the income a property produces and a tax on the value of the property itself to analyze the distribution of the burden of the corporate income tax. We recall first that if the imposition of the tax in no way affected the stock of assets the corporations owned, then corporate profits before tax would remain unchanged, and the burden of the tax would fall on the owners of corporate shares at the time the tax is first imposed. If the total number of shares outstanding were to remain unchanged, this burden would be capitalized in a lower selling price per share of capital stock.

The corporations need not passively accept this decline in the share price of their stock, however. They could mitigate the effect on stockholders by selling off some of their physical assets to noncorporate businesses and use the proceeds to buy up their own stock certificates. Such transactions would be analogous to physical depreciation of their assets and would have an analogous impact of shifting the burden from the stockholders to the consumers of corporate-made products via higher prices received for a smaller supply of output. If the corporations could sell off their physical assets without affecting the price they receive for those assets, then the output of the corporate sector would fall until the price of corporate output had risen sufficiently to pass all of the burden of the tax forward onto consumers. Generally, however, the corporations would find that the price of their physical assets would decline as they attempted to sell off their assets. (Why?) In this case, the proceeds from the sale of its assets will not provide sufficient revenues to buy up enough corporate shares to maintain their pretax price. Owners of corporate shares will, therefore, absorb some of the burden of the tax in the form of reduced stock values, while their customers will also bear some of the burden. In addition, the fact that the market value of physical assets has fallen means that noncorporate owners of capital will have also had their wealth reduced by the imposition of the tax on corporate income.

In the long run, since firms would find it unprofitable to pay more for a newly produced machine than for an equivalent machine already in existence, the corporate income tax will have repercussions on the market for new capital goods. Faced with a lower demand price, capital goods producers will reduce their output of new capital goods. As a consequence, the growth in the nation's stock of capital will be impeded, and future wage earnings reduced.[10]

Monopoly and the Incidence of the Corporate Income Tax

Competition forces a firm to act as a profit maximizer in order to survive. In the short run, the stock of capital that the firm owns is fixed. Consequently, the short-run marginal cost of production is independent of the market value of the firm's capital stock. The imposition of a tax on the firm's property, therefore, does not alter its short-run marginal cost schedule. It does not affect the demand schedule which the firm faces either. If its pretax output maximized its profit, it had to be producing at a rate where marginal revenue equaled marginal cost. Since the tax does not change its marginal revenue or cost curves, given its current stock of capital, the firm cannot profitably raise its price *and* retain the same stock of capital. The only response it can make to the tax is to attempt to sell off his capital. But as we have seen, if almost all potential purchasers of the capital are subject to the same tax, the market value of the capital must decline.

The foregoing result about the incidence of a tax on corporate property is not materially altered by the presence of monopoly so long as the firms with monopoly power are profit maximizers. The only way for a firm, which has been maximizing profits, to attempt to reduce its tax burden is to attempt to sell off its assets. However, a monopoly is not forced by competition to be a profit maximizer. It may operate on any number of principles, such as mark-up pricing, or sales maximization, which may have left it operating in the inelastic portion of its demand curve. If it finds itself in this position at the time the tax is imposed, it may choose to increase its before-tax profits simply by raising its prices. (Why can't the profit-maximizing monopolist take this action?). As a consequence, in a nonprofit maximizing environment, it is possible to observe after-tax profits that exceed profits before the tax was imposed.

While it is theoretically possible for the corporate income tax to be shifted forward by more than 100 percent, the circumstances under which it can occur seem so implausible to most economists that an empirical study by Musgrave and Krzyzaniak that produced this result[11] has been subject to more scrutiny and criticism than almost any other empirical study in the field of economics. There have been sufficient weaknesses exposed in their econometric methods to convince most economists that at least some of the burden of the corporate income tax is borne by owners of capital.

THE VALUE-ADDED TAX (VAT)

● In addition to income, expenditures, wealth, and transactions, value added has been used by some countries as a base upon which to level a tax. Value added at a given stage of production is simply the difference between the value of output at the end of that stage in the productive process and the value of output at the beginning of that stage. The sum of value added over all processes and all stages is then equal to either gross national product or national income, depending on whether output at each stage is valued at output prices or factor cost net of depreciation charges. A tax based on value added measured on output prices is called a "gross-product" value-added tax, because its base is equivalent to gross national product. A tax based on value added measured at factor cost net of depreciation charges is called an "income-type" value-added tax, because its base is equivalent to national income. If firms are allowed to deduct the value of capital equipment purchases in the year they are made from their tax base, the value-added tax is called a "consumption-type" VAT, because the base is equivalent to a tax on final consumption goods only.

In most countries where VAT has been introduced, it has been used to replace turnover, or sales, taxes levied at several stages in the production process. A sales tax levied on transactions that occur before the sale to a final consumer will represent a larger portion of the retail price of a good whose wholesale price net of tax is a large percentage of its retail price than for a good whose wholesale price is a small percentage of its retail price. A sales tax imposed before the retail level, therefore, will tend to raise the cost of products in which retail inventory turns over quickly relative to products where retail inventory turns over slowly. Food turnover is more rapid than most commodities. Furthermore, food purchases represent a larger portion of the total budget of the poor than of the rich. A sales tax imposed before the retail level, therefore, might be more regressive than a retail sales tax would be. Since the VAT of the consumption type has the same base as a retail sales tax, substitution of VAT for sales taxes on transactions made before the retail level may increase the progressivity of the distribution of the tax burden. In addition, even if the tax imposed on value added at one stage in the production process is passed forward to the next stage in the form of a higher price, it does not enter into the tax base at that next stage, since it is not a part of value added at the next stage. In contrast, a sales tax imposed at every stage in the production process at which a transaction occurs treats price increases induced by the tax imposed at an earlier stage as part of the base of the tax imposed at a later stage. That is, a multiple-stage sales tax is pyramided, while a value-added tax is not. Since the degree of pyramiding·is a function of the number of transactions made in the production process, those goods which can be produced relatively effectively by vertically integrated firms will bear a lower effective tax rate than goods that are produced and marketed by nonvertically integrated firms when a multiple-stage sales tax is used.

SOCIAL SECURITY

● In 1935 the Congress passed the Social Security Act. This act established the Old-Age, Survivors and Disability Insurance (OASDI) program in which revenues from an employment tax were to be earmarked for special trust funds out of which retirement, survivors and disability pensions were to be paid to individuals who had "contributed" their tax dollars to the fund. There have been several amendments to the original act that have extended coverage, increased tax rates and benefits, and extended the scope of the system to include medical insurance for the aged. Today the system covers almost all workers, including those who are self-employed.

Although the payments into the social security trust funds are called "contributions" and the funds are called "insurance" trust funds, there are three fundamental differences between private insurance and pension plans and the social security program. First, the "contributions" are not voluntary. Second, factors other than an individual's past "contributions" into the fund determine his "benefits." The benefit schedule is designed in such a way as to provide a minimum "benefit." It also gives a larger portion of the benefits to low-income workers comparable to their contributions than to high-income workers of the same generation. In addition, family size and wage or salary income at the time benefits are received influence the size of the benefits. These redistributive characteristics would not be marketable features of a private pension or insurance plan. (Why?) The third characteristic of the social security system that differentiates it from a private insurance plan is its "pay-as-you-go" policy. A private pension plan must place a large portion of its current revenues in a capital account in order to insure its contributors that the plan will have a sufficient future cash flow from investments to meet its obligations. In contrast, the social security system is designed to finance current benefits out of current receipts. Such a system can provide future benefits whose value exceeds the value of past contributions only so long as the base of the system expands. Now that the coverage of the system includes virtually all employees and self-employed persons, there are only three ways for the base to expand: an expansion of the labor force, an increase in the maximum wage income subject to tax, and a change in the base of financing from wage income to other forms of income.

Although the absence of significant reserves in its trust fund would make a private pension plan unattractive to potential participants, the expanding revenue base and benefit schedules of social security might make the social security system an attractive alternative to well-managed private pension plans. A well-managed pension plan will produce for its contributors a rate of return on their contributions equal to what a prudent investor could have earned. In comparing the taxes that different individuals can expect to pay with the benefits they can expect to receive, Brittain found that if benefits and earnings grew at real annual rates of between 2 and 3 percent per year, the real rate of return to individuals would vary between 2 and 7 percent, depending upon the average earning level, marital status, and age of entry into the labor force of the individual. For most individuals, the expected real rate of return would exceed that which has been historically available from savings accounts, but would be considerably less than the real rate of return available from equity investments.[12] Brittain's calculations suggest, therefore, that the social security system viewed as a public pension plan is not a particularly attractive alternative to privately operated pension plans. In the long run, there would be more benefits to be divided among all beneficiaries if the social security tax revenues were placed in private pension plans than would be available from a continuation of the "pay-as-you-go" principle in an economy which is experiencing less than 3 percent real rate of growth in per capita income.

As a method of income redistribution, the social security system has two basic weaknesses. The first weakness is its revenue base. Because the coverage of the employment tax is practically universal, employees cannot shift the tax they pay forward by changing jobs. Moreover, the employer's contribution, which matches the employee's "contribution," will be treated by the employer as a part of his wage bill, so that the employee ends up effectively paying the total tax bill. Since wage income is less heavily concentrated among high-income groups than is total income which includes income from property, a wage tax has the character of a regressive income tax. The regressivity of the tax base of the social security system is further enhanced by the provision of a maximum wage limit, above which no tax is payable. Even though the combined effect of the tax and benefit schedules is to redistribute income from high-wage earners to low-wage earners of a given generation, the intragenerational redistribution of income would be much greater if the tax base included income from all sources and had no maximum limitation. Except for the requirement that an individual make "contributions" into the system in order to qualify for "benefits," expansion of the tax base for social security would convert the system into one which had the properties of an income tax with negative rates at low incomes. Indeed, some people have suggested that if a negative income tax were adopted, the social security system should be eliminated. Since the employment tax currently is the second largest federal revenue producer, such a switch would significantly increase the progressivity of the federal tax structure.

The second basic weakness of the social security system is that not all families of the same income class are treated equivalently. Consequently, the system appears quite inequitable in operation. For example, a husband and wife receive more than a single person who has paid in the same amount. Treating the size of the family as a variable in the benefit formula is justified on the grounds that two cannot live as cheaply as one. However, this provision penalizes the family in which both husband and wife have worked. If both claim benefits, they are treated as if they were single individuals. This effectively places a discount on the wife's benefits, since she would have been entitled to some benefits even if she had not been employed. Another source of inequity is that the basic unit for tax purposes differs from the basic unit for benefit purposes. The individual is the basic unit for tax purposes. Given the maximum limit on individual taxable wages, a family with a working wife may pay a larger tax out of family income than a family with a single worker that has the same family income. A third source of inequity arises out of the limitations placed on the earned income of beneficiaries. The income limitation was initially designed to encourage older workers to retire so as to "share the available work." As such, it was a desperation move to reduce unemployment. However, other fiscal policies can be followed to reduce unemployment through an expansion of aggregate demand. Therefore, the principal impact of this feature of the system is to penalize those who have qualified for benefits, but wish to continue working.

INDIRECT TAXES

● In Chapter 5 we defined indirect taxes as taxes that are assessed on the volume and/or value of exchanges in particular markets. As should be clear from our discussion of income and property taxes, these taxes *as they operate* are in the nature of excise taxes, since not all sources and/or kinds of income are subject to the same rate of tax. Consequently, these taxes produce substitution effects (in addition to income effects), which induce a reallocation of resources and, consequently, a change in relative prices. The final distribution of the burden of any tax depends on how the structure of prices is changed. But the change in relative prices depends upon quantitative relationships, which often cannot be known a priori. In this section, we present a short discussion of the role of market structure and factor proportions on the final distribution of the burden of an excise tax in order to illustrate this point.

A Widgets Tax

Suppose that widgets are sold in a competitive market and that the inputs required for the production of widgets represent a very small fraction of the markets for those inputs. Then very large changes in the rate of production of widgets would require very small changes in the rate of total supply of the type of inputs used in their production. Because widgets are sold competitively, in the pretax equilibrium the rate of production will be such that the selling price just covers marginal cost for the marginal firm in the industry. If there are no resources specific to the production of widgets (as our assumptions imply), then the cost of production for every firm will be the same, and marginal cost will equal average cost. Since input prices do not change, the long-run marginal costs will be constant, and the long-run supply curve will be infinitely elastic at the initial equilibrium price. The introduction of a tax will reduce the marginal revenue of every firm in the industry at the old price. Consequently, at the old rate of production, average cost will exceed average revenue, and resources will be diverted from the industry. The reduction in output will continue until the market-clearing price exceeds average cost by the amount of the tax. Since, in this case, average cost remained unchanged as output was reduced, the total burden of the adjustment must fall on the buyers of widgets. This is illustrated in Figure 6.5.

If we retain our assumption about the market structure for widgets, but now assume that there is some resource specific to the output of widgets (as, for example, alumina for aluminum), then our answer changes. In the former case, resources released from production could be absorbed in other uses with no change in their prices. Consequently, the rate of production had no impact on the average cost of production in that case. In this case, however, the maximum price per unit that the owner of the resource specific to the production of widgets can charge is the difference between the producers' total receipts and their total costs for other factors of production divided by the number of available units of the specific resource. As production of widgets change, net receipts gross of payment to the specific factor change in the same direction. Consequently, the price of the specific input is directly related to the rate of the industry's output. Therefore, the industry supply curve will slope upward. With an upward-sloping supply curve, a portion of the burden of the tax will be shifted backward onto the owners of the resource which is specific to the production of widgets. This is illustrated in Figure 6.6.[13] In general, because the resource proportions used in a specific industry differ from the resource proportions in the economy as a whole, the average cost of production will be directly related to the rate of output, and a portion of the tax will be paid by owners of those factors used relatively intensively by the industry in question as they find the price of their services falling. (Note that an individual may find his income reduced even if he doesn't work in the activity upon which the tax is levied.)

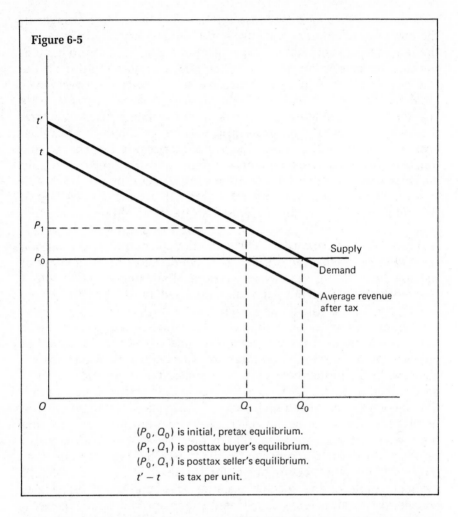

Figure 6-5

(P_0, Q_0) is initial, pretax equilibrium.
(P_1, Q_1) is posttax buyer's equilibrium.
(P_0, Q_1) is posttax seller's equilibrium.
$t' - t$ is tax per unit.

The degree to which the tax is shifted back onto resource owners depends upon the elasticity of the demand curve relative to the supply curve. In our first case, the supply curve was infinitely elastic, and the full burden of the tax was shifted onto consumers. If the supply curve were completely inelastic (indicating that none of the resources had valuable uses elsewhere), all of the burden of the tax would be borne by the resource owners.

Our discussion of the distribution of the burden of a state income tax rested implicitly upon an analysis such as that presented above. Consider the state as a firm selling its products in competition with other states (firms). Each state has certain resources (land) that are specific to its own output and cannot be used in the production of

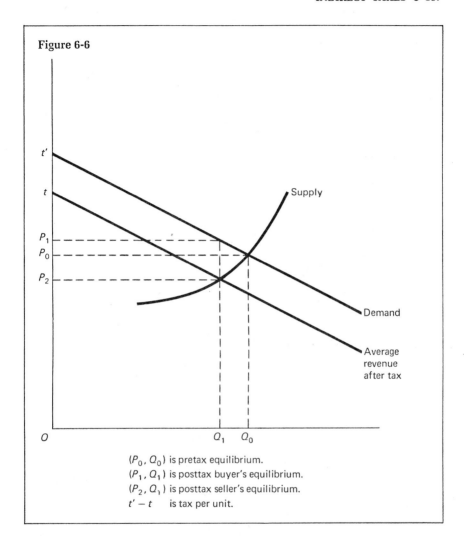

Figure 6-6

(P_0, Q_0) is pretax equilibrium.
(P_1, Q_1) is posttax buyer's equilibrium.
(P_2, Q_1) is posttax seller's equilibrium.
$t' - t$ is tax per unit.

output in other firms. A tax on the revenue generated by the sale of the state's output reduces the most profitable rate of output. As its output is reduced, the net receipts, gross of payments to land in the state falls, and a portion of the burden of the tax is passed back onto owners of land. In the (perhaps not so) extreme circumstances of a small city, where a change in rate of output would have no effect on the selling prices of the products it sold and where all of its capital and labor could eventually find employment elsewhere at their old rates of renumeration, the entire burden of the tax would fall on owners of land. It is in this sense that it is sometimes remarked that all local taxes are ultimately taxes on real estate.

Notes

1. G. Break, "Income Taxes and the Incentives to Work: An Empirical Study," *American Economic Review*, September 1957, p. 549.

2. Thomas Sanders, *Effects of Taxation on Executives*, Boston: Harvard University Press, 1951;
   Robin Barlow, H. Brazer, and J. Morgan, *Economic Behavior of the Affluent*, Washington, D.C.: Brookings Institution, 1966.

3. "Effect of Nonemployment Income and Wage Rates on the Work Incentives of the Poor," *Review of Economics and Statistics*, November 1969.

4. Another aspect of the consumption versus necessary expenditure problem that relates to the income but not the substitution effect of taxes may be mentioned here. There are expenditures necessary for the maintenance of physical and mental well-being and hence indirectly related to productivity. As Pigou saw the problem:

   > Up to a point every £'s worth of any man's purchases of certain sorts of commodities, besides yielding directly satisfaction commensurate with his desire for it, also yields a by-product. This by-product is his own, and perhaps his children's, increased production efficiency. . . . If, in consequence of taxation, his consumption is cut down in such ways that his or his children's efficiency is reduced . . . (then) the ultimate and total sacrifice imposed is larger than the immediate sacrifice. Moreover, it should be noted, the mere fact of a man's spending part of his income on things that do not promote efficiency— "conventional necessaries," and so on—is no proof that cuts in his income, if such are forced upon him, will be made in ways innocuous to efficiency. There will be room for making them in these ways, but a man may easily prefer to hold on to conventional necessaries even at the expense of doing without real necessaries.

   (A. C. Pigou, *Public Finance*, 3rd ed., New York: Macmillan, 1959, pp. 60–61.)

5. For different viewpoints, see N. Kaldor, *An Expenditure Tax*, London: Allen and Unwin, 1955; A. R. Prest, "The Expenditure Tax and Saving," *Economic Journal*, September 1957; R. Goode, *The Individual Income Tax*, Washington, D.C.: Brookings Institution, 1969.

6. Compare the percentage of government revenue collected in income taxes for countries with high and low per capital income. In countries with low per capital income, most of the income tax is paid by civil servants who face withholding by the government prior to wage and salary payment.

7. Suppose the tax rate is t percent. If W_0^A and W_0^B are the before-tax wage rates for jobs A and B, respectively, and W_1^A and W_1^B are the after-tax rates, then $W_1^A = (1-t)W_0^A$, $W_1^B = (1-t)W_0^B$. If $W_0^A = 2W_0^B$, then

$$2 = \frac{W_1{}^A}{W_1{}^B} = \frac{(1-t)W_0{}^A}{(1-t)W_0{}^B} = \frac{W_0{}^A}{W_0{}^B}$$

But

$$\frac{2W_0{}^B - W_0{}^B}{(1-t)2W_0{}^B - (1-t)W_0{}^B} = \frac{1}{1-t}$$

so that the absolute difference is also reduced by t percent as a consequence of the proportional tax.

8. The present value of the first alternative is

$$\sum_{i=1}^{20} \frac{500}{(1+0.05)^i} + \frac{10,000}{(1+0.05)^{20}} = 10,000$$

The present value of the skill alternative is

$$\sum_{i=1}^{20} \frac{x}{(1+0.05)^i}$$

Two investments that are equally attractive must have the same present value. If $x = \$800$, then the present value of the investment in skills will be approximately $9970.

9. Why does the investor require a $105 difference in possible gain to just compensate an equally probable $100 difference in possible loss? Possibly because the marginal utility of income diminishes as income increases. If this is true, then the gain in utility per dollar reduction in possible loss must be greater than the loss in utility per dollar reduction in possible gains. Since the riskier asset, B, has a greater dollar change in possible gains and losses $\{[t(705), t(-500)]$ vs. $[t(600), t(-400)]\}$ than A, it must become relatively more attractive than A.

10. Of course, all taxes reduce disposable income. Since savings are related to disposable income, all taxes will have an impact on the rate of capital accumulation. From the point of view of higher-wage incomes, labor will benefit from those taxes that have the smallest impact on the savings rate. From this point of view, Krzyzaniak has found that it would be in labor's interests to switch from the corporate income tax to an equal-yield tax on wage income. (See M. Krzyzaniak, "The Long-Run Burden of a General Tax on Profits in a Neoclassical World," Public Finance, Vol. XXII, No. 4, 1967, and "The Differential Incidence of Taxes on Profits and on Factor Incomes," Finenzarchives, 1971.)

11. N. Krzyzaniak and R. A. Musgrave, The Shifting of the Corporate Income Tax, Baltimore: Johns Hopkins Press, 1963.

12. J. A. Brittain, "The Real Rate of Interest on Lifetime Contributions Toward Retirement Under Social Security," in Old Age Income Assurance, Compendium of Papers on Problems and Policy Issues in the Public and Private Pension System, Part III, Public Programs, 90th Congress, 1st Session, 1967, pp. 109–114.

13. It is possible to conceptualize the case of a tax on a product produced by a

monopoly by considering the monopolist as supplying a factor which has no alternative uses and hence involves no opportunity costs. The previous analysis of the excise tax then applies. The substitution effect of the tax will lead to some increase in demand price as output is reduced. But the increase in price will be less than the rate of tax, a portion of the adjustment being made by a reduction in the rate of monopoly profit.

Questions for Discussion

1. Many studies of the incidence of various property taxes have assumed that the burden of a tax on a given class of property would be shifted forward to the renters of the property. On the basis of this shifting assumption, most studies have shown the burden of various property taxes, observed one at a time, falls relatively more heavily on the poor than on the wealthy. Why, therefore, do these results not imply that a general property tax based on all classes of property in the country would have the character of a regressive income tax?

2. Two pervasive, unpleasant characteristics of urban areas are (1) the decrease in density as the city grows, thus requiring an increase in per capita expenditures on urban services, and (2) the continued occupation of valuable central area real estate by low-value, run-down buildings. Some economists have argued that by removing the tax on structures and increasing the tax on sites, the city would develop a more dense settlement pattern, and the conversion of valuable sites to highest-valued uses would occur more quickly. What is the rationale for such claims?

3. Why are most local governments heavily dependent on real estate taxes while the federal government is not?

4. *Tax exempt municipal bonds.* Interest income from municipal bonds is not subject to federal income tax. Suppose the tax exemption were removed.
   a. What would happen to the interest cost of local government bond-financed projects?
   b. What would happen to local government tax rates?
   c. Would the after-tax income of the average purchaser of municipal bonds be affected by removal of the exemption?

5. If all assets had the character of default-free, irredeemable bonds with fixed coupon rates, changes in the market value of existing bonds would simply reflect changes in the interest rate. If an individual sells a bond at a capital gain, he could do so only because the interest rate has fallen. But, given a lower interest rate, he will not be able to buy, with the proceeds of his bond sale, a claim to a larger sustained flow of cash receipts than he would have gotten if he simply held onto his old bonds. That is, the change in capital value yields him no change in income. The logic of this example would seem to indicate that *no* taxes should be paid on capital gains. Yet many writers argue that capital gains ought to be more heavily taxed than they currently are. How do you reconcile these views?

6. Some admirers of capitalism have argued that private ownership spurs innovative activity by allowing individuals to keep whatever profits they can generate for themselves by producing better and/or lower-cost products for the market. Critics of capitalism point to the widely unequal distribution of income which such an incentive system can produce. Can you suggest any tax plan that a capitalist country might adopt which would redistribute income without reducing the incentives to innovative activity?

Suggested Readings

George, H., *Progress and Poverty*, New York: Modern Library, 1939.

Goode, R., *The Corporation Income Tax*, New York: Wiley, 1951.

Goode, R., *The Individual Income Tax*, Washington, D.C.: Brookings Institution, 1964.

Gordon, R. J., "Incidence of Corporate Income Tax," *American Economic Review*, Vol. 57, No. 4, September 1967, pp. 731–758.

Harberger, A., "The Incidence of the Corporate Income Tax," *Journal of Political Economy*, Vol. 70, No. 3, June 1962, pp. 215–240.

Kaldor, N., *An Expenditure Tax*, London: Allen and Unwin, 1955.

Krzyzaniak, N., and Musgrave, R. A., *The Shifting of the Corporate Income Tax*, Baltimore: Johns Hopkins Press, 1963.

Morgan, D., *Retail Sales Tax: An Appraisal of New Issues*, Madison: University of Wisconsin Press, 1964.

Netzer, D., *Economics of the Property Tax*, Washington, D.C.: Brookings Institution, 1966.

7

THE PRINTING PRESS

The effect of taxation that is most noticeable to the average person is that it reduces the amount of money he has to spend, while providing the public treasury with more money to spend. An alternative way of providing money for the state's coffers is simply to print it. Furthermore, as we shall argue below, since the economy will function better with currency than without it, financing government purchases by printing additional money may sometimes represent a true alternative to reducing the purchasing power of private individuals, that is, to taxation. The topic to which this chapter is addressed, therefore, is: "When does money creation represent an alternative to taxation and when does it simply represent a form of taxation?"

MONEY

● In a modern economy, the direct exchange of commodities for commodities between any pair of individuals is extremely rare. The reason, of course, is because individuals have become specialized in their productive activities. Consequently, an elaborate network of marketing activities is required to coordinate the exchanges required to balance supplies and demands. The marketing problem of the individual, in his capacity as both seller and buyer, is not simply one of identifying a set of individuals who wish to sell what he wishes to buy and to buy what he wishes to sell. For it is quite likely that these sets are not composed of the same people. In order to remain specialized in production, an individual must participate either directly or indirectly in a system of exchanges that balance out supplies and demands in products other than those in which he himself is interested. We can illustrate this proposition with a simple example. Suppose individual A produces wine and wishes to sell some of it in order to buy some bread, which is produced by individual B. B, however, does not want wine; he wishes to purchase some meat, which is produced by individual C. Unfortunately, C wishes to buy some wine rather than bread, but A does not desire any meat. In this example, no direct bilateral trade is possible, since there are no "double coincidences" or matching of wants. Neither A, B, nor C can find a buyer who has to trade what he wishes to buy. In order to sustain the specialization of labor among A, B, and C, therefore, a more complex marketing system must develop. In our simple example, this might take either of two forms. First, A, B, and C might enter multilateral negotiations, which will produce a common agreement as to how much wine A will ship to C, how much meat C will ship to B, and how much bread B will ship to A. Here, each party takes an active role in determining how much trade takes place among all parties. Clearly, this means of balancing trade by direct, multilateral negotiations is not feasible once the number of parties involved becomes large. A second method of allowing A, B, and C to retain their respective producing specialties is to introduce a broker who establishes a market in one of the commodities. For example, let A become a broker in meat. He will establish a market for meat by agreeing to exchange wine for meat with C. Having acquired meat, A can then resell it to B for bread. In this way, A in his capacity as broker has effected two bilateral trades which could produce the same result as the multilateral agreement described above. He does this by accepting in trade a commodity which he does not really desire—meat, in order to use it for securing a commodity which he does desire. In effect, meat has become a medium of exchange, which allows B and C to deal only indirectly with each other via A's activity as a broker.

Unlike the multilateral trade solution, the brokerage solution does lend itself to extension to large numbers of parties by (possibly) multiplying the number of brokers while maintaining the essential bilateral nature of every exchange. The brokerage function becomes a specialty of its own (or rather a class of specialties) in which individuals specialize in taking the risks of establishing and maintaining markets. The extent of trade flowing through markets depends upon the cost of arranging market transactions.

Two important transactions costs are (1) costs of transportation and handling and (2) costs of bearing the risks attendant with buying merchandise for resale. By the introduction of credit instruments, it is possible to reduce transport and handling costs. For example, rather than accepting delivery of meat from C in exchange for wine, A might secure a transferable promissory note from C to send the bearer on demand a stated number of pounds of meat. Individual A could then exchange this note with B for loaves of bread. In this way, C's promissory note rather than goods, which are more expensive to ship and to handle, becomes the medium of exchange. C's promissory note may, or may not, be as useful a medium of exchange as C's goods. This depends on the faith which B has in C's promise. If B could be certain that C would honor his debt obligation, then he would offer A as favorable terms for the debt instrument as for the meat itself. But if he is not certain that C can and will deliver what he has promised, then B will only accept a claim to meat at a discount from delivery of meat itself. The default risk will, in turn, affect the terms at which A will deal with C. Therefore, if default risk is attached to a credit instrument which is used as the medium of exchange, it will adversely affect the total volume of trade in the same manner as high transportation costs for a commodity medium. Consequently, a credit instrument is an attractive medium of exchange only if the risk of default by its issuer is small.

As the number of individuals participating in market transactions increases and the pattern of trade becomes more complex and indirect, it becomes impossible for any individual to know the reliability of all the other individuals against whom he may acquire claims in exchange for his own produce. Consequently, a complex trading pattern requires the use of a medium of exchange which is *generally* acceptable without discount, that is, money. The government is in a most advantageous position to create such a medium by issuing its own notes in exchange for goods and services and declaring that such notes may be exchanged for cancellation of tax liabilities. Since most individuals have tax liabilities, these notes will become generally acceptable in exchanges between private individuals as well. To further assure that its notes become money, the government may declare them legal tender, thereby legally obliging a creditor to accept them without discount for the cancellation of debt.

In creating a credit instrument which serves as the generally accepted medium of exchange, the government is producing a public good. All traders, whether or not they currently hold money, are better off than they would be if no generally accepted medium existed, since its existence reduces both the costs of commodity handling and the risks of engaging in trade. At the same time, because money plays such an important role in the economy, control of the supply of money gives the government a potentially powerful tool for controlling the level of activity in the economy. We shall develop this aspect of fiscal policy somewhat in the next section and much more fully in Chapter 9.

THE DEMAND AND SUPPLY OF MONEY

● Individuals and business firms do not usually find it convenient or possible to arrange for the simultaneous sale and purchase of commodities. Instead of taking receipts from sales and immediately using them to replenish inventories, business firms find it more convenient and less costly to place relatively large orders at somewhat less frequent intervals than small orders at very frequent intervals. Between the time of sale and the replenishment of inventory, therefore, they hold cash which they may leave idle or lend out for a short period of time. If it is lent out, the firm will earn interest on its investment. Against these earnings, the firm must weigh both the brokerage cost of buying and then selling bonds as it wishes to purchase goods and the risks attendant to holding its assets in the form of bonds. These two factors will generally lead the firm to desire to hold at least some fraction of its financial wealth in the form of money. The size of this fraction will vary inversely with the interest income it will *have to forego* on assets held in the form of money.[1]

Because individuals desire at any given point in time to hold a stock of money, an institution or individual whose financial notes have become accepted as money will find that it can issue notes whose value is in excess of its actual ability to redeem. This is because some fraction of its indebtedness will be held for purposes of facilitating exchanges in the economy. In the United States monetary system, commercial banks have been able to establish their notes (demand deposits against which checks may be drawn) as money by agreeing to pay any holder of their notes legal tender on demand. In fact, there is not enough legal tender in existence for the commercial banks to honor all of their demand notes. But, since only a fraction of their notes outstanding is ever presented for payment in legal tender, banks can maintain the credibility of their claim simply by maintaining an adequate fractional reserve of legal tender to satisfy usual note-redemption requests. Given this need to maintain the credibility of their promise to pay on demand, the stock of demand deposits would, even in the absence of government stipulation, be tied to the stock of government-issued currency. Ultimately, therefore, changes in the supply of money are controlled by government decisions.[2]

While the stock of money in existence must always be held by some set of individuals, there is no logical necessity for anyone to be satisfied with his current holdings. If an individual finds that, at current prices and interest rates, he would be better off holding more commodities and/or bonds and less money than he is currently holding, he will attempt to exchange his cash for other assets. If his excess supply of money is not offset by someone else's excess supplies of other assets, that is, if there is a net excess supply of money in the economy — prices and interest rates will change. As interest rates fall, the cost of holding money falls so as to lead people to wish to hold more money. In addition, the increased demand for commodities will expand the money value of transactions (which equals the average price per transaction multiplied by the number of transactions). This increase in the money value of transactions will lead people to wish to hold more cash to facilitate these transactions. The changes in the interest rate and the money value of output, therefore, both contribute to bringing the demand for money holdings in to line with the stock of money in existence.

INFLATION AND TAXATION

● As long as the government's notes are generally accepted as money, it has the option of securing resources from the private sector either by raising taxes, by borrowing, or by printing more money. When there is excess capacity in the economy, an increase in the supply of money will stimulate production. The resources the government secures will come, therefore (at least partly), from stocks that would not otherwise have been utilized. In this case, output expands while prices may remain unchanged. Here, the financing of government expenditures by issuing more money is a true alternative to taxation. Public output expands without sacrificing private goods. But if the economy is operating at full capacity, resources secured by the government must be sacrificed by private users. This can be accomplished only by taxation or by borrowing. The government is free to print new money in order to pay for its purchases, but when the economy is already at full capacity, the issuance of new money has the effect of raising prices. This inflation of prices reduces the purchasing power of individuals' money holdings and, in effect, is a tax on money holdings. Under conditions of full employment, therefore, there is no alternative to taxation in financing government expenditures.[3]

Anticipated Versus Unanticipated Inflation

If an individual anticipates a general rise in prices, he will revise his plans for the future in light of that expectation. If prices are going to rise, then a dollar available tomorrow will purchase less than a dollar available today. Consequently, potential lenders will see that the opportunity cost of foregoing present purchases will be increased by the anticipated price increase. They will, therefore, demand a higher rate of interest to cover their foregone opportunities. Borrowers, in turn, will be willing to pay the higher rate, since they expect a capital gain via price appreciation on the goods they currently purchase. As a result, the money rate of interest rises to accommodate the same current transfer of resources from lenders to borrowers in exchange for the same future transfer from borrowers to lenders that would have occurred in the absence of a rise in money prices and interest rates.

However, if the inflation is not anticipated, the current money interest rate will not reflect the unanticipated change in future prices. Borrowers will secure a capital gain which is not offset by higher interest payment obligations to lenders. Consequently, lenders will find that they receive a smaller (and borrowers, a larger) command over future resources than they had planned on. In other words, if an unanticipated inflation occurs, wealth will be redistributed between lenders and borrowers.

As a practical matter, neither the onset of an inflation nor its actual rate is ever anticipated by groups who have made long-term commitments a considerable period in advance of the price rise. Pensioners and other annuity holders as well as welfare recipients, whose money income tends not to rise in periods of inflation, are, therefore, groups who tend to suffer from inflation.

Another important area in which an unanticipated inflation will generate wealth redistributions is between wage earners and capital income earners. If a union or an individual enters into a multiyear labor contract with expectations of general price stability, it will find its actual real wage to be less than anticipated. Conversely, companies will find their real rates of return in excess of anticipations. Of course, if the inflation is anticipated, the wage bargain will reflect the expected rate either explicitly in terms of future money wages or implicitly via "cost of living" escalator clauses.

Regardless of whether or not the inflation is anticipated, holders of money at the time prices rise find their command over resources reduced. If the anticipated rise in prices is large, therefore, there will be an incentive to avoid holding the government's notes and other notes whose "moneyness" is tied to their redemption in government issue. Firms will seek alternative media of exchange (for example, use of a foreign currency) which, in general, will be more costly. In cases of hyperinflation, the government's notes and bank certificates based on them will simply lose general acceptability.[4]

Inflation and Growth

As we indicated earlier, when inflation is anticipated, the rate of interest on current loans increases to reflect the fact that such loans will be paid back in a depreciated currency. This increased money interest rate implies a higher opportunity cost of holding cash. At this higher cost, individuals will find it in their interest to attempt to hold a larger portion of their financial wealth in the form of bonds. In order to get borrowers to accept this additional exchange of dollars for indebtedness, lenders will find that the new money rate of interest cannot be sustained at a rate sufficient to cover the initial (preinflation) interest rate plus full compensation for the anticipated depreciation of the value of money. This is because borrowers will only expand their indebtedness if they can profitably put the additional funds to work by expanding their investments in plant and equipment. But, as this expansion occurs, the return to capital is diminished. Therefore, indebtedness will only expand if the new rate of interest, net of compensation for depreciation of the value of money (the real rate of interest), is lower than the initial preinflation rate. Through this "portfolio" effect, therefore, a sustained rate of inflation may generate an increase in the rate of capital accumulation and growth rate of the economy.

Whether inflation is actually a stimulus to growth depends upon whether the portfolio effect is offset, or enhanced, by (1) a change in aggregate savings propensity induced by the wealth redistribution which its onset produces and (2) by the increased costs of making transactions.

SUMMARY

● A modern complex exchange economy requires the existence of a generally accepted medium of exchange, or money. Because the government has tax claims against most individuals, its own notes will be generally acceptable for payment of private as well as public debts.

In periods of unemployment, government purchases financed by expansion of the money supply draw resources from stocks that would otherwise be unemployed. In such circumstances, there will be no pressure on the general price level. Furthermore, an economy whose productive capacity is growing can absorb (limited) increases in the money supply without price inflation. However, if government attempts to finance purchases without resorting to other forms of taxation lead to a too-rapid expansion of the money supply, inflation will result. This inflation is simply a tax on money holdings.

A tax on money holdings will lead to an increased rate of lending and attempts to effect exchanges without using money. A further effect of such a "tax," if it has not been anticipated, is to redistribute wealth from those who in the past had agreed to future fixed-money agreements, such as life insurance purchasers and wage earners with long-term contracts that make no provision for inflation. Furthermore, since inflation is rarely an announced form of taxation, it is difficult for decision makers to know how to plan for it. By making future terms uncertain, the risk of inflation is likely to lead to shorter-planning horizons and the substitution of short- for long-term investments.

Notes

1. There is a large literature on the transaction demand for money. See, for example, W. Baumol, "The Transactions Demand for Cash: An Inventory Theoretic Approach," *Quarterly Journal of Economics*, Vol. 66, November 1952, pp. 545–556; J. Tobin, "The Interest Elasticity of Transactions Demand for Cash," *Review of Economics and Statistics*, Vol. 38, August 1956, pp. 241–247; E. Feige and M. Parkin, "The Optimal Quantity of Money, Bonds, Commodity Inventories, and Capital," *American Economic Review*, Vol. 61, June 1971, pp. 335–349.
2. For a fuller account of money supply creation as well as the role of money substitutes in the U.S. monetary system, see any good text on money and banking.
3. As will be discussed more fully in Chapter 8, current borrowing can be thought of as an obligation to collect future taxes to repay current lenders.
4. Historical instances include the Hungarian inflation of 1945–1946 and the German inflation of 1920–1923.

Questions for Discussion

1. Considering inflation as a tax, what is the nature of its excess burden?
2. If, on equity grounds, inflation is considered a "bad tax," would deflation be considered a "good" form of subsidy?
3. Which policy of diverting resources to public use do you think would have the greater excess burden — an open inflation, or a policy of printing money combined with wage and price controls to prevent the price level from rising?

Suggested Readings

Bailey, M. J., "The Welfare Cost of Inflationary Finance," *Journal of Political Economy*, Vol. 64, 1956, pp. 93–110.

Kessel, R., and Alchian, A., "Effects of Inflation," *Journal of Political Economy*, Vol. 70, 1962, pp. 521–537.

Tobin, J., "Money and Economic Growth," *Econometrica*, Vol. 33, 1965, pp. 671–684.

8

THE NATIONAL DEBT

In a full-employment economy, the government has only two options with respect to financing its current expenditures. It may tax or it may borrow. The government's choice of financing method will determine who bears the burden of the foregone private production which the government's expenditure displaces. In this chapter, we analyze the burden of the debt.

DEBT AND THE INTERGENERATIONAL REDISTRIBUTION OF WEALTH

● Individuals will purchase government bonds voluntarily only if they have some assurance that they will be repaid sometime in the future. That assurance lies ultimately in the ability of the government to raise taxes to meet its annual interest obligations, since as long as it can do so, it will be able to float new issues to replace those that have reached maturity. In this way, the possibility of current deficit financing rests ultimately on the creation of future tax liabilities. Therefore, the choice between raising current taxes and issuing bonds to finance current expenditures is a choice between creating a current tax liability and creating a liability for future taxes that has the same present value.

Even if the same tax system that currently exists were to prevail in the future, deficit financing would not be socially equivalent to raising current taxes to meet current expenditures. The reason, of course, is that while "society" assumes the responsibility of meeting the future tax liabilities when it issues debt, the *membership* of society will be different in the future from what it is today. As a consequence, individuals who are living at the time of debt issue do not face over their lifetimes a future tax liability whose present value is equal to the debt incurred. The generation existing at time of issue will, therefore, act as if its real wealth had been increased by the issuance of bonds instead of current taxes to finance current expenditures. With a (perceived) increase in real wealth, this generation will wish to increase its rate of current consumption. But, since the issuance of government bonds is purely a financial transaction which does not expand the current productive capacity of the economy, this debt-induced increase in consumption must reduce the flow of resources going into new capital formation. In this way, the issuance of debt diverts more resources from current capital formation than would the levying of current taxes to raise the same revenue. Since the capital stock is passed on from generation to generation, the issuance of debt has the effect of a levy on the legacy to be left to the future.

It is important to emphasize that this analysis of the intergenerational impact of deficit financing rests squarely upon the assumption of a full-employment economy. If the economy were operating at less than full employment, it would be possible for the government to secure additional resources without diverting them from either present consumption or investment by running a deficit. The financing of this deficit can occur by increasing the supply of money. For institutional reasons, in a fractional reserve banking system, the increase in the money supply may occur indirectly by the purchase of government bonds by the banking system. In such cases, the public debt is increased, but since no resources are diverted from private investment, this increase in the debt does not transfer wealth from the future to the present generations.

EXTERNAL VERSUS INTERNAL DEBT

● Historically, discussion about the burden a public debt places on future generations has focused upon the tax liabilities it creates in order to pay the interest obligations. According to one point of view, if one treats the future generations as a group, then the necessity to raise taxes to meet the interest obligations can represent a burden only if some portion of the debt is held by foreigners. This is because if the debt is held internally, for every dollar of tax collected from a domestic resident, a dollar in interest payments will be made to a domestic resident so that on balance the necessity to pay interest does not make the group any worse off. However, it is argued, if the taxes collected domestically go to pay interest to foreign owners of the bonds, then domestic taxpayers taken as a group will find their incomes reduced as a result of the existence of the debt.

A second point of view argues that this distinction between the burden of an internally held and of an externally held debt is wholly artificial. According to this view, the important distinction is between bondholder and taxpayer.

Holding a bond is a voluntary act. Paying taxes is not. When the purchaser of the bond sacrifices current command over resources, he must be fully compensated by the promise of a higher future income. The burden of the government expenditures financed by his bond purchase must, therefore, fall upon those who must pay taxes in order to fulfill the obligations of the government to its bondholders be they citizens or foreigners. Furthermore, it is argued, the assertion that interest payments made to foreigners reduces domestic income ignores the obverse fact that at the time the bonds are sold to foreigners, resources are received from abroad which would not otherwise have been available for domestic use. These resources provide for the reduction in domestic income as the foreign bondholders are repaid, so that externally held debt creates no more or less of a burden than does internally held debt.

The analysis of the impact of the debt on the intergenerational distribution of wealth is not fully consistent with either of these views on the burden of the debt. It is inconsistent with the first view, since that view denies that an internally held debt creates a burden on future generations. It is inconsistent with the second view, because that view denies that future holders of the government's bonds are made worse off by the creation of a public debt. The analysis of the intergenerational impact of the debt implies, to the contrary, that the existence of the debt may not only affect the distribution of income at each point in the future, but will also affect the level of income to be distributed.

GROSS VERSUS NET BURDEN AND DEBT POLICY

● The preceding discussion of the burden of the debt served only to show that deficit financing of government expenditures will reduce the current rate of private capital formation without regard to what use the government puts the resources it acquires. If the government places the resources into capital projects which will produce benefits over a substantial period of time, these benefits may be of more value to future generations than the foregone benefits from the private savings which the debt displaces. Taking the position that the rate of growth of the economy is best determined by individual savings decisions, some authors have, therefore, proposed that separate budgets be established for current and capital expenditures. In periods of full employment, the capital budget (and only the capital budget) would be financed by the sale of bonds, whose amortization schedule would correspond to the useful life of the projects that they finance. In this way no net burden would be passed on to any generation, and the debt policy could be called neutral with respect to growth.

Not all observers believe that the growth rate of the economy ought to be determined by individual savings decisions. As we noted in Chapter 4, many authors believe that individuals tend to display positive time preference or discriminate against future consumption possibilities in favor of present consumption. They further believe that such discrimination is unethical and that the government ought to act to compensate for this myopia. According to another view, the market fails to account for the interdependencies that may exist between one generation's level of consumption and another's level of utility, so that a joint savings decision is required for a pareto optimal allocation of resources. Still others argue that many government policies (for example, the corporate income tax, property taxes,) market failures, the inability of individuals to secure educational loans at reasonable rates of interest, and monopoly constraints on expansion of capacity so distort the individual's view of the return to investment that a market-determined rate of saving has no normative significance. Each of these views would support a nonneutral debt policy as an instrument in affecting the aggregate rate of saving.

SUMMARY

● Selling bonds to finance current expenditures shifts the burden of sacrifice of private opportunities from present to future taxpayers. Since not all present taxpayers will also be future taxpayers, this represents a redistribution of wealth from the future to the present generation. This redistribution is effected by a shift from investment to consumption in the current period.

Since the purchase of bonds is a voluntary activity, individuals who agree to their purchase cannot be assumed to have sacrificed anything in giving up claim to use of current resources. They are fully compensated by the acquisition of additional claims (in the form of bonds) to future resource use. It is the future taxpayer, therefore, who bears the burden of the debt. Since future bondholders and taxpayers are not likely to be perfectly paired, the debt will influence the distribution of income at future points in time.

Once it is recognized that debt policy can effect intergenerational transfers, ethical questions arise as to whether the government should manipulate its debt policy to determine the legacy each generation leaves to its progeny.

Questions for Discussion

1. In a growing economy, it is necessary to have a growing supply of money in order to maintain a stable price level. One way of supplying the additional currency is to have the government buy back its bonds with newly printed currency. Alternatively, the government might reduce taxes and finance its deficit by issuing currency. Compare the effects of these policies on the aggregate rate of savings out of full-employment output.

2. A major portion of the U.S. debt was incurred to finance expenditures during World War II. These expenditures did not result in a larger stock of publicly owned capital. Could their financing by bond issue be justified by those who hold that the government should have a neutral debt policy?

3. If it is possible to shift the burden of current government expenditures to future generations by financing those expenditures via the sale of bonds, what (if anything) in the absence of moral restraint prevents each generation from financing all of its government expenditures by increasing the national debt?

4. Should a government, which refrains from issuing new debt because it does not wish to reduce the aggregate rate of savings, prevent its citizens from buying foreign bonds?

Suggested Readings

Buchanan, J., *Public Principles of Public Debt*. Homewood, Ill.: Irwin, 1958.
A critique of the no-future-burden position.

Domar, E. D., "The Burden of the Debt and the National Income," *American Economic Review*, 1944.
Explores the limits on debt expansion generated by increasing interest costs.

Ferguson, J., ed., *Public Debt and Future Generations*, Chapel Hill, N.C.: University of North Carolina Press, 1964.

Thompson, E. A., "Debt Instruments in Macroeconomic and Capital Theory," *American Economic Review*, December 1967, pp. 1196–1210.

9

STABILIZATION POLICY

The only certainty about the future is its
uncertainty.

It is a matter of historical record that there have been periods, sometimes of extended duration, in which capitalistic economies have not
utilized all of the labor that was seeking work. These periods of unemployment result from the failure of markets to coordinate the plans
for action constructed by myriads of individual consumers and suppliers. In a free-market system, planning is highly decentralized. Individuals are connected to one another, and influence the decisions
of one another, only by affecting the prices at which goods and services
are traded.

When ownership of resources is widespread and decision making
decentralized, there is no guarantee that plans will be consistent. The
textile manufacturer must commit resources today for the production of
cloth he *hopes* clothing manufacturers will buy in future periods. And
the clothing manufacturer, in turn, is forced to guess (and bet) today on
what the market will be next season. Individuals perform highly specialized tasks. They depend on others wanting to buy what they have to
sell and wanting to sell what they wish to buy. Those who save, who
decide how much of currently produced goods they wish to make available for reinvestment, are not the same group who decide by how much
the stocks of capital should grow. The only forms of communication
between these groups is indirect, via changes in prices and market
surveys. Such information can be easily misinterpreted. A falling price
indicates excess supply at the old price, but leaves unanswered
whether or not at the now lower price a state of excess supply continues
to exist. Even if at the lower price the quantity people would plan to

buy would be consistent with the quantity offered, *assuming that the price did not change*, people may expect the price to continue to fall and so withhold their offers to buy. In this case, the just established price will not clear the market, and price will continue to decline, thereby fulfilling buyers' expectations.

If, in the aggregate, producers are planning to supply more than purchasers are planning to purchase, so that a general state of excess supply of outputs exists, then producers, finding themselves accumulating unanticipated stocks, will reduce their demand for inputs, creating a condition of general excess supply of labor or general unemployment.

The consequences of this lack of synchronization of plans is twofold. First, resources are being used inefficiently. The same supply of resources could produce goods of greater total value. Secondly, since wages represent the principal source of income to those who work, the burden of the loss in economic value, when aggregate demand is less than aggregate supply, falls most heavily on unemployed wage earners. Thus, while the difference between the aggregate value of full-employment output and the value of output produced with, say, 5 percent of labor unemployed may be close to 5 percent, the loss of value to those 5 percent may be close to 100 percent. That is, the cost of the inefficiency created by a failure of markets to effectively coordinate planning tends to be concentrated on a relatively small percentage of the decision makers involved.

Advocates of central planning have argued that by taking control of resources out of the hands of individuals and consolidating the planning process in a central authority, a central output plan could be constructed so that there was never any unemployed labor. At the crudest level, everyone could simply be arbitrarily assigned jobs. This would eliminate "unemployment" in one sense of the word but would almost certainly not satisfy the conditions of producer efficiency. That is, starting from an arbitrary assignment of resources to productive processes, it would be possible to shuffle the resources around and alter the input proportions so as to produce more of some goods and no less of any others than was formerly produced. During this shuffling-around period, everyone would be "working," would be assigned a job, but they would not be producing as much as they could if the initial allocation were producer efficient. In effect, it will be as if "full employment" were achieved by having some workers digging ditches and then refilling them. Of course, this period of unproductive work could be eliminated if the central planner knew about every production process available to the economy. If he had such a detailed notebook of blueprints at his command, then he could make hypothetical assignments on paper and simulate the effects of reassignments without actually (physically) transferring resources from one process to another. Unfortunately, such detailed, comprehensive knowledge is not generally available to the central planner. Consequently, the trial-and-error groping for the production-possibility frontier must involve some mechanism to transmit such knowledge to the central planning office. This act of knowledge transferal may take considerable time during which resources continue to be used inefficiently.

Even if central planners were able to keep the economy on the production-possibility frontier, there may still be considerable amounts of unproductive work and wasted effort if the goods being produced are not consistent with consumer preferences. Producing the wrong goods efficiently is just as wasteful as producing the right kinds of goods by inefficient processes. Therefore, in both socialist countries with detailed central planning and in capitalist free-market economies, there exists a problem of transmitting information from buyers to those who must make production decisions. When a nation is at war and war production is the top priority, the problem of consumer-good production can be neglected. But in times of peace, the problem of deciding what to produce is as vexatious to a central planner as it is to a New York garment manufacturer.

To recapitulate, detailed central planning does not eliminate unemployment if by unemployment it is meant the production of a non-pareto optimal bundle of goods and services. But the social consequences of the less than full utilization of resources in a centrally planned economy are much different than the consequences of unemployment in a laissez-faire environment. As noted earlier, the effects of laissez-faire unemployment are concentrated in greatly reduced incomes for a relatively small number of people. In a centrally planned economy, the costs of the inefficiencies in production planning are spread over the entire population via the shortages of goods which crop up.

Capitalist countries, after the Great Depression of the 1930s, recognized the need for some kind of national employment policy intervention to prevent the economy from developing extended periods of general excess supply or excess demand for labor while allowing free operation of almost all markets. The theoretical basis for this kind of policy of maintaining consistency between aggregate demand and production plans was set out by John Maynard Keynes in his book, *The General Theory of Employment, Interest and Money.*

In this book, Keynes argued that the adjustment of money wage rates to a *general* state of excess supply in the labor markets could not be expected to increase total employment in the same manner that a decline in the price of an unimportant commodity, say, of tea, may be expected to increase its consumption. Tea producers, themselves, spend only a small fraction of their income on tea. Therefore, a decline in the price of tea, even if it reduces the tea producer's income, will not significantly reduce the producer's demand for his own product. Since the tea price reduction induces everyone else to expand his tea purchases, the net effect of the reduction in the price of tea will be to increase the quantity purchased.

However, a decline in the money price of labor will entail a significant reduction in money incomes. As a consequence of generally smaller money incomes, consumer expenditures for goods and services may fall proportionately with money prices. This would leave the total volume of goods and services purchased at the now lower prices unchanged from the volume purchased at the higher prices. In the aggregate, total expenditures for goods and services could not be divorced from the income people receive from the products and services they sell. Indeed, if one simply looks at the transactions *after they have been completed*, total expenditures on final goods and services will always equal total income payments to factors of production. From a behavioral, rather than accounting, point of view, it is clear that an individual's spending behavior will be closely related to the income he expects to receive.[1] In any given period, of course, an individual or any other decision unit may spend either more or less for goods and services than the income it anticipates receiving. If a decision unit decides to spend less than the income it anticipates, then it must also decide whether to use its net cash flow (savings) to increase its cash holdings or to purchase financial assets. If it decides to expend more on goods and services than can be financed by its income, then the decision unit must either draw down its cash position or borrow. Since a fall in wages and prices reduces income, and since income is a principal determinant of expenditures, Keynes argued that a fall in wages and prices would only stimulate demand for real goods and services if it influenced individuals' savings and borrowing decisions. To analyze the effect of a reduction in wages and prices produced by an excess supply of labor at the going wage rate, therefore, it is necessary to construct a model of the economy in which one could trace the interrelations between a change in the conditions of the labor market and a change in conditions in the financial and commodity markets.

Keynes's great contribution was not only to produce a general equilibrium model within which one could conceivably analyze such relationships, but to produce a model of sufficient simplicity to allow actual estimation or measurement of the relations specified in the model. The importance of being able to carry out analysis with models whose relations have been quantified cannot be overstressed when dealing with policy issues. In an economic system, prices and quantities are simultaneously determined. A change in one market induces changes in others, and these changes, in turn, feed back upon the market in which the initial change was made. In order to predict the final outcome, one must have some quantitative estimate of the impact of all of these indirect effects as well as a measure of the direct effect. The beauty of the Keynesian approach to this problem is that it does allow, in practice, such estimates to be made. In the following sections, we shall develop a Keynesian-type model and use it to explore the implications of alternative policies directed toward maintaining full employment.

A KEYNESIAN GENERAL EQUILIBRIUM MODEL

● We shall suppose that every activity takes place in one of three "markets": (1) the "commodity market," (2) the "financial markets," and (3) the "labor market."

The Commodity Market

We shall first describe the "commodity market." This is the market in which the demand for and the supply of final goods and services are reconciled with each other. If the current rate of planned expenditures is different from the income which would be associated with the sale of current output, then the commodity market is in disequilibrium. This disequilibrium state would reveal itself in the form of unanticipated changes in inventories—excessive inventory accumulation if supply exceeded demand and excessive depletion of inventory if demand exceeded supply. Firms are assumed to adjust their rates of production to restore their appropriate inventory holdings. Changes in production imply changes in income payments to owners of factors of production. Changes in income, in turn, imply changes in expenditures. It is through the changes in output, therefore, that the market moves toward an equilibrium. Equilibrium is achieved when planned expenditures for final goods and services (which are identified with the aggregate demand for output given a constant price level) equal income from sales of output.

If, for the sake of simplicity, we assume no foreign transactions, then we can subdivide planned expenditures E_{pL} into planned consumption expenditures C, planned investment (that is, planned changes in inventories, plant, and equipment) I_{pL}, and planned government purchases G. We can express aggregate demand as:

$$E_{pL} = C + I_{pL} + G \tag{1}$$

Total income Y is always equal to total expenditures. This is simply an accounting identity:

$$Y \equiv E \tag{2}$$

Some portion of total expenditures may be unplanned, however. In our model, these are unintended inventory changes, I_{up}. Therefore, total realized expenditures can be written as

$$E = E_{pL} + I_{up} \tag{3}$$

This implies $Y = E_p + I_{up}$. As we described above, whenever unplanned inventory changes occur, $I_{up} \neq 0$, output and income change. Therefore, only *in equilibrium* will income equal planned expenditures. We express this equilibrium condition as

$$E_p = C + I_{pL} + G = Y \tag{4}$$

As we noted earlier, a basic determinant of what consumers plan to spend is their income. Of course, not all of their income is available for private purchases. The government must be paid taxes before individuals can make private purchases. Tax revenues are themselves responsive to changes in income. Letting T equal total taxes collected, we can approximate this relationship by the linear expression:

$$T = T_0 + tY \tag{5}$$

where t is a measure of the responsiveness of tax collections to changes in aggregate income.[2] Planned consumption expenditures can then be related to disposable income $Y - T$ by the expression:

$$C = P \cdot \alpha + \beta(Y - T) \tag{6}$$

where P is the price level; α is a constant; and β is the marginal propensity to consume out of disposable income. Various studies of consumer behavior have produced estimates of the value of marginal propensity to consume as being less than, but close to, 1.

If we substitute the value of T from Equation (5) into Equation (6), we can write

$$C = P \cdot \alpha - \beta T_0 + (\beta - \beta t)Y \tag{6'}$$

The second component of planned private expenditures, planned investment, represents an adjustment of the capital stock toward its optimal level. The optimal stock of capital to combine with a given quantity of labor depends on sales expectations and the interest rate. A reduction in the interest rate would, *ceteris paribus,* increase the present value of an investment. This would increase the desired stock of capital and lead to a planned expansion of the current rate of investment. The relation between the planned rate of investment and the rate of interest can be approximated by the linear expression:

$$I_{pL} = P(\psi + v \cdot r) \tag{7}$$

where v is a measure of the responsiveness of investment spending to changes in the rate of interest.

The public component (government expenditures) of demand for commodities is determined by the budget. As such, if the government desires, it can use its expenditure rate as a policy variable to influence aggregate demand. We may express the policy relatedness of government expenditures by the expression,

$$G = P \cdot \overline{G} \tag{8}$$

where $\overline{G}$ is the volume of goods government plans to purchase.

Using Equations (6'), (7), and (8) to express the components of planned expenditure, we can now rewrite the commodity market equilibrium condition, Equation (4), as:

$$Y = E_{pL} = C + I_{pL} + G = P \cdot \alpha - \beta T_0 + (\beta - \beta t)Y \\ + P(\psi + v \cdot r) + P \cdot \overline{G} \tag{4'}$$

Collecting terms, this can be rewritten as

$$Y = \frac{P}{1 - \beta + \beta t} \left[(\alpha + \psi + \overline{G}) - \frac{\beta T_0}{P} + v \cdot r \right] \tag{4''}$$

Since the volume of money income Y is simply the volume of output y multiplied by the price level P, we may rewrite Equation (4'') in terms of the volume of output consistent with equilibrium in the commodity market. Dividing both sides of Equation (4'') by the price level P yields

$$y = \frac{1}{1 - \beta + \beta t} \left[(\alpha + \psi + \overline{G}) - \frac{\beta T_0}{P} + v \cdot r \right] \tag{4'''}$$

The Interdependence Between y and r

Equation (4''') clearly states that the level of aggregate output, which is consistent with equilibrium in the commodity market, depends on the rate of interest. There is a presumed negative relation between the rate of interest and the level of planned investment. Therefore, we assume $v < 0$. Since planned investment is one component of aggregate demand, aggregate demand will be inversely related to the rate of interest. Equation (4''') reveals this in the term $v/(1 - \beta + \beta t)$. This quantity represents the rate at which the equilibrium level of aggregate demand will vary with variations in the rate of interest.[3] Since v is a negative number, Equation (4''') implies that y is inversely related to r.

In Figure 9.1, we represent this relationship by the curve EE'. The quantity

$$\frac{1}{1 - \beta + \beta t}\left[(\alpha + \psi + \overline{G}) - \frac{\beta T_0}{P}\right]$$

is represented by the y intercept of EE', while the quantity $v/(1 - \beta + \beta t)$ is represented by the slope of EE'. Note that the position and shape of the curve are, therefore, determined by all of the parameters of the expenditure function $(\alpha, \beta, T_0, t, \overline{G}, v)$ and the price level. There is, therefore, a different EE' curve for each possible set of values for these parameters. Given a set of values for these parameters, each point on the corresponding EE' curve represents a possible equilibrium in the commodity market at the given price level. Furthermore, at any point to the right of EE', such as point A, the rate of interest is too high to sustain aggregate spending at the associated rate of output. There is an excess supply of commodities; unplanned inventories accumulate; and businesses find it profitable to reduce their rate of output. At any point to the left, such as B, the opposite is true. Aggregate expenditures ex-

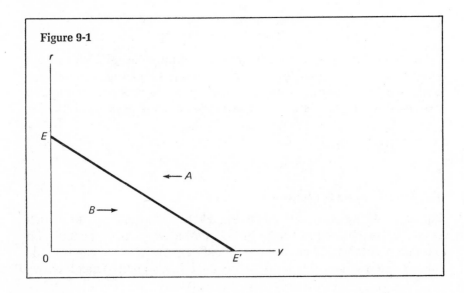

Figure 9-1

ceed the current rate of output, and firms will find it profitable to expand their rates of production.

All of the parameters of the EE' curve (α, β, ψ, v, T_0, t, $\overline{G}$) can be estimated independently of any knowledge of what the equilibrium level of the rate of interest and of aggregate demand will be. The parameters α and β can be estimated by studying the past association between consumption spending and income. Similarly, ψ and v can be estimated by studying past investment behavior. The parameters T_0 and t can be estimated by analysis of past tax revenue records, and $\overline{G}$ can be derived directly from government budgets. These estimated parameters, of course, only determine the position and slope of the EE' curve. But to predict the equilibrium level of aggregate demand for a given price level, one must also be able to predict the rate of interest. That is, a prediction of the equilibrium level of aggregate expenditures means not simply locating the EE' curve, but also specifying a particular point on that curve. Unlike the other variables that enter into the expenditure function, however, the rate of interest cannot be predicted independently of any knowledge of y. The rate of interest represents the price that borrowers must pay lenders for the use of their money. This price will vary according to the amounts people wish to borrow and lend. The amount people wish to lend will depend, in part, on how much income they receive. Therefore, the rate of interest cannot be predicted independently of the level of income. For this reason, taking the price level as given, Equation (4′′′) represents a single equation in two unknowns, r, y. To determine what the actual equilibrium r and y will be, we must develop another equation which relates these two variables. As our discussion suggests, the natural place to find such an equation is in the financial markets since, on the one hand, spending decisions must be financed, while, on the other, the amount of finance available to individuals who wish to spend more than their income will depend, in part, on the incomes of those who will be net lenders. We turn now, therefore, to the financial sectors of our model.

The Financial Markets

At any given point in time, there is a certain stock of money available in the economy. Individuals who possess funds can either hold the money for their own use or lend it out. People who wish to finance expenditures beyond their current cash holdings are assumed to issue "bonds," and people who do not wish currently to hold money for their own use purchase these bonds. In this way, an excess supply of money in the money market is assumed to be associated with an excess demand for bonds, so that if one financial market is in equilibrium, so is the other. Therefore, it is necessary to explore the equilibrium conditions in only one of the financial markets. Because we have already discussed the determinants of the demand and supply of money at some length in Chapter 7, we shall formally introduce only the money market into our analysis.

As we noted in Chapter 7, not all of the debt instruments that are generally used as money are issued by the central government. Nevertheless, the necessity to assure the general acceptability of private debt instruments restricts private bank created money to some fraction of public issue of legal tender. Ultimately, therefore, the total stock of money in existence can be controlled by public policy. We represent this policy determination by writing

$$M^s = \overline{M} \tag{9}$$

The supply of money M^s is exogenously determined by public policy.

On the other side of the market, we have the demand for money balances. People wish to hold cash to meet current and future transaction needs. The dollar volume of transactions in the economy will be positively related to the volume of physical output y and the price level at which the output will be sold, P. On the other hand, cash yields no interest. Therefore, the higher the rate of return on bonds, *ceteris paribus*, the less money an individual would wish to hold. Therefore, we can approximate the demand for money as

$$L^D = P(k \cdot y + m \cdot r) \tag{10}$$

where k is a measure of the responsiveness of the demand for money to changes in y, and m (which is a negative number) is a measure of the responsiveness of the demand for money to changes in the rate of interest.

When the financial markets are in equilibrium, the quantity of money people wish to hold will just equal the amount that is actually in existence. We express this equilibrium condition as

$$\overline{M} = P(ky + mr) \tag{11}$$

Since $m < 0$ and $k > 0$, Equation (11) indicates that for a given price level, the volume of money income consistent with equilibrium in the financial markets is directly related to the rate of interest.

Diagrammatically, Equation (11) can be plotted as the *LM* curve in Figure 9.2.

There is one such curve for each given set of money-supply and money-demand parameters. ($\overline{M}/Pk$ is the y intercept, and m/k is the slope of the *LM* curve.) Given a set of values for the parameters and given the price level, each point on the corresponding *LM* curve represents a possible equilibrium in the financial markets. At any point to

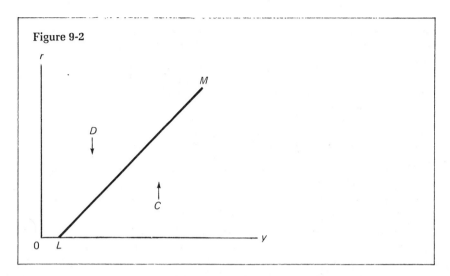

Figure 9-2

the right of the LM curve, such as point C, the rate of spending and associated rate of borrowing are too high to sustain the associated rate of interest. There is an excess demand for money at a point like C, causing people to bid up the interest rate. At any point to the left of the LM curve, such as D, the rate of spending and associated rate of borrowing are too low to sustain the current interest rate; there is an excess supply of money, and the interest rate will tend to fall.

Since changes in the rate of interest will affect investment and, hence, aggregate demand, while changes in the level of income and spending will affect the quantity of money people wish to hold, the economy will not be in equilibrium unless both the commodity market and the financial markets are in equilibrium simultaneously. To find a level of income and rate of interest consistent with equilibrium in both markets, we use Equations (4''') and (11) to solve simultaneously for the equilibrium rate of interest r* and output y*.

Substituting the value of r from Equation (11) into Equation (4''') yields

$$y^* = \frac{1}{(1 - \beta + \beta t) + \dfrac{vk}{m}} \left[(\alpha + \psi + \overline{G}) + \frac{1}{P} \left(\frac{v}{m} \overline{M} - \beta T_0 \right) \right] \qquad (12)$$

Substituting the value of y from Equation (11) into Equation (4''') yields

$$r^* = \frac{(1 - \beta + \beta t)}{\dfrac{m}{k}(1 - \beta + \beta t) + kv} \left[\frac{\overline{M}}{kP} + \frac{\beta T_0}{(1 - \beta + \beta t)P} - \frac{(\alpha + \psi + \overline{G})}{1 - \beta + \beta t} \right] \qquad (13)$$

The diagrammatic equivalent of solving for r^* and y^* simultaneously is to combine the EE' curve of Figure 9.1 with the LM curve of Figure 9.2 and to find their intersection. At the intersection, there are no forces tending to change the values of the variables; hence it is the point of equilibrium associated with a given price level P.

The Interdependence Between Output and the Price Level

Equation (12) indicates that the volume of output, which is consistent with equilibrium in the commodity and financial markets, depends on the price level. Changes in the price level have two effects. First, the revenue from some taxes, notably property taxes, is not strongly related to current levels of money income. A change in the price level, which changes the money income associated with a given volume of output, therefore changes disposable real income $(y - T/p)$. An increase in the price level raises real disposable income, and a fall in the price level decreases real disposable income. (See Figure 9.3.) Diagrammatically, a change in the price level shifts the y intercept of the EE' curve in the same direction as the change in prices. At the same time, a change in the price level changes the volume of real money balances, M/p. An increase in the price level would, therefore, shift the y intercept of the LM curve to the left, and a decrease in the price level would shift the LM curve to the right. Therefore, a change in the price level shifts the EE' and LM curves in opposite directions. The net impact of price level changes on the commodity and financial markets, therefore, depends on which shift is more important. As Equation (12) indicates, if $(v/m)\overline{M}$ is greater than βT_0, the net impact of a price change is to change the level of real income consistent with equilibrium in the commodity market in the direction opposite to the price change. Conversely, if $(v/m)\overline{M}$ is less than βT_0, then y is positively related to P.

In order to find the equilibrium output and price level, it is necessary to develop another equation relating y to P. Since output cannot be produced without input, a natural place to look for this relation is in the "labor market."

The Labor Market

We assume that business firms' output and input decisions are guided by the profit motive. Profit maximization requires that additional workers be hired up to the point at which the value of the marginal product of labor equals the wage rate. (Why?) We further assume that the marginal product of labor diminishes as the quantity of labor used

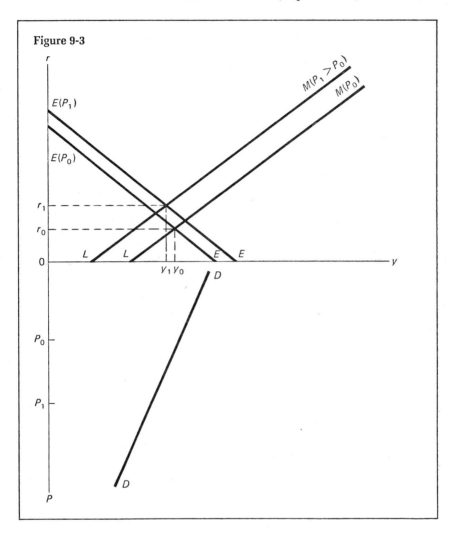

Figure 9-3

increases. We may then approximate the relationship between output and labor input by the relation:

$$y = AN^a \tag{14}$$

where N is the quantity of labor used; A is a constant greater than zero; and $0 < a < 1$.

From Equation (14), the marginal product of labor MP_L is ay/N. If firms are maximizing profits, then

$$\frac{Pay}{N} = W \tag{15}$$

or

$$N^D = \frac{Pay}{W} \tag{15'}$$

Ordinarily, workers will offer to sacrifice more of their potential leisure time only if by doing so they increase their command over goods. Since the real wage rate W/P represents the rate at which workers can transform leisure into goods, we may approximate the labor supply function by the relation

$$N^s = Z \cdot \left(\frac{W}{P}\right) \tag{16}$$

where Z is a positive constant.

The quantity of labor seeking work at a given real wage W/P need not, of course, be equal to the quantity firms wish to hire on those terms. If the quantity seeking employment on those terms differs from the quantity businesses wish to employ, then there will be market pressure exerted on the wage rate to change. A change in the wage rate will change production costs and will, therefore, ultimately cause a change in the price level in the same direction as the change in wage rates. If the labor market clears, so that there is no excess demand or supply of labor, then

$$N^D = N^S$$

or $\hspace{9cm}$ (17)

$$\frac{Pay}{W} = Z\frac{W}{P}$$

Collecting terms and simplifying, we see that

$$\frac{W}{P} = \left(\frac{ay}{Z}\right)^{1/2} \tag{17'}$$

Equation (17') says that the market-clearing real wage rate depends only upon the rate of output.

Substituting Equation (17') into Equation (15) yields the quantity of labor hired when the labor market clears:

$$N^* = (aZy)^{1/2} \tag{15''}$$

If the labor market clears, there is no *involuntary* unemployment. N^* is, therefore, the *full-employment* level of employment.

Substituting Equation (15'') into the production function, Equation

(14), yields the volume of output that will induce sufficient demand to clear the labor market.

$$y_f = [A(aZ)^{a/2}]^{2/(2+a)} \tag{14'}$$

Equation (14') indicates that the full-employment level of output is determined solely by the parameters of the production function and of the labor supply function. These parameters reflect the current state of knowledge of production processes, the volume and character of the nation's capital stock, the size and age distribution of the population, and the rate at which individuals are willing to trade leisure for goods. Each of these dimensions of the economic environment may be sensitive to *specific* governmental policies, but none of them is likely to be much affected by a change in the size of the total government budget, to a change in the size of the government debt, or to a change in the money supply. This is why they are treated as parameters in an aggregative model. (Question: What specific policies might affect the age distribution of the capital stock? Of the population? Of the response to real wage rate change?)

If money wage rates always rose when the aggregate demand for labor exceeded the supply *and always fell* when the aggregate supply of labor exceeded the demand, then the market-clearing equation, Equation (14'), would be the aggregate supply function for the economy. However, there are good reasons for expecting the money wage rate to be unresponsive to conditions of aggregate excess supply of labor. Labor is not a homogeneous commodity, nor is it perfectly mobile. Consequently, there is not simply one labor market, but many, many labor markets. Even in conditions of aggregate excess supply, there will be many of these labor markets where there is excess demand. Each labor group will resist a reduction in its wages if it does not believe that the wages of competing groups have also fallen. But market information is neither free nor instantaneously available. It can only be acquired by search. Consequently, it will take time for a group to recognize that the change in market conditions is general, and not specific. During this time, they will resist wage reductions.[4]

We may characterize this resistance by assuming that for any level of the demand for labor less than N^*, the money wage rate is fixed at W_0. Given this assumption, the actual level of employment will be equal to the quantity of labor demanded or N^*, whichever is less. We may express this as

$$N = \frac{Pay}{W_0} \quad \text{for } P \cdot y < Py_f \tag{18}$$

Substituting Equation (18) into the production function, Equation (14), yields the aggregate supply function:

$$y = \left[A\left(\frac{Pa}{W_0}\right)^a\right]^{1/(a-1)} \qquad \text{for } y < y_f \qquad (14'')$$

Equation (14) indicates that aggregate supply of output is an increasing function of the price level until full employment is attained. At full employment, further increases in the price level produce corresponding increases in the money wage rate, leaving the real wage rate and output supplied unchanged. (See Figure 9.4.)

Aggregate Demand and Supply

Although the principles of their derivation differ from those that underlay demand-and-supply equations for a single commodity, we may call Equations (12) and (14″) the aggregate demand and the aggregate supply equations of the economy. Together, they summarize all of the conditions that determine the behavior of the economy. We may, therefore, analyze the impact of changes in monetary and fiscal policies on prices and on the rates of output and employment by determining how such policy changes shift the position of the curves that represent these

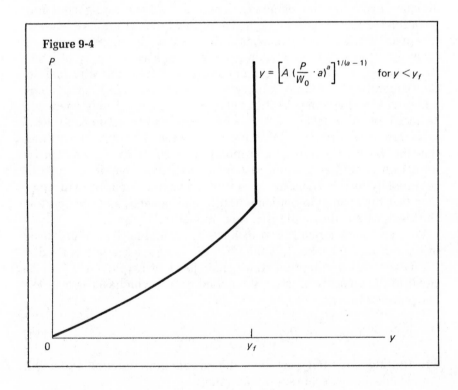

Figure 9-4

$$y = \left[A\left(\frac{P}{W_0} \cdot a\right)^a\right]^{1/(a-1)} \qquad \text{for } y < y_f$$

equations. Before we carry out the analysis of policy changes, however, it may be useful to discuss some general characteristics of an economy described by this model.

First, let us suppose that the economy has achieved an equilibrium state, where aggregate demand equals aggregate supply (points A, B, and C in Figure 9.5(a), (b), (c), respectively). If the level of aggregate demand is temporarily reduced, by a decline in the rate of investment spending which is, after a lag, offset by an increase in government spending, will the economy return to the initial equilibrium? In other words, does the economy have a stable equilibrium? As long as the demand curve is downward sloping, as in Figure 9.5(a), the answer to this question is yes. However, if the demand curve is upward sloping in the neighborhood of equilibrium, as in Figure 9.5(b) and (c), the answer may be no.[5] The question of the stability of the system is of obvious importance in evaluating fiscal policy for two reasons. First, if the system is unstable, then attempts to control the level of aggregate demand will be insufficient to control prices and employment levels. An unstable system requires direct intervention in price and output decisions in order to control price and employment levels. Secondly, as we indicated earlier, the structure of taxes in the economy influences the slope of the aggregate demand curve. Fiscal policy can, therefore, help to create, or to avoid, system instability and the need for direct controls on prices and output.

A second characteristic of the economy described by our model is the fact that the full-employment level of output is not necessarily the equilibrium level of output. The price mechanism does not necessarily clear all markets. One obvious reason for the possibility of a less-than-full-employment equilibrium is the downward rigidity of the wage rate which accounts for the shape of the aggregate supply curve in the less-than-full-employment region of output. A less obvious reason is that the aggregate demand curve may "bend backward," so aggregate demand does not equal aggregate supply at the full-employment rate of output. (See Figure 9.6.) If we return to Equation (4′′′), we see that the output demanded depends upon both the price level and the rate of interest. According to Equation (13), the rate of interest is also dependent upon the price level. Consequently, a change in the price level changes the quantity of output directly, by its effect on disposable income, and indirectly, by its effect on the rate of interest. Moreover, it is this indirect effect that produces the negative relation between the demand for output and the price level. This indirect effect operates only so long as a decline in the price level reduces the rate of interest. However, the rate of interest cannot fall below zero, so that at a sufficiently low price level, a further decline in the price level will have

Figure 9-5

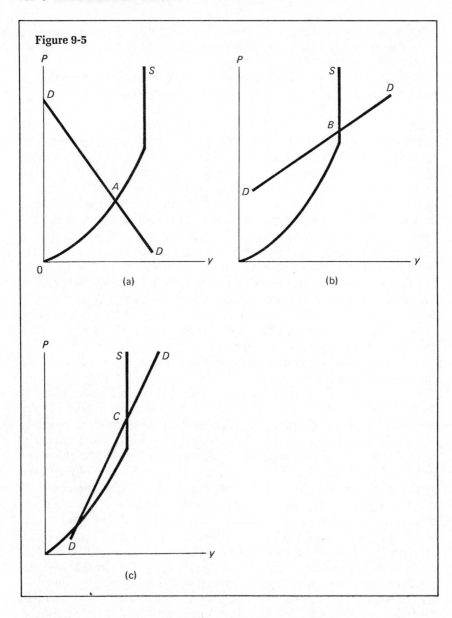

(a)

(b)

(c)

no effect on the interest rate. At this price level, the aggregate demand curve bends backward. Furthermore, as Equation (13) indicates, the price level at which the interest rate goes to zero is positively related to the money supply. Consequently, if the economy finds itself caught in this "liquidity trap," increases in the money supply can generate

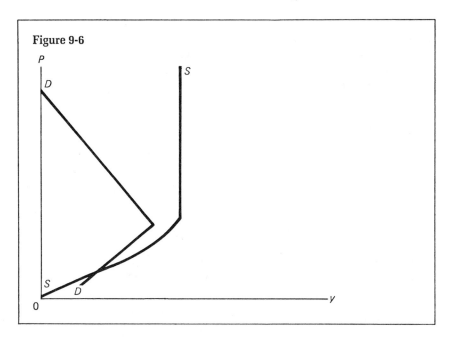

Figure 9-6

increases in the price level, but have no impact upon the maximum
rate of output demanded.

A third characteristic of the economy represented by our model is
the fact that increases in the rate of output and employment induced
by increases in aggregate demand necessarily raise the price level.
Producers will expand employment only if the real wage rate falls. If
money wages are rigid downward, a decline in real wages requires a
rising price level. As a result, in an economy characterized by wage
rigidity, the path to full employment via changes in aggregate demand
must be an inflationary path. It is wishful thinking to believe that the
unemployment rate can be reduced without inflation.

A fourth characteristic of our model economy is its probable inflationary bias. A temporary increase in aggregate demand raises prices
and wages at full employment. Once aggregate demand is reduced to
its former level, a legacy of higher wages persists. At these higher
wages, the demand for labor is reduced. In order to restore full employment, therefore, the government will have to raise the level of aggregate
demand back to the highest level achieved. This *validation process*
converts every temporary increase in aggregate demand into a permanent increase. Moreover, since no one knows with certainty what the
full-employment real wage is, various groups will continually "test"
the system by raising their wage demands. If these wage demands produce a significant drop in employment, the government may be com-

pelled to raise aggregate demand sufficiently to "validate" the wage increase. The combined circumstances of uncertainty, wage rigidity, and a government committed to full employment are almost certain to produce a creeping inflation.

POLICY INSTRUMENTS

● Within a macroeconomic context, the government has three general instruments at its command by which it can move the economy toward desired goals. These instruments are the level of government spending, the level of taxation, and the stock of money in existence. Each of these instrumental variables affects the level of aggregate demand in the economy and, hence, the level of output, employment, and the price level. However, each instrument affects aggregate demand in a different way: A change in taxes influences the level of consumer demand; a change in the money supply induces a change in the interest rate which, in turn, influences the level of investment goods demand; a change in government spending directly affects the level of demand for government-purchased commodities. Moreover, any change in aggregate demand changes income and interest rates. These changes induce further changes in aggregate demand. Since their initial impacts differ, we must expect the total impact of a given change in the dollar magnitude of different instrumental variables to differ. Our aggregate demand equation,

$$y = \frac{1}{1 - \beta + \beta t + \dfrac{vk}{m}} \left[\alpha + \psi + \overline{G} + \frac{1}{P}\left(\frac{v\overline{M}}{m} - \beta T_0 \right) \right] \tag{12}$$

represents the relationship that exists between the equilibrium level of output demanded at a given price and our instrumental variables $(\overline{G}, \overline{M}, T_0, t)$. We may, therefore, use it to determine the total (direct and indirect) impact on the quantity of output demanded at a given price level of a given change in each of our policy instruments.

Suppose

$$y^1 = \frac{1}{1 - \beta + \beta t + \dfrac{vk}{m}} \left[\alpha + \psi + \overline{G}^1 + \frac{1}{P}\left(\frac{v\overline{M}^1}{m} - \beta T_0^1 \right) \right] \tag{19}$$

and

$$y^2 = \frac{1}{1 - \beta + \beta t + \dfrac{vk}{m}} \left[\alpha + \psi + \overline{G}^2 + \frac{1}{P}\left(\frac{v\overline{M}^2}{m} - \beta T_0^2 \right) \right] \tag{20}$$

where y^i, G^i, M^i, and T_0^i are specific values of these variables. Then, subtracting Equation (19) from Equation (20) yields

$$\Delta y \equiv y^2 - y^1 = \cfrac{1}{1 - \beta + \beta t + \cfrac{vk}{m}}$$
$$\left\{ (\overline{G}^2 - \overline{G}^1) + \frac{1}{P} \left[\frac{v}{m} (\overline{M}^2 - \overline{M}^1) - (T_0^2 - T_0^1) \right] \right\} \quad (21)$$

If we have changed only the level of government spending (so that $\overline{M}^2 = \overline{M}^1$ and $T_0^2 = T_0^1$), Equation (21) reduces to

$$\Delta y = \cfrac{1}{1 - \beta + \beta t + \cfrac{vk}{m}} \Delta \overline{G} \quad (22)$$

Equation 22 indicates that the total impact on aggregate demand is a multiple of the change in government demand. The size of the government expenditure multiplier

$$\cfrac{1}{1 - \beta + \beta t + \cfrac{vk}{m}}$$

is dependent upon the responsiveness of investment and to interest rate changes (v) and of the demand for money to interest rate changes (m). The reason these parameters enter the multiplier is that a change in government spending, which is not accompanied by changes in tax rates, will change the government's indebtedness. This changes the total volume of bonds in existence and, therefore, the rate of interest. If the demand for money were highly unresponsive to interest rate changes (implying a small value of m), the appearance of additional bonds on the market to finance the government deficit would create a large increase in the rate of interest. The change in interest rate would then induce a change in investment demand to partially offset the impact of the change in government spending. In the limit, as m approached a value of zero, the government spending multiplier would also approach zero. Conversely, the greater the absolute value of m, the larger the government spending multiplier.

If only T_0 varies, so that $\overline{G}^2 = \overline{G}^1$, $\overline{M}^2 = \overline{M}^1$, Equation (21) reduces to the tax multiplier:

$$\frac{\Delta Y}{\Delta T_0} = - \cfrac{\dfrac{\beta}{P}}{1 - \beta + \beta t + \cfrac{vk}{m}} \quad (23)$$

The money multiplier can be deduced from Equation (21) by setting $G^2 = G^1$ and $T_0{}^2 = T_0{}^1$ to yield

$$\Delta Y = \frac{1}{k + (1 - \beta + \beta t)\dfrac{m}{v}} \cdot \frac{\Delta M}{P} \tag{24}$$

The size of the money multiplier

$$\frac{1}{k + (1 - \beta + \beta t)\dfrac{m}{v}}$$

is also a function of m and v. The relationship between the money multiplier and the interest responsiveness of the demand for money is just the reverse of that of the government spending multiplier. As the absolute value of m increases, the value of the money multiplier declines. In the limit, as $(m) \to \infty$, the money multiplier approaches zero.

Equation (24) also indicates that the money multiplier is positively related to v. If the rate of investment were unrelated to the interest rate (implying $v = 0$), then a change in the money supply would have no impact on aggregate demand.

Our comparison of the equations for the expenditure and money supply multipliers indicates that the effects of fiscal policy are strongest when conditions are most unfavorable for stimulus of demand via changes in the money supply. For this reason, considerable econometric effort has been expended in attempting to estimate the values of v and m. The earliest studies tended to indicate that the responsiveness of investment to changes in the interest rate to be quite small. Later studies, using better econometric techniques, have produced somewhat higher estimates. Similarly, studies of the response of the demand for money to interest rate changes seem to rule out extreme values.[6] These studies, therefore, suggest that the government almost always is free to pursue many different combinations of expenditure, tax, and monetary policy changes in order to generate a given impact on aggregate expenditures.

GOALS AND TOOLS: THE THEORY OF ECONOMIC POLICY

● If our only goal were to regulate the volume of aggregate demand, then we might be indifferent to the particular choice of monetary and fiscal policy employed. But, as we have already noted, each policy instrument has a different impact on the composition of activities in the economy. The division of resources among private consumption, private capital formation, and public goods depends upon the particular combination of policy used to control aggregate demand. Similarly, the size of the public debt and the balance of international payments are dependent upon the way aggregate demand is controlled. Typically, there is a public interest in these dimensions of the economy as well as in its current size. A concern for growth may establish a target rate of investment; a concern for social balance, a target rate of government purchases; a concern for the future, a target level of public debt; a concern for international monetary stability, a target balance of payments.

It is intuitively obvious that as the number of targets increases, the freedom of the policy maker to choose a set of instruments is reduced. For example, since taxes are related to income, any change in aggregate income will change tax revenues. Unless government expenditures change by the amount taxes change, the size of the debt will be altered. Moreover, except for specific parameter combinations, a change in government expenditures does not usually result in an equal change in tax revenues. Therefore, if one target of policy is to leave the size of the debt unaltered, then the policy maker is not free to use one, and only one, instrument to control aggregate demand. He must use at least two instruments. But he is still free to choose which two, or which combination of three instruments to choose subject to the condition that the change in size of the government debt is zero.

If for purposes of illustration we simplify our model by dropping the labor market and assuming the price level is fixed exogenously, a change in aggregate demand will be equivalent to a change in output. Equations (22) to (24) will then represent the relations between changes in our policy variables and changes in output. Using these relations, we can characterize the policy maker's problem as finding a solution to the following set of equations:

$$\frac{1}{1 - \beta + \beta t + \frac{vk}{m}} \left\{ d\bar{G} + \frac{vm}{P} d\bar{M} - \frac{\beta}{P} dT_0 \right\} = d\bar{y} \qquad \text{(i)}$$

$$d\bar{G} - dT_0 - td\bar{y} = 0 \qquad \text{(ii)}$$

where $d\bar{y}$ is the target change in output we wish to achieve, and $d\bar{G}$, dT_0, and $d\bar{M}$ are the changes in policy instruments whose values must satisfy the target conditions.

Since we have more unknowns than equations, we are free to arbitrarily choose any one of the instrument variable values and then solve for the other two values. If we expand the number of targets, we further reduce the discretion of the policy maker. For example, if he must not only maintain the size of the debt, but also maintain the volume of private investment, then he must choose dG, dT_0, and dM in such a way that the following equations are satisfied:

$$\frac{1}{1 - \beta + \beta t + \dfrac{vk}{m}} \left(d\overline{G} + \frac{vm}{P} d\overline{M} - \frac{\beta}{P} dT_0 \right) = d\overline{y} \tag{i}$$

$$d\overline{G} - dT_0 - td\overline{y} = 0 \tag{ii}$$

$$v\left[\frac{dM}{mP} - \frac{k}{m} d\overline{y} \right] = 0^7 \tag{iii}$$

We now have three linear equations in three unknowns. The policy maker has lost all discretion by the addition of this third target since, if Equations (i), (ii), and (iii) are independent, there is only one combination of instrumental values that is consistent with these target equations.

There is no reason why the number of policy targets a society wishes to achieve should be less than or equal to the number of policy instruments its government has at its disposal. However, if the number of targets exceeds the number of instruments, it will often be logically impossible to simultaneously achieve all the targets. The reason for this is that each target adds an equation to the policy maker's "problem." If there are more equations than unknowns, the equation system may be overdetermined. For example, since Equations (i), (ii), and (iii) are consistent with one, and only one, combination of tax, expenditure and money supply change, if we prespecify an expenditure target

$$dG = dG \tag{iv}$$

we shall not be able to simultaneously satisfy our other target equations unless dG just happens to be consistent with the value of dG that the other policy targets require.

The Social Welfare Function

Presumably, the targets of fiscal and monetary policy reflect the constituency perceptions of political representatives of the welfare judgments of their constituencies. As long as the number of available policy instruments exceeds the stated policy targets, the policy maker need not consider trade-offs or the relative significance of achieving different targets, for he may be able to achieve all of them. But when the number of targets exceeds the number of instruments, the problem of determining the magnitude of the instrumental variables must be reformulated in terms of a problem of maximizing a social welfare function subject to the constraints created by the structure of the economy. In such an approach, the target values do not enter exogenously. They are determined simultaneously with the values of the instrumental variables. The practical difficulty in implementing this approach is that it presumes that a social welfare function not only exists, but can be estimated. Yet, as we have seen in Chapter 3, a social welfare function may not exist. Furthermore, issues are seldom presented to legislatures in a way which would facilitate the determination of the relative weights they attach to the pursuit of different policy goals.

The Problem of Lags

If wages and prices were highly responsive to conditions of excess supply and excess demand, there would be no need to establish a target level of aggregate demand. The markets would automatically, and quickly, adjust to any movements away from full employment. As we noted above, a principal cause of wage and price rigidity is the cost and difficulty which individuals face in trying to determine just what changes have taken place in the various markets in which they might participate. The underlying rationale for adopting full employment as a target objective of government policy, therefore, rests on the following proposition: The amount of information necessary to recognize the need of a change in government policy in order to move toward a full-employment equilibrium is less detailed and more readily available than the information needed by individuals to change their decisions in a way which would move the economy toward a full-employment equilibrium. Put differently, there is less uncertainty about the value of aggregates than of the components that comprise those aggregates. Government policy is based on estimates of the aggregates (aggregate consumption, investment, and so on), while individual decisions must be based upon knowledge of the components. It is its presumed ability to base decisions on more easily attainable and less error-prone information that gives government an advantage over the sum of individual adjustments in moving the market toward a full-employment equilibrium.

The government may have an advantage with respect to gathering relevant information, but the information that it gathers is never complete nor current. Policy makers must rely upon various indicators constructed on sampled evidence such as the consumer price index, the wholesale price index, reported unemployment rates, production indices, inventory indices, and so on, which are subject to sampling error and often give conflicting signals as to what the general state of the economy actually is.

The recognition lag, that is, the time elapsed between a change in aggregate conditions and the recognition of a need to make a policy response, is not the only delay incurred in the stabilization process. After recognition of a need for a policy change, a second lag occurs, while a decision as to the appropriate response is formulated and enacted. The length of this "inside" lag depends upon the institutional framework within which the policy is formulated. In the United States, changes in the money supply are under the control of the Federal Reserve Board of Governors, who need not appeal to the Congress but may act on their own initiative. Changes in fiscal policy, on the other hand, often require formulation and passage of legislation by the Congress. Given the difference in the sizes of the decision-making groups, it is not surprising that the inside lag for fiscal policy changes is longer than for monetary policy revision.

A third lag, which our model conceals because its equations lack a time dimension, is the reaction time of the economy to changes in the policy parameters. Various econometric estimates of these lags have been made, and there is considerable disagreement among the results, but a general result is that the outside lag of fiscal policy is shorter than the response to changes in the money supply. These lags create a problem because by the time a policy change is made, the underlying conditions may have changed in such a way as to require precisely the opposite response. The policy change would, therefore, be destabilizing rather than stabilizing.[8]

Automatic Stabilizers

Not all fiscal responses to changes in aggregate demand require legislative approval. Certain institutional arrangements have the character of automatic stabilizers. An automatic stabilizer adjusts the rate of flow of funds into and out of the spending stream in the opposite direction to any change in the aggregate rate of spending. If aggregate expenditure is rising, an automatic stabilizer reduces the inflow or increases the outflow of funds; if aggregate expenditure is falling, an automatic stabilizer increases the inflow or reduces the outflow of funds. Two American fiscal institutions which have this character are (1) unemployment insurance and (2) the income tax. Unemployment insurance is financed by contributions of employers based on the number of employees on their books and their history of layoffs. As employment increases, the flow of funds into the pool automatically increases and the outflow decreases, thereby drawing funds out of the spending flow. As employment falls off, unemployment compensation payments increase while employers' contributions decrease, thereby injecting additional funds into the economy.

In a similar manner, the rate of tax withdrawals from the spending stream automatically expands and contracts with expansion and contractions of the rate of aggregate expenditure. In addition, under a progressive tax system, the marginal rate of tax t is directly related to the level of aggregate expenditure. This provides an accelerated response to changes in aggregate expenditure.

Fiscal Drag

In an economy where potential output is growing as a result of capital formation, population growth, and technical progress, maintenance of full employment requires a continuous expansion of aggregate demand. Within a growth context, automatic stabilizers act as a drag against the stimulus to aggregate demand which is required to keep the economy growing at or near its potential rate of growth. An automatic stabilizer reduces the response of the economy to changes in the volume of aggregate demand. The size of the monetary and fiscal multipliers [Equations (24), (23), and (22)] is inversely related to the marginal tax rate. As a result, the magnitude of the change in instrumental variables needed to keep the economy near the full-employment growth path is greater the greater the reliance placed upon automatic stabilizers to control short-run fluctuations in aggregate demand.

Rules Versus Authority

It is possible to predict the future values of some parameters in a growing economy with a reasonable degree of accuracy. Demographic characteristics of a society, for example, the rate of growth of the population and the age distribution, typically do not change dramatically or unpredictably. The propensity to consume seems quite stable over time. So does the distribution of income. But other parameters, especially the volume of investment which is unrelated to interest rates, and the rate of technical progress to which it is related, appear quite unpredictable. Some newly discovered technical processes induce large spurts in investment, which may be highly concentrated in time. The advent of the railroad, mass production of automobiles, the transistor, and the jet engine were accompanied by investment booms whose time, magnitude, and duration could not have been easily predicted. What the technology of the future will be, the rate at which it will be introduced, and the volume of investment it will stimulate are matters of pure conjecture. We may, of course, make some "guesstimates" with respect to the near-term future. But extrapolation of the past seems a much less satisfactory method of estimating future values of the investment and production-function parameters than of estimating the parameters of the consumption function.

The necessity of relying upon "expert opinion" in judging how the investment and production functions will change from year to year means that estimation of the gap between the full-employment target and the volume of aggregate demand in the absence of a change in the value of the policy maker's instrumental variables falls somewhere between the realm of "art" and the realm of "science." Given the climate of uncertainty and imperfect knowledge within which the policy maker must operate, and given the lags between a change in conditions which call for a policy response and the impact of a policy change made in recognition of that change, a considerable debate has developed about the appropriate conduct of fiscal and monetary policy.[9]

One side of the debate takes the position that the policy maker's authority *to change the rate of change* of instrumental variables at his discretion should be severely limited. According to this view, a policy rule should establish the growth rate of instrumental variables according to the implied requirements of maintaining the *trend* rate of growth of potential output. This policy rule, which sets the growth rate of the instrumental variables, should only be changed whenever it has become clear that the trend in the growth path of potential output has changed. Such a policy would prevent the policy maker from attempting to keep the actual path of aggregate demand from straying from the actual path of potential output. It accepts a certain amount of price instability and unemployment as the inevitable consequence of living in a world of uncertainty. Furthermore, proponents of policy "rules" believe that the lags involved in the operation of policy tend to be so long and unpredictable that attempts to continuously maintain full employment are not only fruitless, but are also likely to increase the actual size of the fluctuations experienced.

The opposite side takes issue with the limitation of the policy maker's authority to change policy at his discretion. They point out that the policy maker must use his own judgment in judging what rates of change of the instrumental variables are consistent with the trend of aggregate demand matching the trend of potential output. Furthermore, they point out that the argument that a policy rule establishes some trend rate of growth in the value of instrumental variables places the burden of short-run stabilization upon movements in prices and interest rates as well as the automatic stabilization features of the fiscal system. It can be shown, however, that depending upon the structure of lags within the economy, automatic stabilizers such as the income tax can be destabilizing.[10] Furthermore, it can be shown that under certain circumstances, a policy which moderates movements in interest rates can increase the speed with which the economy moves toward its equilibrium value. The frequency and/or magnitude of fluctuations about the equilibrium may, therefore, be greater when the money supply grows at some trend rate than if policy action were taken to "lean" against the movements in interest rates.[11] Without adequate knowledge of the structure of the lags within the economy, therefore, it is not possible to judge whether a policy rule setting rates of growth of instrumental variable values or discretionary movements in these variables designed to counteract movements in the economy, will be more likely to mitigate the fluctuations the economy experiences. Given a lack of such knowledge, proponents of discretionary policy argue that authority to make policy changes should be vested in those whose "expert judgment" must serve as a substitute for more definitive statistical knowledge.

The Coordination of Stabilization Policies

We have been speaking as if there were a single policy maker who is responsible for setting the values of our instrumental variables in a coordinated fashion. While the interrelated nature of various segments of the economy suggests that control over monetary and fiscal variables be consolidated into the hands of a single authority, the institutional and political structure of the United States has, in fact, produced a wide dispersal of control over these variables.

The United States has a federal structure in which state and local governments have autonomy in fiscal matters. In order to control the overall volume of government spending, therefore, the federal government must take account of the volume of nonfederal government spending. Similarly, the tax revenues collected by the nonfederal governments must be accounted for in setting the overall tax schedule for the economy.

While the federal government may estimate the behavior of state and local governments, it cannot know with certainty just what their fiscal actions will be. The federal structure of government, therefore, increases uncertainty about spending aggregates and makes the task of pursuing a stabilization policy more difficult.

The federal fiscal authorities not only share control of fiscal instruments with state and local governments, but have no direct control over the money supply. The money supply is controlled by the Board of

Governors of the Federal Reserve System, a legally independent group which is free to pursue any monetary policy it desires. Since the Fed may take independent action, simultaneous pursuit of several goals such as a balanced federal budget, a given volume of government spending, and a stimulation of aggregate demand may be outside the abilities of federal fiscal authorities.

A further complication in developing a coordinated stabilization policy is created by the desire of the Treasury to minimize the cost of managing the outstanding debt. Typically, the interest rate paid on short-term debt is lower than the interest rate paid on long-term debt. However, the longer the date to maturity, the less frequently must the debt be refinanced. Therefore, as interest rates fall, the Treasury has an incentive to refinance its debt by substituting longer-term for shorter-term bonds. Since short-term bonds are closer substitutes for money than are long-term bonds, the Treasury's action of stretching out the maturity structure of the outstanding debt will induce individuals to increase their desired cash holdings in order to compensate for the reduced liquidity of their portfolios. Since interest rates typically move in a procyclical fashion, rising as aggregate demand rises, falling as aggregate demand falls, the action of the Treasury's debt management activities must be accounted for in determining the appropriate values of the other instrumental variables.[12]

SUMMARY

● Both theoretical analysis and historical experience confirm the possibility that a free-market system will reach an equilibrium at less than full employment. The government can influence the level of aggregate demand by changing the volume of tax collections, the volume of government spending, and the supply of money in the economy. Such changes influence not only the overall level of activity, but also its composition. The appropriate choice of policy to regulate the volume of aggregate spending will be influenced by a consideration of the desired composition of activities and other social goals. The dynamic properties of the economy may also be affected by the nature of the fiscal system and the particular policy rules adopted in pursuit of fiscal objectives.

The actual ability of the government to moderate fluctuations in aggregate demand depends upon the quality of the information it gathers, the speed with which it can come to a decision, and the lags among the formulation of a policy response, its political execution, and its impact upon the economy. Its ability also depends upon the number of other policy objectives it wishes to pursue and the degree to which it can coordinate the decisions of various agents who have control of policy instruments.

APPENDIX: THE DIFFERENTIAL INCIDENCE OF GENERAL TAXES

● In describing the labor market in this chapter, the effects of taxes on the demand for and supply of labor were ignored. In this appendix, we shall take these effects into account. We shall then explore the impact of substituting a general retail sales tax for an income tax, in such a way as to leave the rate of tax on aggregate income unchanged, upon the equilibrium rate of output and upon the general price level.

We may assume that the price level P is price inclusive of sales tax. The output price which matters to firms in deciding upon the quantity of labor is, however, the output price net of tax. If θ is the rate of sales tax, and P' designates the output price net of tax, then

$$P' + \theta P' \equiv P \tag{A.1}$$

or

$$P' = \frac{P}{1 + \theta}$$

The profit-maximization condition, Equation (15), which determines the relationship between the quantity of labor demanded and the real wage rate W/P, must, therefore, be modified to read

$$\frac{P'ay}{N} = \frac{P}{1+\theta} \frac{ay}{N} = W \tag{A.2}$$

This modified profit-maximization condition then alters the demand for labor function to read as

$$N^D = \frac{ay}{1+\theta} \frac{P}{W} \tag{A.3}$$

As Equation (A.3) indicates, the quantity of labor demanded at any real wage rate is inversely related to the rate of sales tax. Conversely, the real wage rate, which would call forth a demand for any given quantity of labor, is inversely related to the rate of sales tax.

Just as the demand for labor is derived from a profit-maximization condition, the supply of labor is derived from a utility-maximization condition. As discussed in Chapter 6, individuals are interested in equalizing their marginal returns from work and leisure. This condition is satisfied when the individual's personal rate of substitution of income for leisure is equal to their after-income-tax real wage rate. The labor supply function should, therefore, be modified to read

$$N^s = Z \cdot \left(\frac{W}{P}\right)^A = Z \cdot \left(\frac{W}{P}\right)(1 - \rho) \tag{A.4}$$

where $(W/P)^A$ is the after-tax real wage rate and ρ is the rate of income tax.

As Equation (A.4) indicates, the real wage rate required to call forth any given supply of labor is directly related to the rate of income tax.

Using Equations (A.3) and (A.4), we may rewrite the labor-market-clearing condition $N^D = N^S$ as

$$\frac{\alpha y}{1 + \theta} \frac{P}{W} = Z \cdot \frac{W}{P}(1 - \rho) \tag{A.5}$$

Collecting terms and simplifying, we see that

$$\left(\frac{\alpha y}{Z}\right)^{1/2} \left[\frac{1}{(1 + \theta)(1 - \rho)}\right]^{1/2} = \frac{W}{P} \tag{A.5'}$$

Equation (A.5') indicates that the market-clearing real wage rate depends not only upon the level of output, but also upon the magnitude of the income tax rate relative to the sales tax rate. Conversely, Equation (A.5') together with Equation (A.3) and the production function imply that the *full-employment* level of output and employment depend upon the magnitude of the income tax rate relative to the sales tax rate.

In order to assess the impact of a change in the tax structure upon the economy, we wish to abstract from the impact of such a change on the aggregate tax parameter t in the aggregate expenditure function. We observe that the total tax function, Equation (5), may be rewritten:

$$T = T_0 + tY = T_0 + (\theta + \rho)P'y = T_0 + \frac{(\theta + \rho)}{1 + \theta} Py = T_0 + \left(\frac{\theta + \rho}{1 + \theta}\right)Y \tag{A.6}$$

Therefore, the aggregate marginal tax rate t can be expressed as

$$t = \frac{\theta + \rho}{1 + \theta} \tag{A.6'}$$

Variations in θ, $d\theta$, and ρ, $d\rho$, which leave the value of t unchanged, must satisfy the relation

$$d\rho = -\left[\frac{1 - \rho}{1 + \theta}\right]d\theta \tag{A.7}$$

We are now in a position to answer the following question: What happens to the division of after-tax income between wage earners and profit recipients when a sales tax is substituted for an income tax in such a way as to leave the aggregate rate of tax and the full-employment level of income unchanged?

To answer this question, we must first calculate

$$d\left(\frac{W}{P}\right)_{dy=0} = \frac{1}{2}\frac{W}{P}\left[\frac{1}{1-\rho}\,d\rho - \frac{1}{1+\theta}\,d\theta\right] \tag{A.8}$$

By constraining the variations in ρ and θ to satisfy Equation (A.7), Equation (A.8) may be modified to

$$d\left(\frac{W}{P}\right)_{\substack{dy=0 \\ dt=0}} = \frac{1}{2}\frac{W}{P}\left[-\frac{2}{1+\theta}\,d\theta\right] = -\frac{W}{P}\frac{1}{1+\theta}\,d\theta \tag{A.8'}$$

Equation (A.8') indicates that a substitution of a sales tax for an income tax, which leaves the rate of output and the aggregate tax rate unchanged, must reduce the before-income-tax real wage rate. Of course, labor's after-tax income depends on the after-tax real wage rate. The total variation in after-tax real wage is related to the variations in the before-tax real wage and the income tax rate by

$$d\left(\frac{W}{P}\right)^A_{dy=0} = (1-\rho)d\left(\frac{W}{P}\right) - \frac{W}{P}\,d\rho \tag{A.9}$$

When the variations in ρ and θ satisfy condition (A.7), Equation (A.9) is modified to

$$d\left(\frac{W}{P}\right)^A_{\substack{dt=0 \\ dy=0}} = (1-\rho)\left(-\frac{W}{P}\right)\left(\frac{1}{1+\theta}\right)d\theta - \frac{W}{P}\left[-\left(\frac{1-\rho}{1+\theta}\right)d\theta\right] = 0 \tag{A.9'}$$

As Equation (A.9') indicates, when a sales tax is substituted for an income tax of equal tax yield, the effective after-tax income of labor is unchanged. Since aggregate after-tax income is unchanged and labor's after-tax income is unchanged, profit earner's after-tax income must be unchanged. Our analysis indicates, therefore, that the incidence of a general sales tax, in terms of functional income shares, is equivalent to the incidence of a proportional income tax of equal yield when the economy is at full employment.

Two extensions of the analysis are left as exercises. First, what happens to the general price level when a sales tax is substituted for an income tax at full employment? Second, suppose the money wage is rigid downward, and the economy is at a less-than-full-employment equilibrium. Show that the substitution of a sales tax for an income tax must raise the general price level and reduce the equilibrium level of employment. (*Hint:* Show that the real wage must fall; then, since the money wage is fixed, the price level must rise. Since aggregate demand is a function of t, not θ and ρ, the position of the aggregate demand curve remains unchanged. An increased price level must, therefore, imply a decreased rate of output and employment.)

Notes

1. Our laws do not permit an individual to pass debts on to his children as an inheritance. Consequently, lenders will tend to force potential borrowers to plan their lifetime rate of spending in accordance with their lifetime income. The correspondence between yearly spending and yearly income, can, of course, be much weaker. Considerable work has gone into attempting to describe how the lifetime constraint interacts with current income receipts to influence current spending decisions. See, for example, M. Friedman, *A Theory of the Consumption Function*, National Bureau of Economic Research, Princeton, N.J.: Princeton University Press, 1957; F. Modigliani and R. Brumberg, "Utility Analysis and the Consumption Function: An Interpretation of Cross Section Data," in K. Kurihara, ed., *Post Keynesian Economics*, New Brunswick, N.J.: Rutgers University Press, 1954.

2. The increase in tax revenue generated by a given increase in aggregate income clearly depends upon how that increase in income was distributed over various income groups. We ignore this complication by implicitly assuming that any increase in income does not change the income distribution. In a similar fashion, all of our other behavior equations ignore distribution effects.

3. Given any linear expression between two variables (Y, X) say $Y = a + bX$, the coefficient of X, b, is equal to the ratio of the change in Y to the change in X. To see this, let Y^1 be the value of Y when X has the value X^1, and Y^2 be the value of Y when X has the value X^2. Then we have

$$Y^1 = a + bX^1 \tag{1}$$

$$Y^2 = a + bX^2 \tag{2}$$

Subtracting Equation (1) from Equation (2) yields $Y^2 - Y^1 = b(X^2 - X^1)$, or

$$\frac{Y^2 - Y^1}{X^2 - X^1} = \frac{\Delta Y}{\Delta X} = b$$

4. Much of the recent theoretical work on the so-called Phillips curve, or the relation of the rate of unemployment to the rate of price change, is based on this search problem. A good (but difficult) collection of recent work is in E. Phelps, ed., *Microeconomic Foundations of Employment and Inflation Theory*, New York: Norton, 1970.

5. For a discussion of the stability properties of such models, see Bert Hansen, *A Survey of General Equilibrium Systems*, New York: McGraw-Hill, 1970, ch. 2.

6. For a review of this literature, see, for example, R. Teigen, "The Demand

and Supply of Money," in W. Smith and R. Teigen, eds., *Readings in Money, National Income, and Stabilization Policy,* Homewood, Ill.: Irwin, 1965, and T. Mayer, *Monetary Policy in the United States,* New York: Random House, 1968, esp. chs. 3 and 4.

7. $I = \psi + v \cdot r$. Therefore, $dI = v \cdot dr$. From Equation (11), $r = (\overline{M}/mP) - (k/m)y$, assuming P is constant, $dr = (dM/mP) - (k/m)dy$.

8. Extensive studies of the various lag structures are reported in *Stabilization Policies,* Research Studies Prepared for the Commission on Money and Credit, Englewood Cliffs, N.J.: Prentice-Hall, 1963.

9. For a discussion of the choices between automatic versus discretionary policy and monetary versus fiscal policy, see M. Friedman and W. Heller, *Monetary Versus Fiscal Policy: A Dialogue,* New York: Norton, 1969.

10. See W. J. Baumol, "Pitfalls in Contracyclical Policies: Some Tools and Results," *Review of Economics and Statistics,* Vol. 43, February 1961, pp. 21–26.

11. M. Lovell and E. Prescott, "Money, Multiplier Accelerator Interaction, and the Business Cycle," *Southern Economic Journal,* Vol. 35, 1968, pp. 60–72.

12. For a fuller discussion of the problem of debt management, see James Tobin, "An Essay on the Principles of Debt Management," Yale University, Cowles Foundation Paper No. 195, 1963.

Questions for Discussion

1. In our model, we made the simplifying assumption that the economy engaged in no foreign trade. We could introduce a foreign trade component into the commodity market by letting aggregate demand for domestic output be augmented by the difference between exports X and imports M. Then the planned expenditures function would be written.

$$E_{pL} = C + I_{pL} + G + (X - M)$$

Suppose that export demand were unaffected by domestic income or interest rates. Then $X = P \cdot \overline{X}$.
Suppose further that demand for imports did depend on domestic income. Then $M = z \cdot Y$.
   a. Write the new equation for equilibrium in the commodity market when exports and imports are expressed as above.
   b. Does the existence of the foreign sector increase or reduce the impact of a given change in government spending on domestic income?
   c. How would you expect z to vary with the size of the domestic economy?

2. Equation (12) indicates that the equilibrium level of income could be increased by an increase in private investment spending ψ.

   If this is so, why do private businesses not increase their rates of investment whenever the economy's unemployment rate is increasing, thereby increasing income and the demand for their own products? For a discussion of this question, see Chapter 11.

3. a. Explain why, if the supply of labor is directly related to the real wage rate, that once the economy has found a level of money income and

money wage rate at which the demand for labor equals the supply, any further increase in aggregate demand will increase prices but not output. (This is the so-called excess-demand inflation.)

b. Prices seem to continue to rise even after the excess-demand pressures on the price level have been removed. How might the difficulty facing individuals of obtaining and interpreting information about changes in market conditions account for such a phenomenon?

4. In the popular press, it is often asserted that an increased budget deficit is a sign of an expansionary fiscal policy. Is this necessarily true?

Suggested Readings

Allen, R. G. D., *Macro-Economic Theory, A Mathematical Treatment*, New York: St. Martins, 1967, chs. 5, 9, 17, and 18.
Provides a mathematical introduction to dynamic macroeconomic models and stabilization policy.

Commission on Money and Credit, *Stabilization Policies*, Englewood Cliffs, N.J.: Prentice-Hall, 1963.
A set of studies on the quantitative effects of fiscal and monetary policy actions.

Friedman, M., and Heller, W., *Monetary Versus Fiscal Policy: A Dialogue*, New York: Norton, 1969.
A lively discussion of the choices between automatic versus discretionary policy and the relative effectiveness of monetary and fiscal policy.

Hansen, B., *The Economic Theory of Fiscal Policy*, Cambridge, Mass.: Harvard University Press, 1958, Part I, "General Theory of Fiscal Policy."
Contains a good discussion of the relationship between targets and instruments in shaping fiscal policy.

Peacock, A., and Shaw, G., *The Economic Theory of Fiscal Policy*, New York: St. Martins, 1971.
Contains an analysis of fiscal policy issues within a multiregional, multiproduct framework.

In addition,

The Annual Report of the Council of Economic Advisers contains a review of the performance of the economy and a discussion of current issues of fiscal policy.

The student who is interested in alternative formulations of a macroeconomic model and more extensive discussion of their characteristics and underlying behavior assumptions should consult a good text on macroeconomic theory. In addition to the text by R. G. D. Allen cited above, some others are:

Ackley, G., *Macroeconomic Theory*, New York: Macmillan, 1961.

Bailey, M., *National Income and the Price Level: A Study in Macroeconomic Theory*, 2nd ed., New York: McGraw-Hill, 1971.

Branson, W., *Macroeconomic Theory and Policy*, New York: Harper & Row, 1972.

10

THE REGULATION OF PUBLIC UTILITIES

What the regulatory commissions are trying to do is difficult to discover; what
effect these commissions actually have is,
to a large extent, unknown; when it can
be discovered, it is often absurd.

Ronald Coase

The "invisible hand" of competition, *when it works well*, serves to shape or regulate private activity to serve three social purposes. First, it leads producers to seek out those methods of production that minimize the cost of production.[1] The more inefficient producer is driven out by his less inefficient competitors. Secondly, in the absence of externalities, competition leads to a pattern of outputs that exhausts the possibilities of expanding the total gains from trade. This is just another way of saying that a competitive equilibrium is pareto optimal. A third way in which competition shapes private activity to serve a social purpose is by limiting the power of the individual to force his will on a larger group. If effective competition exists, no one individual or firm can extort the public by threat of a discontinuance of service. Effective competition also limits the ability of any seller to discriminate against various buyers and of any buyer to discriminate against various sellers.

When competition on either side of a market is weak, the party who is in the monopoly position faces less constraints on his behavior. He is free to make decisions, which improve his well-being at the expense of those with whom he deals. We do not mean to imply that competition makes men altruistic, while the lack of it makes them egotistic. Competition does not influence behavior by changing a man's psyche, but rather by changing the environment within which he acts.[2] We may assume that, regardless of the degree of competition, production decisions of private firms are guided by the possibility of changes in output contributing to its own profits. In making output decisions, the firm sets the change in revenue against the change in cost. Production is expanded if the revenue change exceeds the cost change. Production is contracted if the cost change exceeds the revenue change. The degree of competition plays a role in this calculation by affecting the change in revenue the firm can anticipate from its decision. No firm is free from all competitive constraints. It must, at a minimum, compete with firms producing goods for other markets for the consumer's dollars. It is this interindustry competition that produces downward sloping industry-demand curves. Most firms do not face the entire industry-demand curve, but face intraindustry competition. This intraindustry competition makes the demand for any one firm's output even more sensitive to the price it charges. In the limit, as intraindustry competition increases, each individual firm's selling price becomes completely divorced from its own production decisions. Even most monopolies do not have complete control of prices set within their own industry. If they face the potential competition of their own buyers, then they must set the same selling price for all buyers. The less control a firm has over its market, the smaller the fraction of the total gains from trades that it makes will it be able to secure for itself. Of course, the difference between the total expenditures its customers would have been willing to make and the revenues the firm actually receives — that is, the consumer surplus — does not affect the firm's production decisions; only the contribution to the firm's receipts enters its decision calculus. As we discussed in Chapter 1, the paradoxical consequence of these facts is that if producers are faced with such effective competition that they have absolutely no control over the price they can receive, they will make output decisions which maximize the total possible gains from trade; but if a firm has something more than zero but less than complete control over its price setting, then its best interests are inconsistent with maximizing the total gains from trade.

In Chapter 1, we characterized the inefficiency of a monopoly trading system in terms of the difference between the monopolist's rate of substitution of the monopoly good for other goods and the rate of substitution of his customers. We did this in order to demonstrate that the "social waste" associated with monopoly does not necessarily relate to the way in which the monopolist produces the output which he chooses to produce; rather, the "waste" stems from too much of society's resources being devoted to the production of products which are less highly valued by society than the monopoly goods into which they could be converted. The waste arises because the monopolist produces too little, not because he produces inefficiently. In fact, in some circumstances, a firm may be able to secure a monopoly precisely because a single firm can produce a given output more cheaply than if that output were divided among several competing firms. In these circumstances, competition will not flower, and society must look to other methods of control. In this chapter, we address ourselves to the public control of such monopolies.

THE COOPERATIVE VERSUS THE MONOPOLY

● Rather than dealing with a monopolist, consumers of a product could form a cooperative to supplant the monopolist as their source of supply. The distinctive difference between these two modes of organization will be in the objectives of the management. Under the monopoly form, the management's objective is to secure the largest possible gains from trade for the *seller* of the product. But, since in a cooperative the sellers and buyers are coextensive, the objective is to maximize the *sum* of the gains from trade that accrue to the group in both their capacities as seller *and* buyer. This difference in objective will lead to a very different evaluation of the desirability of expanding output. Whether monopoly or cooperative, an expanded output can only be marketed by a reduction in selling price. This means that the additional revenues the organization takes in from expanding output will, therefore, equal the change in output times the new price plus the (negative) change in price times its former output. These two quantities are represented by the areas of Q_0ABQ_1 and of P_0CAP_1 in Figure 10.1. From the point of view of the monopolist, P_0CAP_1 in revenues is lost by extending trade. Consequently, the monopolist acts as if P_0CAP_1 were a part of the cost it must bear if it expands output. But from the point of view of the cooperative, these revenues are not lost to the organization by virtue of the price reduction; they are merely "returned" to the membership in the form of a consumer surplus. This difference in perspective with respect to revenues lost by price reductions will lead the cooperative to expand production beyond the point the monopolist would find most profitable. The monopolist will expand output only so long as the addition to profits is positive. But the cooperative will expand output as long as the *sum* of the addition to consumer surplus plus the addition to the profits of the firm is positive.

If, from a social point of view, the division of the gains from trade between the monopoly and its customers is immaterial, then the objective of public regulation ought to be to induce the monopoly to behave as if it were a cooperative. For the cooperative's objective is to maximize the total gains from trade in its market. But as we shall presently observe, in some cases the cooperative's objective cannot be achieved simply by imposing public regulations on the operation of a private monopoly. In practice, regulatory commissions' stated objec-

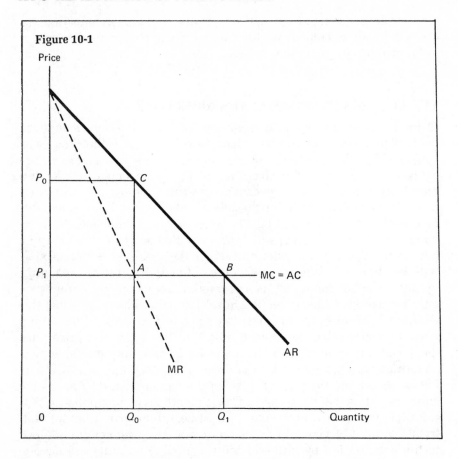

Figure 10-1

tives have not been expressed in terms of maximizing the total gains from trade, but rather in terms of controlling the monopolist's share of such gains. In the following sections, we shall explore some of the difficulties of implementation and implications for resource use of regulations designed to serve this purpose.

INCREASING RETURNS AS A BARRIER TO COMPETITION

● An important fact of life is that the large-scale enterprise often has a competitive advantage over the small-scale enterprise. As long as the advantages of scale are small relative to the size of the market, competition can still flourish. For example, the supermarkets have displaced the mom-and-pop store as the typical unit of retail food distribution, but the market for food is large enough to accommodate effective competition among various chain stores. The problem of finding a substitute for "regulation by competition" arises when the plant with the lowest average cost of production is capable of producing most of the output which would be demanded at a price equal to its minimum average cost. We can illustrate how such conditions effectively eliminate competition by means of Figure 10.2. In this figure, OD is the market-demand curve. The curves AC_1 and AC_2 represent the average-cost curves associated with two different plant sizes. The first producer monopolizes the market by choosing a plant of size two and operating at the output level Q_M. He sets his price at P_M, where he earns a monopoly profit $P_M D''EC_M$. If a second entrant, drawn by the lure of above normal returns, attempts to enter with a plant of size one, the original

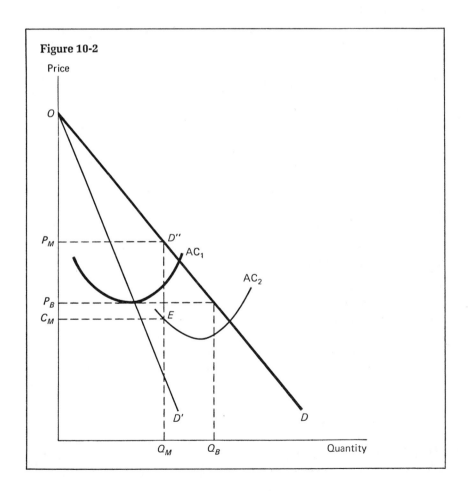

Figure 10-2

entrant can increase his output just above Q_B. The market price will fall below P_B. But P_B is the lowest selling price that would possibly allow the second entrant to cover his costs with plant size one. Therefore, the entrant would be squeezed out. If the new entrant attempts to enter with plant of size two, then they must share the market. But if they share the market, then each faces a demand curve OD' $(= \frac{1}{2}OD)$. As drawn, facing a demand curve OD', there is no rate of output from plant size two that can be sold at a high enough price to cover costs. Under these circumstances, the first entrant into the market can, by choosing the lower average-cost plant, secure a natural advantage over any subsequent entrants and effectively keep them out.

Scale economies, or declining average costs of production, usually are associated with activities that require a large fixed expenditure in order to produce any output at all combined with very low additional costs incurred to serve additional customers. Most prominent in this regard are transportation, communication, and energy distribution systems. A railroad or pipeline company must undertake a huge outlay in construction costs before any commodities move over their systems, but the cost of moving commodities once the line is constructed is quite low. There are high costs of wiring up a city and establishing a switching system, but once such investments are in place, additional calls can be accommodated at very little additional expense. Consequently, fixed costs represent a large portion of total costs. The larger the volume over which these fixed costs can be spread, the lower the average total cost. Such cost conditions create "natural" monopolies. That is, under such conditions, provision of the service by a single firm is the most efficient means of provision.

NATURAL MONOPOLIES AND PUBLIC POLICY

● In discussing public policy response to monopoly based on natural cost advantages of large-scale production, it is necessary to distinguish between those cases where the market-demand curve lies to the right of the minimum possible average cost of production, as in Figure 10.3(a), and those cases in which it lies to the left as in Figure 10.3(b). In Figure 10.3(a), the monopolist's profit-maximizing output is M, at which marginal revenue equals marginal cost. His profits are represented by the area $P_M C_M ED$, and the consumer surplus by $OP_M D$. The output which will maximize the sum of the consumer surplus plus producer's profit, our cooperative's criterion, is Q, where price equals marginal cost. (Why?) If the government were to take the control of price away from the firm and tell it to sell all of the output it could

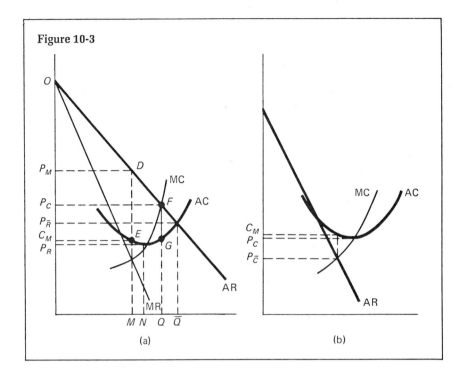

Figure 10-3

(a)

(b)

profitably sell at the price P_C, the firm would produce Q receiving a profit over all costs (which include a normal return on capital) of $(F - G) \times Q$. Obviously, the same result would obtain if the managers were told to produce Q at minimum cost and sell it on the open market to the highest bidders. Therefore, in this case a pure (monopoly) profit will still accrue to the firm even if it sells the socially most profitable output on the open market.

The average person's complaint with monopoly rests with its ability to earn a greater-than-normal return on its investment. If the government wishes to control both the rate of output of the monopoly (assume exhaustion of all gains from trade) and its rate of return (eliminate monopoly profits), it will need to adopt two separate controls. For example, it may set the price at P_C, where the marginal cost curve intersects the demand curve and also set a fixed "license fee" equal to the monopoly profits that could be earned at that price. The purpose of the license fee is to use a lump sum tax which will not effect the marginal profitability calculations of the firm; setting the price makes average revenue and marginal revenue equal from the point of view of the firm. Both kinds of policy are required. If only one is used, either resources will be used inefficiently or monopoly profits will be retained by the firm. However, in the United States, the power to raise taxes rests with Congress. Public utility commissions are, therefore, restricted to price setting in their attempts to regulate the behavior of privately owned monopolies. Public utility commissions have been mandated to utilize their price-setting power to allow regulated firms to just earn a return sufficient to cover the opportunity cost of attracting funds, while securing output at the lowest possible price for consumers. This regulatory criterion has come to be known as the "fair-rate-of-return" doctrine. As the problem illustrated in Figure 10.3(a) shows, application of this criterion is inconsistent with maximizing the gains from extending trade.

REGULATION AND NONPRICE RATIONING

● Application of the fair-rate-of-return doctrine not only precludes the possibility of inducing a monopoly to choose the output rate that a cooperative would choose, but may also prevent efficient distribution of the output that is produced. Returning to the situation illustrated in Figure 10.3(a), the lowest achievable price that allows the firm to earn a normal return is P_r. But if the commission sets the selling price at P_r, the firm can only supply N units without loss, while its customers will wish to purchase a much larger quantity. The commission cannot force the company to sell more than N units at a price P_r, since to do so would force the firm to incur losses.[3] Consequently, if the commission sets the price equal to the minimum achievable average cost of production, some form of nonprice rationing must be used to allocate the firm's output among its customers.

The problem of nonprice rationing frequently occurs in regulated industries whose selling price is administratively determined. Regulatory rate making is a tedious business, complicated by the necessity of determining the value of the assets of the firm, or rate base upon which the total returns are to be adjusted to yield a fair rate of return. The central problem of rate-base determination is that there is no generally accepted method of valuing a firm's assets for purpose of regulatory proceedings. Different measures such as actual cost of assets when purchased, reproduction cost, market value have all been used to establish a rate base. Since there is no necessary correspondence among these three measures, there is room for extensive legal argument as to which measure is "appropriate" for rate-making purposes. For this reason, regulatory hearings are held infrequently, and rates are established for considerable periods of time. While rates change infrequently, demand-and-cost conditions cannot be perfectly forecast in advance. If a firm underestimates the growth in demand in planning its plant expansion, it may well find itself with insufficient capacity to meet all of the demand forthcoming at the regulated price and still make its "fair" rate of return. It may petition the commission to raise its prices temporarily in order to ration the quantity it would be willing to sell at the regulated price. But the commission is likely to deny its petition, for if it were granted, this would raise the firm's rate of return above the fair rate. In effect, if the petition is granted, the firm is rewarded for underestimating demand when it makes its plant capacity extension decisions. Granting such a petition might, therefore, set a precedent which would provide the regulated firm with an incentive to consistently underestimate the growth in demand. On the other hand, it is not generally possible to force the regulated firm to meet the demand forthcoming at the regulated price if this would force the firm to incur losses. To do so, the commission would have to prove that the firm could have been reasonably expected to make better cost-and-demand estimates than it presented at the last regulatory hearing. But by providing such proof, the commission would (1) be admitting that it was not inquisitive enough at its previous hearings and (2) have to know more about the industry which it is regulating than the firm itself. Neither condition is likely to be met.[4] Consequently, the firm must resort to nonprice rationing whenever demand exceeds the "fair-rate-of-return" output associated with the regulatory price.

Brownouts, or a general reduction in electrical voltage, inability to get dial tones, reduced water pressure are all methods of nonprice rationing which have been used to meet allegedly unexpected excess demands in various parts of the country. Since voltage reduction damages some electrical equipment more than it does others, and access to a clear line is more valuable for some purposes than others, such methods of nonprice rationing inefficiently allocate the available supply. Moreover, as our illustrative situation in Figure 10.3(a) illustrates, nonprice rationing can be a chronic result of applying the fair-rate-of-return doctrine to rate making, not merely the result of imperfect forecasting.[5]

Suppose that demand and cost could be accurately forecast, the problem of continuous nonprice rationing could be avoided by setting the price where the cost curve intersects the demand curve. The firm will then (in the absence of random fluctuations in cost and demand) just be able to sell all of the output it would wish to produce at the given price. This rule eliminates the problem of nonprice rationing, but may result, as in the case illustrated in Figure 10.3(a), in an excessive output relative to the socially optimal output. The fair-rate-of-return doctrine, when applied by a commission that has no taxing power creates an insoluble dilemma. If society is not to waste its resources through overextension of capacity or via the use of nonprice rationing devices, it cannot constrain the profits of a private monopoly.

THE SUBSIDIZATION OF A REGULATED MONOPOLY

● Figure 10.3(b) is similar to 10.3(a) except the demand curve of the former cuts the average-cost curve to the left of the point of minimum average cost. This apparently small difference makes a very substantial difference in terms of appropriate regulation. If the regulatory agency sets the price equal to the minimum possible average price P_C, the firm will not voluntarily produce anything since any quantity it could sell at that price would produce insufficient revenues to cover total costs. But from the point of view of maximizing the total gains from trade, even P_C is too high a price to charge, since P_C exceeds the price at which demand price and marginal cost are equal. The conflict between securing the efficient output and avoiding monopoly profits is the opposite of case illustrated in Figure 10.3(a). In this case, the efficient output will be produced only if the firm is subsidized by the amount $(C_M - P_{\bar{C}})$ per unit sold; otherwise, the firm cannot meet its expenses. The necessity of raising revenues to pay this subsidy has created a considerable controversy among economists about the desirability of attempting to regulate output by the price-equal-marginal-cost rule. We survey this controversy in the next section.

SHOULD PRICE EQUAL MARGINAL COST?

● The argument for setting price equal to marginal cost in order to achieve the most efficient level of output rests upon the assumption that the market prices of the inputs represent the highest price anyone in the economy would pay for their use. Given this assumption, if output in a given industry is less than that where price equals marginal cost, the total value of resources could be increased by increasing the output of that industry and reducing the output of others. Conversely, if output in a given industry is greater than that where price equals marginal cost, then the total value of resources could be increased by releasing some inputs for use in other activities where their value marginal product was higher. However, if the prices of inputs do not reflect their highest value in alternative uses, then the price-equal-marginal-cost (as measured by market prices) rule will lead to a diversion of resources from higher- to lower-valued uses. As we saw in Chapter 5, when tax receipts are based upon the volume of particular kinds of exchanges, the value to a producer of extending his output is the price per unit net of tax, while the value to his customers is the price per unit gross of tax. Since it is the producer who purchases the inputs, it is the value of the output to the producers that determines his maximum offer price for inputs. If his output is subject to tax, then this is necessarily less than the value his customers would place on the inputs. Taxes, therefore, lead to inefficient resource allocation, the extent of the inefficiency being called the excess burden or deadweight loss. The necessity of raising taxes to pay the loss if a utility operates according to the price-equal-marginal-cost rule, therefore, poses a serious dilemma. If you wish to avoid the deadweight loss of additional taxes, then price must be set above marginal cost. But if price is set above marginal cost, then some consumers of this product may be willing to pay more for additional resources than necessary to fully compensate others for reduction in output of other goods and services. In such circumstances, it is not possible to choose decision rules that will lead to an efficient allocation of resources. Rather, the policy problem is to choose the combination of regulations that will lead to the smallest degree of inefficiency.

The Measurement of Deadweight Losses

Before we can consider various proposals for minimizing the deadweight loss implied by the structure of the problem depicted in Figure 10.3(b), we must discuss the nature of the measurement of such losses. The notion of efficiency, which we developed in Chapter 1, rested on the pareto ordering principle. According to that principle, situation A was socially preferred to B if at least one person was better off in A than B and no one was worse off. It is not possible to order by this principle a switch from C to D if in making the switch there are both gainers and losers. But in the policy problem we wish to consider, any switch will have an impact on prices in other markets and consequently affect the distribution of the gains from trade in those markets. It is not possible, therefore, to discuss the gain in efficiency attributable to the changes induced by a policy in terms of the pareto ordering. The pareto ordering implies no interpersonal comparisons of utility. But if there are both gainers and losers, then some kind of weighting must be adopted in order to judge whether the gains exceed the losses. Once such a weighting scheme is adopted, then it is possible to judge one situation as being more or less inefficient than another.

One kind of weighting scheme is to take the distribution of the gains from trade *before* the policy switch as a bench mark and ask if, in terms of that distribution, the gainers from the switch *could* compensate the losers so that the losers were no worse off than before and (the gainers) still profit from the policy change. This is the Hicks-Kaldor compensation principle for judging the potential improvement in efficiency of resource use.[6] It is only a criterion for *potential* improvement, since the principle does not require that the losers actually be compensated, only that they *could* be. We illustrate the Hicks-Kaldor principle in Figure 10.4.

In Figure 10.4, we assume that the economy produces two goods A and B. The demand curves for A and B before the policy switch are represented in Panel 1. The equilibrium prices are P_A and P_B, represent-

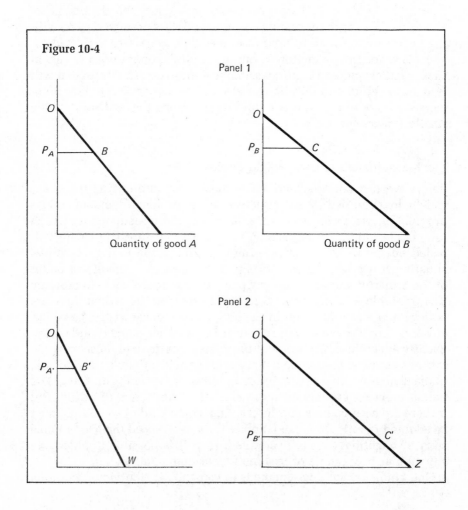

ing a consumer surplus of P_ABO for consumers of A and P_BCO for consumers of B. For simplicity, we assume that the policy switch does not affect the total gains secured by producers so that only the changes in the size of the various consumer surpluses are relevant. The demand curves for A and B after the policy switch are represented in Panel 2 by the curves OW and OZ; the new equilibrium prices are $P_A{}'$, $P_B{}'$, and the new consumer surpluses $P_A{}'B'O$ and $P_B{}'C'O$, respectively. If $P_A{}'B'O +$ $P_B{}'C'O > P_ABO + P_BCO$ (as is readily apparent in the diagram shown), then the policy switch passes the Hicks-Kaldor test, since the *total* gains from trade are larger after the switch than before.

Of course, those people who have relatively strong preferences for good A will actually be harmed, since the decrease in the price of B does not fully compensate them for the increase in the price of A. However, it is not practical to attempt to arrange additional compensation, since no one knows the amounts by which various specific individuals have gained or lost by the policy switch. Many proponents of the compensation principle argue that if the principle is applied to a large number of policy switches, then on the "principle" of the equal division of ignorance, it should turn out that on average everyone will be a gainer even if no attempt at redistribution is made after each policy switch.

Several types of criticism have been addressed to the application of the compensation principle in judging a switch in policy. First, the choice of the bench-mark distribution for judging the possibility of compensating the losers is arbitrary. Tibor Scitovsky suggested that the distribution of gains from trade *after* the policy switch be used as the bench mark.[7] The compensation test based on this bench mark would be: The policy switch is desirable if there is no redistribution of income before the switch which everyone would prefer to the result of the policy switch. The rationale of this test is that if the test is not satisfied, it would be possible for the potential losers from the switch to bribe the potential gainers not to make the switch and (the potential losers) still be better off than if the switch were made. Scitovsky then showed that a policy switch that satisfied the Hicks-Kaldor compensation test need not satisfy this second test. We illustrate this possibility in Figure 10.5.

In Figure 10.5, the left side of Panel 1 reproduces Panel 2 in Figure 10.4. The right side represents the conditions in the market for good C, a market which is not in any way affected by the proposed policy switch represented in Figure 10.4. Panel 2 in Figure 10.5 represents the demand-and-price conditions which would prevail in markets A, B, and C if the potential losers bribed the potential gainers not to make the policy switch. As can be seen, the sum of the consumer surpluses in Panel 2 of Figure 10.5 is larger than the sum of consumer surpluses generated by the policy switch as represented in Panel 1.

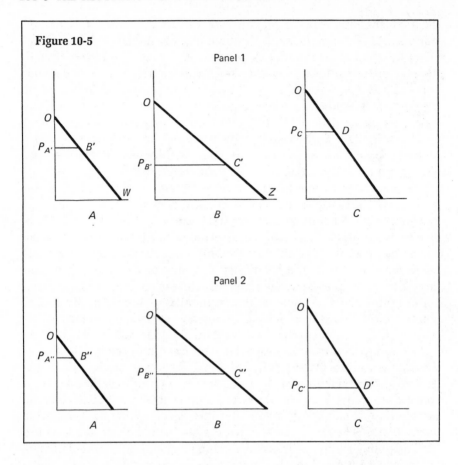

Figure 10-5

Since it seems just as reasonable to require that the losers not be able to bribe the gainers in order to avoid the tax as to require that the gainers be able to compensate the losers for the imposition of the tax, Scitovsky suggested that when both tests could not be satisfied or violated, then no judgment be rendered as to the desirability of the tax-subsidy proposal. If Scitovsky's suggestion is not to imply a presumption in favor of the status quo, then it must be interpreted as meaning that when the tests give conflicting indications, society should be indifferent between adopting and not adopting the tax-subsidy proposal.

Samuelson has argued that the Scitovsky double test is still inadequate, since it arbitrarily assumes that either the preswitch or postswitch distribution of wealth is (are) ethically acceptable bench marks.[8] His criterion would be that the policy be adopted if it passes the compensation test against any conceivable bench-mark distribution of wealth. Unlike the Hicks-Kaldor-Scitovsky (H-K-S) formulation, however, the Samuelson principle seems to require more information for its application than is feasible to require in making a policy decision in situations where the output of one good is expanded at the cost of reduced outputs of other goods. Nevertheless, consideration of the Samuelson position serves to remind the policy maker that considerations of efficiency cannot be separated from considerations of equity. Both the pre- and postswitch distributions of wealth may be so unacceptable that satisfaction of the Hicks-Kaldor-Scitovsky criteria is irrelevant.

As stated earlier, the advocates of the H-K-S principle recognize that it would not be feasible to actually make the indicated compensations after each policy switch. Rather, they rely upon the consistent application of the principle to a large number of policy proposals to assure that everyone gains from its application. The objection to this argument is that it is an argument from ignorance. There is no basis in ignorance for believing that the "law of large numbers" will hold so that after some finite number of policy switches, the probability that everyone would be a gainer would be close to 1. But it is this assumed probability that makes application of the principle intuitively attractive.

Perhaps the deepest criticism of the H-K-S principle is that when more than two alternatives are compared, it may produce an inconsistent ordering of the alternatives. This intransitivity property is illustrated by the following example taken from Kenneth Arrow's book *Social Choice and Individual Values*.[9] Suppose there are two individuals, I and II, and two commodities, A and B. Individual I ranks bundles of A and B which he will receive in the following descending order:

A	B
2.1	1.0
1.0	2.0
2.4	.7
1.7	1.3
2.0	1.0

Furthermore, there is no bundle which has less than 0.9 units of good B that is at least as good, from individual I's point of view, as (2.0, 1.0). Individual II's ranking is:

A	B
1.4	1.4
1.0	2.0
1.6	1.3
1.8	1.1
2.0	1.0

Furthermore, from individual II's point of view, there is no bundle which has less than 1.2 units of the second commodity that is at least as good as (1.0, 2.0).

A social state is described by listing individual I's bundle of A and B and individual II's bundle of A and B in that state. Suppose that it is possible by various policy switches to attain any one of the following social states:

Social State	I		II	
	A	B	A	B
x	2.0	1.0	2.0	1.0
y	1.7	1.3	1.8	1.1
z	1.0	2.0	1.0	2.0

Comparing x with y, the Hicks-Kaldor test indicates y is preferred to x since both individuals I and II prefer y to x. However, both individuals I and II prefer a state w where individual I has the bundle (2.4, 0.7) and II has (1.0, 2.0) to y. Furthermore, since there are 4 units of A and 2 units of B in state x, state w can be reached from x by a redistribution of goods. Therefore, the switch from x to y does not satisfy the Scitovsky test, and x must be socially indifferent to y. Similarly, if y is compared with z, the H-K test indicates that z be preferred to y. But both individuals I and II prefer state w' where individual I has bundle (2.1, 1.0) and II has bundle (1.4, 1.4) to z. Furthermore, since there are 3.5 units of A and 2.4 units of B in y, w' can be reached from y by a redistribution of the goods. Therefore, the switch from y to z would not satisfy the Scitovsky test and, therefore, y is considered to be socially indifferent to z. If the double test leads to consistent results, then all three social states should be equally acceptable (or unacceptable). However, z is preferred to x (by the H-K test), and x is not preferred to z (by the Scitovsky test), since starting from x there are only 2 units of B in toto, while any social state preferred to z by both parties would require at least 2.1 units of B. The H-K-S double test would, therefore, indicate that z was both (indirectly) no better than x (since z is no better than y, which is no better than x) and (directly) better than x. It is difficult to know what a rational policy decision is when the test upon which it is based produces contradictions.

In summary, a measure of the gains and losses from any given policy switch depends upon the weights attached to changes in the levels of preference of the individuals affected. The choice of a bench-mark distribution of wealth implies a choice of weights. But as the preceding discussion of the compensation tests indicates, there is no measuring scheme that would be acceptable in all situations. Individual policy situations must, therefore, be considered individually, and common sense rather than a well-defined measuring rod must serve to test the reasonableness of the policy considered.

SELF-FINANCING OF PUBLIC UTILITY OPERATIONS

● Earlier, we argued that average-cost pricing of public utility operations led to an inefficient allocation of resources. That would be a strong argument against ever using such a pricing policy if other methods of control always led to more desirable results. But the remarks of the preceding sections caution us not to make such judgments on a priori grounds. Average-cost pricing as a method of control has two desirable traits.

1. Users pay, and nonusers do not pay for the service. There is no redistribution of wealth implied by the method of control. This minimizes potential political conflicts.

2. Since the operations must be self-financing, the average-cost pricing rule tends to prevent excessive expansion of capacity. The owners of the utility cannot ask the government to bail them out when they overestimate the rate of expansion of demand.

In some cases, the demand curve may not intersect the average-cost curve. Many mass-transit systems seem to be in this position. With demand declining as more people switch to automobiles, transit authorities find fare box receipts cannot keep pace with rising costs. In these cases, there is no price that will produce sufficient revenues to cover costs. Nevertheless, the total amount consumers would be willing to pay for a given output may exceed the total cost of providing that output. This case is illustrated in Figure 10.6. In this figure, when output Q_0 is produced, the total cost would equal C_0Q_0, which is greater than the total revenue P_0Q_0 that could be earned if that output was sold

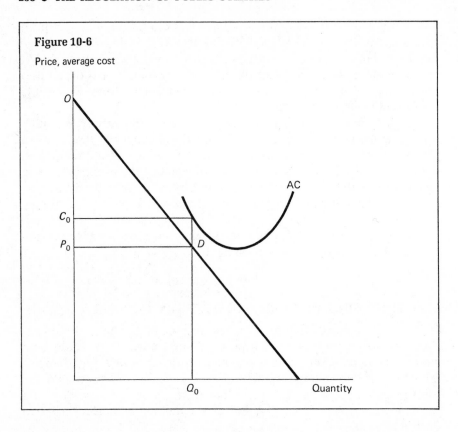

Figure 10-6

Price, average cost

Quantity

at the market-clearing price. Nevertheless, the consumer surplus OP_0D associated with the market-clearing price P_0 is so large that the loss $(C_0 - P_0)Q_0$ could, in principle, be covered by lump sum charges (or licenses) for the privilege of consuming any quantity at all. The lump sum charge would have the effect of making the unit cost highest for those who use the service least and lowest for those who use it most. It is, in effect, a method of establishing a discriminatory pricing policy in order to capture larger revenues from the sale of a given output. The success of a discriminatory policy depends upon the inability of buyers to recontract among themselves. In the case of an electrical utility where retransmission from one buyer to another would be costly, the power-generating firm does not have to worry about recontracting. On the other hand, if municipal bus lines were to attempt lump sum plus individual fare tariffs (for example, requiring both purchase of a monthly riding permit and a fare box token), many riders would probably share a common permit, thereby restricting the revenue-generating potential of such a scheme. The firm could attempt to make the permits nontransferable, but actually enforcing such a clause is likely to be quite expensive.

A second difficulty with using a two-part tariff to increase revenues is that demand may be most elastic for those who use the service relatively infrequently. But effective price discrimination requires that the highest price be charged to users with the least elastic demands. Since riders who use the service least frequently pay the highest effective price per trip, a high permit fee may actually reduce total revenues.

In some cases, therefore, services that can be sold (and are therefore not public goods) and that are potentially profitable will, nevertheless, require public subsidy if they are to be provided.

WHAT CAN REGULATORS REGULATE?

● No authority can directly control all of the variables that affect the performance of the regulated firm unless it is involved in the day-to-day management of the firm. (Even the owners of firms find it difficult to maintain cost and quality controls.) The typical regulatory agency when faced with a request for a change in rates can do little more than ask if the new rates will generate an excessive rate of return. It is in no position to judge if the firm would obtain the same profit results from reducing costs. By fixing the maximum allowable rate of return, the authority reduces incentives to maintain pressure on costs. If the price is fixed, but the rate of return is not, the firms will tend to alter the non-price component of its service (such as maintenance services, and so on) so as to partially offset the impact of price regulation on its rate of return. The fact that there are many dimensions of a service other than price over which a regulatory authority has no effective control implies that the regulatory commission might not even be able to prevent the regulated firm from earning the same rate of return it would have had in the absence of regulation. Indeed, a study by Stigler and Friedland of rates of return to regulated and unregulated electrical utilities found no statistically significant difference between them.[10]

REGULATION IN THE PUBLIC INTEREST?

● Stigler and Friedland offer two explanations for the apparently insignificant impact of regulation on the return of a utility. First, they argue, as above, that regulation of output price still gives the firm considerable control over exercising whatever monopoly position it possesses. Secondly, they conjecture that the typical electrical utility's monopoly power is severely constrained by the existence of competition from both other locally provided power sources and from the desire of utilities in other locations to attract a larger industrial base.

When we combine the Stigler-Friedland result that regulation does not necessarily reduce monopoly profits with our earlier analysis of the effects of regulation on the efficiency of resource allocation, we are led to ask who benefits from regulation. One disturbing thesis, which seems to have considerable circumstantial support, is that an industry seeks out regulation in order to increase or maintain the profits of the firms extant when regulation is first imposed. The regulatory powers of the state can be used to benefit firms in an industry in two ways. First, the existing firms may seek regulation in order to limit the number of new entrants into the industry or the expansion of competitive industries. For example, transmission of television signals by cable into major marketing areas, which would effectively increase the range of viewing alternatives open to the public and reduce the monopoly rents of over-the-air broadcasters, has been systematically discriminated against in rulings of the Federal Communications Commission. Similarly, the FCC has placed substantial roadblocks in the path of pay-television development, further reducing the competitive challenges to the commercial broadcasting systems.

Secondly, regulation may allow an industry to maintain a price structure that would otherwise be eroded by the presence of competitive pressures. The railroad industry in the period prior to the formation of the Interstate Commerce Commission (ICC) was characterized by individual monopolies on short-haul business and competition among railroads on long-haul business. The railroads attempted to form a cartel on the long-haul Midwest grain market to east coast business, but the pressures for cheating were so strong that the cartel could not hold long-haul rates much, if at all, above the cost of long-haul service. The pressure for formation of the Interstate Commerce Commission came from those groups who principally used short-haul service or were otherwise exposed to a monopoly situation. These groups felt that they were being unfairly discriminated against and should be receiving the same rates as shippers in markets where transport competition was vigorous.

After the ICC was organized, the railroads followed a policy of lowering some short-haul rates to through rates on some lines, while *raising* through rates (long-haul rates) on others so as to conform with the commission's mandate to make through and local rates "comparable." The net effect was to raise rates above those that would be set by competition in long-haul business, while forcing the industry to sacrifice some monopoly profits on short-haul lines. In studying the early impact of the ICC, MacAvoy concludes, that on balance, profits of the trunk-line industries expanded as a result of regulation which strengthened the ability of the cartel to set long-haul rates.[11]

SUMMARY

● The existence of significant economies of scale in the provision of a service or production of a product weakens the regulatory forces of competition and has fostered the development of nonmarket regulatory institutions. These institutions must operate within a legal framework, which both prevents them from levying taxes or granting subsidies and from imposing constraints upon the firms under their jurisdiction which would deprive these firms of a "fair" rate of return on their investments. Attempts to operate within this framework have led regulatory commissions to adopt policies that do *not* force the private firms to act in a way which is consistent with maximizing the total gains from trade, minimizing the cost of providing service, or necessarily reduce monopoly profits. This is not to say that regulation has had no effect. There is evidence that the policies of regulatory commissions sometimes contribute to the monopoly profits of the industries they regulate and alter the distribution of gains from trade among various classes of consumers. It is because the commissions do have the power to affect the distribution of gains from trade that various interest groups have sought to have such commissions established. But just how they will work may perhaps be more readily understood in terms of the interests and political strengths of the groups they affect than in terms of any generally stated criteria of efficiency or equity. A full understanding of regulatory phenomena must wait upon the construction of a theory of the politics of regulation.

Notes

1. This is subject, of course, to the proviso that all of the inputs used by the firm are priced at their social marginal value.
2. Of course, we do not mean to deny that the shape of economic institutions may mold the character of those who participate in them. But such forces are evolutionary in character and do not work instantaneously.
3. Forcing a firm to incur losses has been interpreted as confiscation of property, which is prohibited by the 5th Amendment to the U.S. Constitution.
4. A classic example of the inability of regulatory commissions to effectively challenge a firm's cost-and-demand estimates was the open admission in 1971 by the Federal Communications Commission that it would simply

accept American Telephone and Telegraph's own estimates which required a $5 million expenditure to produce because the commission lacked the resources to challenge them.

5. This seems to be the case in the chronic "shortage" of natural gas. For a discussion, see P. MacAvoy, "The Rationale for Regulation of Gas Field Prices," in P. MacAvoy, ed., *The Crisis of the Regulatory Commissions*, New York: Norton, 1970.

6. J. R. Hicks, "Foundations of Welfare Economics," *Economic Journal*, Vol. 49, 1939; N. Kaldor, "Welfare Propositions of Economics and Interpersonal Comparisons of Utility," *Economic Journal*, Vol. 49, 1939.

7. T. Scitovsky, "A Note on Welfare Propositions in Economics," *The Review of Economic Studies*, Vol. 9, November 1941, pp. 77–88.

8. P. A. Samuelson, "Evaluation of Real National Income," *Oxford Economic Papers* (N.S.), Vol. 2, January 1950, pp. 1–29.

9. Kenneth Arrow, *Social Choice and Individual Values*, New York: Wiley, 1951, ch. 4.

10. G. J. Stigler and C. Friedland, "What Can Regulators Regulate? The Case of Electricity," *Journal of Law and Economics*, October 1962.

11. P. MacAvoy, *The Economic Effects of Regulation: The Trunkline Railroad Cartels and the I.C.C. Before 1900*, Cambridge, Mass.: M.I.T. Press, 1962.

Questions for Discussion

1. In the early 1960s, several U.S. manufacturers of equipment for the electrical utility industry were found guilty of a conspiracy to violate the antitrust laws. Why might utilities whose rate base was replacement cost wish to *encourage* such practices on the part of their suppliers? This possibility is discussed in F. M. Westfield, "Regulation and Conspiracy," *American Economic Review*, Vol. LV, June 1965, pp. 424–443.

2. Why are the major utility companies not organized as cooperatives rather than as profit-making private firms?

3. Changes in technology have, in recent years, made electricity competitive with gas as a heating source if the electricity is sold at a bulk rate above marginal but below average cost. This has encouraged competition between local gas and electrical utilities for servicing large establishments such as office buildings.

   One group argues that the utility commission should prevent such competition on the grounds that if the electrical utility had to offer all of its customers service at the same cost per unit as it offers bulk users, it would have to go out of business. Bulk pricing is discriminatory, according to this view, and should not be allowed. Another group argues that as long as the bulk user pays a rate in excess of marginal cost, no social purpose would be served by preventing him from choosing all electrical service if he so desires.

   With what point of view do you agree?

4. Suppose you knew that the effective price faced by automobile drivers for road services was less than the marginal cost of providing them with such services. How might this fact influence the pricing policy that you would choose to finance and control the use of a mass-transit system?

Suggested Readings

Coase, R. H., "The Marginal Cost Controversy," *Economica,* Vol. 13, August 1946, pp. 169–182.

Coase, R. H., "The Theory of Public Utility Pricing and its Application," *Bell Journal of Economics and Management Science,* Vol. 1, Spring 1970.

Dupuit, Jules, "On the Measurement of the Utility of Public Works," reprinted in K. Arrow and T. Scitovsky, eds., *Readings in Welfare Economics,* Homewood, Ill.: Irwin, 1969, pp. 255–283.

Henderson, A., "The Pricing of Public Utility Undertakings," reprinted in K. Arrow and T. Scitovsky, *op. cit.,* pp. 541–561.

Hotelling, H., "The General Welfare in Relation to Problems of Taxation and of Railway and Utility Rates," reprinted in K. Arrow and T. Scitovsky, *op. cit.,* pp. 284–308.

Meade, J. E., "Price and Output Policy of State Enterprise," *Economic Journal,* Vol. 54, December 1944, pp. 321–328.

Mohring, H., "The Peak Load Problem with Increasing Returns and Pricing Constraints," *American Economic Review,* Vol. 60, 1970, pp. 693–705.

Ruggles, N. D., "Recent Developments in the Theory of Marginal Cost Pricing," *Review of Economic Studies,* Vol. 27, 1949–1950, pp. 107–126.

11

FISCAL FEDERALISM

Governments differ from other social institutions by the fact of their monopoly of the power of legal coercion. The arguments presented in this book for government participation in the economy have rested implicitly on the assumption that forcing individuals to act against their perceived interests in particular circumstances would produce a net social benefit. Whether or not this is so may depend importantly on the structure of government and its attendant costs of decision making. In this chapter, we analyze how the level of government at which policies are formulated to deal with the problems of equity, stabilization, and efficiency is likely to influence the net benefit derived from the implementation of those policies.

THE RESPONSIBILITY
FOR REDISTRIBUTIVE POLICY

The Pressure for an Income Redistribution Policy

The orderly functioning of a free-market system presupposes an institutional framework which defines property rights and enforces contracts. Because of the inherent conflict of individual interest in any division of property rights, coercion is a necessary tool of any institution charged with this responsibility. It is, therefore, natural to place such assignments within a legal framework.

In a capitalist system, the distribution of wealth depends not only on the distribution of property rights, but also upon the values that the market places on various types of property. Changes in prices, over which no individual may have any control or forewarning, transfer wealth from one group of individuals to another. It is no comfort to textile workers and plant owners to know that they retain ownership of their skills and plants when foreign competition has depreciated their market value. Nor are the employees and owners of aerospace firms particularly solaced by the knowledge that a transfer of resources out of their industry will better serve the nation's changed priorities. From their point of view, they have been deprived of some portion of their wealth as effectively as if their property were stolen.

While society does not condone theft of property, and may express sympathy for its victims, in general, there is no collective provision for compensation in the (likely) event that the goods are not recovered. The reason for this is simple. Individuals may purchase in the market insurance against loss by theft. Thus, the individual has access to an instrument of compensation without recourse to state action. However, in the case of possible loss of wealth induced by relative price changes, there is no private insurance market available in which the individual might participate. (Question: What necessary conditions for the formation of a private insurance market are not met in the case of loss via changes in relative prices?) The failure of a private market to provide this type of insurance would generate pressure for a continuing government redistributive policy even in the event that everyone was agreed as to the equity of the initial distribution of property rights.[1]

The Institutional Response

Insecurity of wealth arising out of changes in relative prices is an attribute peculiar to an economy where individuals have become highly specialized in the range of productive activities they pursue and, as a consequence, highly dependent upon an elaborate market system to provide themselves with the range of commodities they consume. In a highly integrated economy, many markets are national in scope. Moreover, changes in one industrial sector will induce changes in many others. Therefore, the effects of market changes will permeate throughout the national economy with no assurance that the regional distribution of gainers will coincide with the regional distribution of losers. It follows that if each region or locality were to attempt to fully compensate the losers out of the gains to the gainers within its own region, there may be some regions which could not do so. Considered as separate insurance "companies," each regional "company" will have the incentive to pool its risks with every other regional "company" so as to reduce the likelihood of being unable to meet its obligations. Indeed, in this case, since the sum of gains over all gainers must be at least equal to the sum of losses over all losers, the probability of being able to meet all claims can be increased to 1 for each region if all regions pool their risks. Obviously, an effective method of accomplishing this is to make policy for income redistribution a responsibility of a supraregional government, thereby assuring regional coordination of income redistribution policies.

In fact, income redistribution schemes are not organized like insurance pools. Payments into insurance pools are made before any knowledge that the insured-against event has incurred. But government income redistribution schemes, which take more from the "rich" than from the "poor" only after the "rich" and "poor" have been identified, are built into the tax structure. As a consequence, a man who would have been willing to purchase insurance against his becoming poor, prior to any knowledge as to whether or not he would in fact so become, will, upon becoming rich, no longer see the utility of his participation in such an insurance scheme. This means that if there are separate regional policies of income redistribution, the rich will tend to migrate toward those areas whose tax scheme is least redistributional in impact, while the poor will migrate in the opposite direction. Separate regional income redistributional policies can, therefore, lead to migration flows, which will tend to segregate people by income class and reduce the degree to which income redistribution can, in fact, be achieved. This prospect, therefore, further reinforces the argument that an income redistribution policy to compensate for differences in market advantages should be the responsibility of the national government.

A change in the pattern of income distributions among areas will have fiscal implications of its own. As an illustration, consider the situation of an area whose growth has been achieved partly by the in-migration from other areas of low-income workers who are attracted by the availability of better-wage opportunities in this area than in the area from which they came. Suppose that this in-migration has led to an increase in the proportion of low-income families in the area. As a consequence, while the total tax base is expanding, the per capita tax base is declining. Therefore, unless the per capita cost of providing the initial level of public services declines with population growth as rapidly as the per capita tax base declines, it will not be possible for this area to maintain its service levels to its initial inhabitants without an increase in their tax rates. Alternatively, if it maintains its initial tax rates, it must lower its standards of service. In either case, the initial inhabitants will experience a reduction in their real incomes through the change in the effective price to them of public services. This in-migration-induced "price" increase may have the further effect of inducing an out-migration of population which may further increase the proportion of low-income people who remain to face even higher effective prices of public services.[2]

The fiscal facts on redistributive programs in the United States reflect the practical necessity for effective redistributional policy to be financed at the highest level of government. George Break notes that by 1966 over 90 percent of all transfer and subsidy expenditures were made by the federal government.[3] These redistributive expenditures have been channeled through a variety of institutions. Federal funds for some programs such as aid to dependent children are channeled directly through existing state and local welfare agencies. In other instances, administration of the program remains a federal responsibility as in the federal farm price support program. In still other cases, new quasi-governmental bodies such as the Appalachian Regional Commission take responsibility for designing and directing the content of a redistributive program, while its financing remains a federal prerogative. In recent years, federal programs directed toward improving the economic opportunities of the poor, such as Head Start and the Youth Corps, have been administered by private corporations and quasi-private institutions such as universities under federal contract. The philosophy underlying this separation of fiscal from administrative responsibility has been that decentralized design and implementation of policies designed to improve the economic position of the poor will lead to more effective programs than would otherwise be the case. This philosophy (expressed in a rather different context) is nicely summarized by Walter Heller when he says, "There is enough money at the center, i.e., in our federal government to *finance* our national programs but there is not enough wisdom to *administer* them centrally. So we rely heavily on states and localities as service stations to carry out the centrally financed functions."[4]

A more comprehensive way of achieving decentralized responsibility for the execution of federally financed redistributive programs would be to pass the funds directly to the poor in the form of a cash grant with each recipient free to spend the money in any way he wishes.

The essential argument for bypassing bureaucratic provision of services to the poor is that individuals with sufficient income could secure those services in the private sector. These direct cash transfers, which could take the form of a guaranteed annual income or a negative income tax, would also effectively establish income maintenance as a right rather than as contingent upon use of the funds in a bureaucratically improved manner.[5]

STABILIZATION POLICY

● In the depth of the depression of 1929–1933, Henry Ford announced that he was raising wages and not laying off workers in spite of the fact that he could not profitably pay these wages or utilize his labor force at current levels of demand. Ford did this because he believed that if workers received higher incomes, they would spend more and thus generate the increased demand needed to employ them profitably. In one sense, Ford was right. If incomes expand, this would expand aggregate demand. If all businessmen undertook sufficient borrowing to finance the initial exogenous increase in incomes, then Ford's expectations would be realized. However, this was not what happened. Ford's plan failed because most businessmen realized that the feedback from their own outlays to expenditures on their own products was quite weak. No individual firm could expect, say, a 1-percent increase in its outlays to produce, of its own accord, a 1-percent increase in demand for its own product, even though if all firms together were to expand outlays by 1 percent, the impact on demand for each of their firms, via the multiplier process, might be considerably in excess of 1 percent. Indeed, since each firm would share the fruits of an expanded aggregate demand even if it did not contribute to the exogenous increase in outlays which could trigger such an expansion, there was much to gain and little to lose from waiting for demand to increase *before committing* itself to a larger wage bill. (Compare the position of the individual firm in a generally depressed economy with that of an individual property owner in a blighted area.)

Just as there is too little feedback on the sales of an individual firm to encourage it to expand its outlays in the face of a generally depressed economy, so, too, is the impact of any particular state or local government too weak to unilaterally pursue a stabilization policy. The existence of a national economy, therefore, makes the execution of stabilization policy a function of a national government.

GOVERNMENT ORGANIZATION AND THE
EFFICIENT ALLOCATION OF RESOURCES

● Up to this point, we have argued that stabilization and redistributive policies must, as a matter of practical necessity, be objects of central government control in an economy composed of highly interrelated regions. If these were the only economic functions of government, then it would follow from our comments that we should expect over time to see the role of the central government expand and the role of regional governments contract as improvements in transportation and communication bound the fates of separate regions ever more closely together.

While the existence of a single government would expedite the execution of stabilization and redistributive policies, the absence of regional and local governments would result in a larger loss in efficiency caused by (1) the existence of unexploited potentially profitable resource reallocations and (2) more resources used in achieving resource reallocation than would be sustained if decentralized decision making could occur through the existence of a multiplicity of governments.

The first kind of value loss, via misallocation of resources, is intimately related to the second, the value lost because resources are used up in reallocating resources. This second kind of costs, which we may call transactions costs, are those required to collect, transmit, and decode the information about preferences, resource availabilities, and technical possibilities which is necessary to direct resources from lower- to higher-valued uses. As we discussed in Chapter 2, when many different individuals would acquire some utility from the same good, irrespective of who owns it, but no one individual would acquire enough utility to make the purchase on his own, no information will be transmitted to the market about the value of that good to the group unless that group has some way of communicating among itself outside of the market. Such communication is necessary in order to determine a collective decision as to the bid the group will submit in the market. The existence of interdependencies, therefore, requires the maintenance of nonmarket collective decision-making institutions if markets are to receive and respond to information relative to them. But such institutions require the use of resources in order to operate. Therefore, it does not make sense to attempt to transmit information via these institutions to the market unless the value gained by having the market respond to this information is greater than the value of resources used up in the process.

The reason that many types of collective decisions regarding the transmission of such information are made through a *government* is that governments need not rely upon the voluntary assent of all of the people involved in any particular decision. By dropping the rule of unanimity, decisions may be reached much more quickly. Application of the coercive power of government is, therefore, a possible technique for reducing transaction costs. Of course, as we noted in Chapter 3, a movement away from the rule of unanimity may result in purchasing a reduction in transaction costs at the expense of allowing some individuals to impose costs on others via the political process. Nevertheless, as Buchanan and Tullock argue, the gains from savings in transaction costs—and the reduction of value losses from uncompensated externalities—may be so large as to offset for each individual the expected costs which will be imposed upon him via the political process.

More pertinent to our argument, however, is the reduction in transaction costs, which can be achieved if the collective decision-making group, with respect to a given class of decisions, is limited to those individuals whose interest in the group decision will be *relevant at the margin*. By this, we mean that if an individual is to participate in the collective decision process (or to have his preferences considered in the final decision), there must be sufficient reason to believe that if his interests were represented, the group decision might possibly be different than if they were not represented. If this condition is met, we shall say that the individual's interests are *pareto relevant*; and if not, they will then be *pareto irrelevant*. Clearly, if an individual's interests in a particular decision are pareto irrelevant, there is no reason to have the decision-making mechanism devote resources to process any specific information relative to his interests. The only information required is that these interests are not likely to be pareto relevant. Since the cost of any decision-making apparatus depends on the amount of information it must process, by restricting the membership in the decision-making body to the group whose interests are pareto relevant, significant economies may be achieved.

An individual's interest in a particular decision may be pareto relevant for either of two reasons. First, the benefits he will receive as a result of the decision may be dependent on the decisions reached. For example, if expected savings in an individual's medical expenses increase continuously as the level of sulfur dioxide concentration in the atmosphere is reduced, then the total benefit an individual will receive from adoption of a policy of sulfur dioxide reduction will depend on the target level chosen, and the interests of each individual so affected would be pareto relevant. Conversely, if the benefits an individual would receive were invariant with respect to small changes in the decision, then that individual's interests would be pareto irrelevant. For example, each of us may be interested in seeing that every person has at least a minimum caloric intake, but none of us may be interested in how far above this minimum any individual other than members of our own family achieves. Suppose we observe that there is no one who, on his own initiative, has attained a caloric intake below the minimum. Then the interests of everyone other than any particular individual are pareto irrelevant with respect to that individual's caloric-intake decision.

The second way that an individual's interests may be pareto relevant to a decision is if the cost he must bear will be dependent upon the decision reached. Using our example of minimum caloric intake, every other persons' interests would be to see that your caloric intake did not exceed the minimum if it was required that each pay a fraction of the cost of whatever caloric intake you achieve. In other words, an individual whose interests in a particular decision would otherwise be pareto irrelevant will become pareto relevant if the cost he bears is sensitive to the decision.

As we argued above, transaction costs can be reduced if participation in a given decision is restricted to those individuals whose interest in that decision is pareto relevant. Furthermore, we have noted that the size of the pareto relevant group will be influenced by the way the costs of the decision are distributed. An effective way of reducing the size of the pareto relevant group is to adopt the following rule: *Only those individuals whose interests would be relevant even if they bore no cost as a result of the decision must bear the cost of the decision.* This is, in fact, the Wicksellian marginal benefit principle of taxation discussed in Chapter 5. Because many externalities, which give rise to pressure for collective action, tend to be relatively concentrated geographically, pareto relevant groups as determined by the Wicksellian principle will similarly be concentrated geographically. Concretely, marginal benefits from reduction in air pollution within a given airshed are likely to be available only to those persons who live within that airshed. A small park is of benefit to those who are conveniently located with respect to it; similarly, fire and police units, sewage systems, local traffic distribution systems, and so on, all have effective geographical boundaries so that the beneficiaries of these publicly provided services will tend either to live, or to own property, in the areas in which these services are concentrated. The organizational implication of these geographical concentrations is that economy of transaction costs can be achieved by establishing a large number of separate governmental institutions, each of whose jurisdiction is such that it imposes taxes upon only those persons who receive marginal benefits from its activities. This organizational embodiment of the Wicksellian principle is what Mancur Olson has called "fiscal equivalence."[6]

The principle of fiscal equivalence assigns fiscal responsibility for provision of a service in which there is a collective interest to the smallest possible pareto relevant group. (Prove this statement.) If the group with fiscal responsibility were any smaller, the likelihood is that the outlay made for provision of the service would not be sufficient to equate the sum of the marginal benefits over all beneficiaries with the costs of providing further increments of the service. To illustrate the problem that arises when fiscally responsible groups are smaller than those required for fiscal equivalence, consider the situation of several independent municipalities who belong to a common airshed.[7]

Each municipality within the airshed may be quite aware that the quality of air they receive is influenced not only by their own expenditures on air-quality improvement, but upon the expenditures of their neighbors as well. Consequently, in determining how much expenditure to make, municipality A must guess the level of expenditure all of its neighbors will make. Given that guess, municipality A will decide to make expenditures of its own until it has equated the marginal cost of its expenditures to the marginal benefits it receives. In so doing, each municipality ignores the benefits of its expenditure that accrue to others because they do not share in its costs. If, on the other hand, each municipality shared in the costs of providing the marginal benefits it received, then municipality A would, given the same initial outlay of the others, expand its expenditures until its unreimbursed marginal cost was equal to the benefits it received. In effect, the absence of this type of cost-sharing mechanism leads each municipality to overestimate the social marginal cost of improving air quality by the amount of the unreimbursed marginal benefits it supplies to others.

It is important to note that each municipality is sharing in the *total* cost of providing improvements in air quality if it decides *on its own* to make some expenditure, given its estimate of what the others will do. It is the fact that each is *on its own* in financing its own actions, which leads to the inefficient allocation of resources to improvement in air quality in the airshed. Efficiency is not insured by every method of cost sharing, only by a method which imposes on each actor the *social marginal cost* of his actions. This is one of the attributes of the principle of fiscal equivalence.

DEPARTURES FROM FISCAL EQUIVALENCE

● In many states, an important debate is now taking place as to whether or not the concept of fault should be eliminated from automobile insurance policies.[8] One of the arguments that supporters of no-fault automobile insurance muster against the current form of liability law is the large cost of the litigative apparatus necessary to assign fault. By moving to a no-fault system, these administrative costs, they argue, could be substantially reduced. On the other side of the argument, proponents of the liability concept argue that the liability feature of insurance provides the individual driver with an incentive to take steps to reduce the likelihood of his becoming involved in an accident. Furthermore, the incentive to reduce accident risks provided by the liability clause serves this purpose better than specific injunctions or safety standards (for example, all cars must be equipped with a standard-quality brake system; no one may drive a private vehicle where public transit is available, and so on), because it will lead those who can most easily reduce accident risks to undertake the largest reductions, thereby minimizing the total cost of achieving any specific reduction in the accident rate. A central issue in the debate, therefore, is whether or not the benefits derived from a liability system, which attempts to present each driver with the incentive to internalize the costs his decisions might otherwise impose on others, are worth the cost of the administrative apparatus required to achieve that purpose.

A similar issue arises when one considers whether or not it might be more desirable to adopt a system with fewer governments and, therefore, a less expensive administrative structure than the system of (possibly) single function governments implied by the fiscal equivalence principle. In our air pollution example, one method of assuring that all beneficiaries of actions taken to improve air quality share in the marginal costs of undertaking such actions would be to form a separate governmental unit encompassing all inhabitants of the airshed with the power to tax all inhabitants. An alternative to such a single-purpose government, with its attendant costs of election and administration, would be to have each community authorize some officer of its already-existing government to act as its agent in negotiating an airshed-quality improvement compact with agents of the other communities.

The fundamental difference between attempting to manage air quality by establishing a government for that purpose and by establishing a compact among several governments is that a compact would be binding only upon those municipalities that consented to its terms, while a government's decision would be binding upon all who lay within its jurisdiction. The principal attractiveness of the regional compact solution to a coordinated regional policy is that each community can assure itself of some portion of the gains from a coordinated policy, whereas under the governmental method of coordination, it is possible for some communities to bear a net loss. Against this advantage must be set the difference in transaction costs of arriving at a regional policy via the two methods. As we noted in Chapter 3, the rule of unanimity (as required by the compact method) provides an incentive for extensive negotiations and strategic maneuvering. Moreover, as we saw in Question 2 of that chapter, situations may arise in which each community can gain if a bargain can be struck, but it may not be possible to propose any compact from which none of the proposed members withdraws. A possible method of resolving such a paradox is to alter the bargaining situation by increasing the number of issues dealt with simultaneously. By expanding the "game," it may be possible to alter the payoffs to various coalitions and thereby generate conditions for a stable coalition. For example, the original circumstances of Question 2, Chapter 3, were that the joint savings to any pair from a sewage system consolidation were 2.5 with the excluded community gaining nothing, while the joint savings to a coalition of all three communities were 3. In this situation, there is always some subset of communities that can do better for its members by breaking away from a proposed coalition no matter what coalition is proposed. Suppose there were some second activity from which gains from cooperation could be made (for example, consolidation of vocational-training facilities) and that the joint savings to any pair from this activity would be 1.5, while the joint savings to a coalition of all three would be 3. If the school jointure is negotiated separately, all three communities will agree, since each can receive some portion of 3, which is greater than it could receive in any proposed coalition of only two communities. Instead of treating the sewage and school issues separately, however, let them be treated as a single package. Then if all three communities agree simultaneously to both the sewage and school jointures, the total gains will be 6. If the arrangements call for these gains to be divided equally among all three communities, then each pair will receive 4 from this arrangement. Since 4 is the maximum any pair can get by excluding the third community, there will be no incentive for any pair to break away from the proposed arrangement. Thus, by treating several issues simultaneously, it may be possible to reach an accord that could not be obtained by piecemeal bargaining. But as the number of issues that affect several communities expands, the fixed costs of establishing a multipurpose regional government become less important, and, therefore, the formation of such a government may represent a less expensive mode of coordinating the interests and actions of several interdependent groups than the use of intergroup compacts.

Multipurpose regional governments have two advantages over a set of single-purpose governments. Because they are multipurpose, they (1) minimize costs of maintaining a governmental apparatus and (2) provide a vehicle through which the trading of votes on issues that affect different groups somewhat differently can take place. The principal disadvantage of a regional multipurpose government is that its geographic boundary of jurisdiction is likely to be larger than that required to encompass the smallest pareto relevant group on many of the issues for which it has jurisdiction. This is because it is unlikely that the smallest pareto relevant groups on any two issues will be composed of the same set of people. As a consequence, the legislation which is passed may not be tailored to the preferences of any particular group that such legislation materially affects. For instance, if setting of air standards becomes a state responsibility because there are no smaller regional governments which encompass airsheds, the tendency will be to set a single standard of air quality for all of the airsheds within the state, even though if there were some mechanism to differentiate their preferences, people living in different airsheds might opt for quite different quality standards. Clearly, it is desirable, other things being equal, to let different groups choose different standards of air quality and other public goods if they so desire. Centralization of decision making leads to a loss of diversification, which must be set against the savings in transaction costs. It is often argued that uniformity of air-quality standards and other public service levels is a *desirable* rather than an undesirable attribute of public-goods provision because, if communities within one airshed wished to have higher standards than those in other airsheds, they would face the loss of their industrial base. This, it is alleged, raises the potential cost to that set of communities of achieving a high-quality environment and prevents them from actually trying to raise their standards. The rebuttal to this position is that the possibility of industrial migration can be met by granting appropriate tax relief so that the only thing that would prevent a community from adopting higher standards than others would be its unwillingness to pay for the improvements it wishes to secure.[9]

We may summarize the discussion of this section as follows: Strict adherence to the principle of fiscal equivalence will tend to insure that the pattern of provision of public goods corresponds to the preferences of the population. However, the only political mechanism that will necessarily embody the principle is a set of single-function governments. One must weigh the costs of maintaining and processing information through such a system relative to a system which uses either fewer (multipurpose) governments and/or regional compacts or both against its evident superiority in differentiating among groups. The outcome of such a calculus is likely to be that neither strict adherence to the fiscal equivalence principle nor complete centralization of decision making is likely to produce the largest net benefits achievable from a system of nonmarket communication.

SOME ORGANIZATIONAL DIMENSIONS
OF THE URBAN CRISIS

● No organizational or political structure is likely to be equally well suited to all possible environments within which it may be required to function. New situations call forth demands for new forms of government and a shifting of responsibilities among established governmental units. In the 1930s, local governments found their tax receipts falling and demands for public assistance increasing. With their borrowing capacities limited by their shrinking property tax bases, and with little ability to tax other forms of wealth, local governments were simply not capable of retaining the fiscal responsibility for all social welfare services which had historically been theirs. The federal government assumed fiscal responsibility for income maintenance through such devices as the WPA, public assistance, and old age and survivors insurance which, through its eligibility and income limitation provisions, embodies substantial elements of income redistribution.

As Table 11.1 shows, today the financing of direct income transfer programs, public assistance, unemployment insurance, and old age and retirement insurance is preponderantly a federal responsibility. Nevertheless, today, as in the 1930s, local governments, especially of the large cities, are again caught in a set of circumstances with which they do not have the financial resources to cope. In part, the problems facing urban governments stem from the inequality of income distribution, and in part, they stem from an inadequate organizational structure for coordination of metropolitan-wide services.

Income Inequality

As we noted earlier in this chapter, when political boundaries are fixed but the population is mobile, an influx of low-income families into an area will both increase the per capita tax burden of the jurisdiction into which they migrate and induce an out-migration of the relatively wealthy. In our largest metropolitan areas, this is precisely the pattern of migration that has occurred. The urban cores have become the residences of the poor, while the rich have left for the suburbs. If the basic responsibilities of local governments were for the provision of community services such as police and fire protection, local parks, street and sewage maintenance, the increasing absolute income of city residents would be sufficient to provide adequate services. But city governments are still charged with a substantial fiscal responsibility for public assistance, education, and health and hospital services. These categories of expenditure are especially important to the poor,

Table 11.1

Government Expenditures by Function (Billion $)

Function	1965 Federal	1965 State and Local	1969 Federal	1969 State and Local	Percent Change Federal	Percent Change State and Local
Defense and state affairs	54.5	—	84.2	0.2	54	—
Administration	4.1	8.2	4.6	11.9	12	32
Econ. development	18.1	9.1	20.8	13.8	14	51
Space	5.6	—	4.0	—	28	—
Transportation	5.4	7.6	6.2	11.0	14	44
Agriculture	4.4	0.6	7.0	0.9	59	50
Natural resources	1.9	0.5	7.4	0.7	26	40
Postal	0.8	—	1.2	—	50	—
Utilities	—	0.4	—	1.2	—	200
Social development	4.3	35.1	9.8	54.7	127	—
Elem. and sec. schools	0.4	22.2	2.2	32.6	450	46
Higher educ.	0.4	4.6	1.2	10.1	300	119
Other educ.	0.4	1.3	1.3	7.2	225	—
Hospital and sanitation	2.5	7.1	3.3	10.0	32	29
Housing and com. dev.	0.6	−0.1	1.8	−0.2	300	−100
Community services	0.3	6.3	0.4	9.8	33	55
Police and correction	0.1	3.7	0.1	6.1	—	64
Fire	—	1.4	—	2.0	—	42
Recreation	0.2	1.2	0.3	1.7	50	41
Transfer to persons	30.8	3.2	53.3	6.4	73	100
Public assistance	3.4	3.2	7.3	6.3	114	100
Unemployment	2.3	—	2.2	—	−4	—
Old age and retirement	19.7	—	35.4	—	79	—
Veterans	5.4	—	8.4	0.1	55	—
Interest or debt	8.3	0.6	13.3	0.1	60	—
Other	2.9	−0.1	4.9	3.7		
Total exp.	123.4	62.5	191.3	106.6	55	

Source: U.S. Bureau of Census, Governmental Finances.

who are heavily dependent on public hospitals and who look to quality public education as a lever to equal economic opportunity for their children. They also are both quantitatively the most important services in municipal budgets and those showing the fastest rates of growth in expenditures.

In spite of increased federal and state participation in the financing of these welfare-related services, the major metropolitan areas have not been able to meet the rising costs of education and public assistance without raising tax rates and further prodding an out-migration of the more affluent to suburban enclaves in which their tax dollars produce more services for themselves.

Local financing of welfare-related services may have been well suited to an age when city limits coincided with the effective limits of metropolitan activity, for metropolitan areas represent important concentrations of wealth. But the advent of the automobile and the growth of population have extended the metropolitan areas beyond the jurisdictional limits of even our largest cities. Consequently, the same local governments and social institutions, which were able to cope with infusions of poor immigrant workers of earlier decades, have lost their ability to tap as large a fraction of the wealth which, in those former years, supported the schools and social services that were necessary to integrate those earlier migrants into an urban society and provide them opportunity for social and economic mobility within that society. The increased physical mobility of the population has made local financing of social services, which are redistributive in intent, a self-defeating process. It seems inevitable that a serious attempt to provide adequate opportunities for education and health care for all people will require either federal underwriting of some minimum standards of educational and medical services or a serious attempt to raise minimum personal income levels so that these services can be adequately financed by private or local initiative.

Inadequate Organization

Although many urban problems are merely the symptomatic manifestations of poverty concentrated in urban areas, the elimination of poverty would not necessarily do much toward alleviating problems such as congestion whose roots lie in organizational failures. As we noted in Chapter 2, the absence of peak-load pricing on urban roadway services results in distorting the relative cost of mass and private transportation from the individual's point of view. In the absence of such a pricing policy, it is not appropriate to divide responsibility for road system expansion, mass transit, and transport-related services among autonomous agencies, for the price system will not coordinate their decisions and guide resources to their most efficient uses. Profitability (or minimum subsidy) of mass transit is not an appropriate social criterion in such circumstances. The fact that the highway trust fund may be producing surpluses is not an adequate signal for free-way expansion if those surpluses are generated by taxes that subsidize peak-hour users who place the burden on the capacity of the current system. But in the absence of coordinated transportation system planning, and given the presence of a strong highway- oriented lobby, cities are likely to continue to sacrifice an ever-increasing portion of their most valuable real estate to the private auto without making a significant impact upon the level of congestion in the central areas.

If problems such as congestion and pollution seem to require a greater degree of organizational centralization than they have hitherto experienced, improvements in the quality of publicly supported education seem to require the opposite. The public school systems have been object of chronic complaint for many, many years. Given the nature of the service they produce, it is inevitable that administrators of school systems be under attack. For what constitutes a good education and how that education is best achieved are matters of general and philosophic dispute. An effective way to minimize such complaints would be to provide a variety of choices of schooling types, so that parents might better match their choices with their preferences. In order to exercise a choice of school under most existing arrangements, the family must either make the character of the local school an important element in their residential choice or pay a 100 percent premium for sending their children to private schools or other schools outside the neighborhood. These are artificial barriers created by institutional arrangements for local financing and public operation of schools, which were more appropriate to an earlier age.

One essential argument for requiring a person to pay taxes to support his local public school even if he were to send his children elsewhere was that the public schools were to act as a redistributive device. But as the population has become more mobile and the rich and poor have become increasingly segregated by political jurisdiction, this objective can only be achieved by federal financing. With federal financing, there would be no point to penalizing the family that chose to send its child to a school in a political district different from its residence.

In large-city school systems, parents' freedom of choice within the public school system is practically restricted by administrative edict to the neighborhood school. To allow children to attend any school in the system might mean that the physical capacities of some facilities would be enormously overtaxed, while others were underutilized. The school administration is faced with the task of matching students with seats. This task is equivalent to the task any producer has of distributing his output among his customers. In ordinary markets, a shift in demand that cannot immediately be met by a change in the pattern of supply is met by the establishment of price differentials to ration the available supply. The price system cannot currently be used in the public school educational marketplace, because individual schools do not receive funds directly from parents, but rather receive their budgets from the school taxing body. There is, of course, no logical reason why this must be so. Each parent might receive vouchers from the state to be spent on education. These vouchers would themselves be financed, by taxation.[10] With a voucher system, the way in which parents chose to spend their vouchers would provide direction as to the types of school programs that will elicit the greatest support and hence provide a guide to the board's allocation of resources so that overcrowding and underutilized facilities are only temporarily phenomena. For consumer expenditures to effectively guide the boards' decision, of course, they must actually have a range of alternatives from which to choose. Individual schools would have to be given considerably more discretion than they now typically have in choosing curriculum, materials, and staff before there would appear sufficient diversity to permit a market to work effectively in indicating a pattern of education that corresponds to the preferences of the people.[11]

Notes

1. As a practical matter, the government cannot, even at a given instant in time, with given prices, adopt a complete assignment of property rights, since there are some types of property which the government cannot control, for example, native intellect and ability at birth, differences in family attitude toward children, and so on, all of which will influence the distribution of income at given prices, but cannot be known by the state and compensated for in the laws which define the system of property rights.

2. We have been assuming here that the provision of (some) public services will be financed out of local taxes. The argument as to why this should be so appears later in this chapter.

3. "The Changing Roles of Government," in Julius Margolis, ed., The Analysis of Public Output, N.B.E.R., 1970, p. 194.

4. "A Reappraisal of Revenue Sharing," in H. Perloff and P. Nathan, eds., Revenue Sharing and the City, Baltimore, Md.: Johns Hopkins Press, 1968, pp. 17–18.

5. The federal tax structure, embodying a degree of progressivity in its effective marginal rates, also serves as a redistributive, risk-sharing mechanism. The adopting of a negative income tax can be viewed simply as a method of increasing the degree of progressivity of the tax structure.

6. ". . . The Principle of 'Fiscal Equivalence': The Division of Responsibilities among Different Levels of Government," American Economic Review, Papers and Proceedings, May 1969, pp. 479–487.

7. For example, the St. Louis–East St. Louis region or metropolitan New York City regions in which the airshed stretches over state boundaries.

8. For a detailed discussion of the various elements entering into the controversy surrounding automobile accident law, see Guido Calabresi, *The Costs of Accidents, A Legal and Economic Analysis*, New Haven, Conn.: Yale University Press, 1970.

9. For an elaboration of this point, see G. Stigler, "The Tenable Range of Functions of Local Government," in *Federal Expenditures for Growth and Stability*, Joint Economic Committee, 85th Congress, 1st session, 1957.

10. See, for example, Milton Friedman, "The Role of Government in Education," *Capitalism and Freedom*, Chicago: University of Chicago Press, 1962, pp. 85–107.

11. For an interesting discussion of the problems and promises of school decentralization, see Anthony Downs, "Competition and Community Schools," in *Community Control of Schools*, Henry Levin, ed.

Questions for Discussion

1. *Pollution control: a local or national problem?* Suppose there are two communities widely separated from each other which have adopted different pollution standards. Waste or pollution is an inevitable by-product of the production of desired output. Assume that the waste or pollution produced in an area increases more rapidly than desired output. The production-possibility frontier in each community is illustrated in Figure 11.1.

a. Prove that a larger total output of desired goods (summed over both

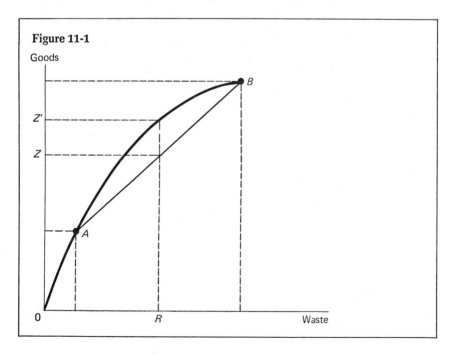

Figure 11-1

communities) will be produced for a given total volume of waste produced if each community produces the same volume of waste than if they produce different amounts of waste.

b. Suppose each community's pollution standard refers to the amount of waste *disposed of* in its area and not to the amount produced. Prove that if both wastes and goods are transportable without cost, pareto optimality requires that the same volume of waste be produced in each area.

c. Prove that if wastes are *not* transportable, and if communities have different preferences with respect to goods and environmental quality, then pareto optimality generally requires that the volume of waste produced in each area differ.

d. Does pareto optimality require a uniform pollution standard for both communities?

2. *Revenue sharing and the social costs of movement.* Many local public services have high fixed system costs set by the interest burden of their large initial capital outlays, and low incremental costs because of their operating characteristics (for example, water and sewage systems, drainage systems, streets, electrical, telephone, and gas lines, and so on). Suppose the quality of service such systems provide individuals is, for a given level of initial construction outlay, inversely related to the level of demands placed upon them. That is, such systems are subject to congestion phenomena, which are directly related to the number of persons served by the system. Under these conditions, explain why community A, which is experiencing a net in-migration of former residents of community B, might wish to share its own tax revenues with community B.

3. Many revenue-sharing proposals contain provisions which would reduce a local government's share if that government chose to reduce its own tax collections in response to receipt of funds from the federal government. Under what assumptions is such a provision consistent with the fiscal equivalence principle?

4. Prove that under simple majority rule, with fixed local tax shares, a matching intergovernmental grant will never produce a smaller local public budget than will a lump sum grant of equal amount. *Hint:* Prove that every voter whose most-preferred level of expenditure in the matching grant circumstances is less than or equal to the median of the most-preferred levels would never vote, under the lump sum grant condition, for a larger expenditure than the majority's choice under the conditional grant. Since this group comprises a majority, the assertion to be proved will be established. For a discussion of this problem, see D. Bradford and W. Oates, "Towards a Predictive Theory of Intergovernmental Grants," *American Economic Review,* Vol. 61, May 1971, pp. 440–448.

Suggested Readings

Break, George, *Intergovernmental Fiscal Relations in the United States,* Washington, D.C.: Brookings Institution, 1967.

Breton, A., "A Theory of Government Grants," *Canadian Journal of Economics and Political Science*, Vol. 31, May 1965, pp. 175–187.

Buchanan, James, *The Demand and Supply of Public Goods*, Skokie, Ill.: Rand McNally, 1968, esp. chs. 8 and 9.

Maxwell, James, *Financing State and Local Governments*, Washington, D.C.: Brookings Institution, 1965.

Oates, Wallace, "The Theory of Public Finance in a Federal System," *Canadian Journal of Economics and Political Science*, Vol. 54, February 1969, pp. 37–54.

Oates, Wallace, *Fiscal Federalism*. New York: Harcourt Brace Jovanovich, 1972.

Olson, Mancur, "The Principle of Fiscal Equivalence: The Division of Responsibilities Among Different Levels of Government," *American Economic Review*, Vol. 30, May 1969, pp. 479–487.

Pauly, Mark, "Optimality, 'Public' Goods and Local Governments: A General Theoretical Analysis," *Journal of Political Economy*, Vol. 24, May 1970, pp. 572–585.

Rothenberg, Jerome, "Local Decentralization and the Theory of Optimal Government," in the *Analysis of Public Output*, Julius Margolis, ed., New York: National Bureau of Economic Research, 1970.

Sigler, George, "Tenable Range of Functions of Local Government," in *Federal Expenditures for Growth and Stability*, Joint Economic Committee, 85th Congress, 1st Session, 1957.

Tiebout, Charles M., "A Pure Theory of Local Expenditures," *Journal of Political Economy*, Vol. 64, October 1956, pp. 416–424.

Warren, Richard E., *Government in Metropolitan Regions: A Reappraisal of Fractionated Political Organization*. Davis, California: Institute of Governmental Affairs, University of California, 1966.

ANSWER SECTION

CHAPTER 1

Question 1

a. 75 percent, regardless of ownership. At any rate less than 75 percent, the coal owner is worse off, and the landowner is no better off. Consequently, 75 percent is pareto superior to any rate less than 75 percent. Any rate in excess of 75 percent is not pareto superior to the 75-percent rate, since the landowner will be made worse off. Consequently, there is no rate which is pareto superior to the 75-percent rate. Hence the 75-percent rate is pareto optimal.

b. Jones would like to see at least 25 percent of the coal remain in the ground. But since he has no effective way of compensating Smith for the profits Smith would forego by leaving this coal unmined, Smith finds it in his own interest to mine out 100 percent of the coal.

c. If Smith could sell mining rights to Jones, Jones would now be able to effectively express his interest in having some coal left unmined by making Smith an offer. The minimum acceptable offer to Smith for 25 percent of the coal would be $50, the maximum acceptable offer from Jones's point of view is $60. Consequently, a mutually profitable trade could be arranged to guarantee that 25 percent of the coal is left in the ground. (Question: Suppose land, but not coal, could be bought and sold. Could any mutually profitable trade take place that would tend to insure that at least 25 percent of the coal remained in the ground?)

d. The existence of 100 landowners instead of one converts the problem of leaving sufficient coal unmined into a *public-good* problem. No one individual landowner now has a sufficient interest to make a bid for the coal on his own. A bid for the coal must come from a coalition of the landowners. However, since the minimum-size coalition which could put together a bid in excess of $50 is less than 100, each individual will have an incentive to *free-load*, that is, remain outside the coalition of contributors while deriving benefits from the coalition's expenditures. If each individual attempts to free-load, however, the minimum-size coalition will not be formed, and Smith will have no incentive to keep 25 percent unmined.

These coalition problems are further discussed in Chapters 2 and 3.

Question 2

a. Profit per unit is the difference between the price per unit of a commodity and its cost per unit. *If* the price of a commodity represents the rate at which individuals are willing to substitute a composite of other goods for this commodity and if the *cost* represents the rate at which society can transform this commodity into units of a composite of other goods, then the existence of profit, that is, price greater than cost, indicates that there exists an allocation which has more of the profitable commodity and less of other commodities that is pareto superior to the current allocation. To see this, let the price of the composite equal 1. Then if $RCS_{\text{composite for good } y} = P_y/1 = P_y$ and if the marginal cost of y in terms of the composite, (which equals the rate of transformation of y into the composite, $RPT_{y \text{ into } c}$), then $P_y > C_y$ implies $RCS_{\text{composite for good } y} > RPT_{y \text{ into } c}$. This inequality implies that a one-unit reduction in the composite will release sufficient resources for the production of y to produce more than enough y to compensate for the reduction in the composite bundle of other goods. The existence of profit on the marginal units of some goods is, therefore, both an indication that resources are not being utilized efficiently and a guide to their more efficient use.

When total profits are maximized, the profit on the marginal unit is zero. This, in turn, is equivalent to the necessary conditions for the exhaustion of mutually profitable reallocations *when the prices in the system reflect the relative marginal valuations people place on goods in their possession.* If a socialist, or any other system, can develop institutions (for example, markets) which will enable it to develop prices that are reflective of the relative marginal valuations people place on goods, then it can guide production to more efficient uses by requiring or inducing producers to shift resources from activities with lower marginal profits to those with higher marginal profits.

b. Yes, *if* all markets are highly competitive. However, this is a big "if." As was discussed earlier, private profit maximization by a monopolist inhibits exhaustion of all mutually profitable trades. In a capitalist system, marginal profits not only serve to *signal* the desirability of reallocating resources, they also serve as the *inducement* to such reallocation, since the individual who responds to the signal gets to keep a disproportionate share of the profits his response generates. In a socialist system, incentives may take other forms.

Question 3

The monopolist is interested in the gains from trade which accrue to him as a supplier in the market. Members of a cooperative have an interest not only in the gains which accrue to them as suppliers, but also those gains which accrue

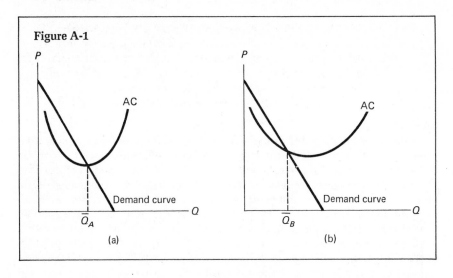

Figure A-1

(a)

(b)

to them as buyers in the market. Consequently, while a monopolist views a price reduction as *reducing* the profits he could have earned on units which would have been sold at a higher price, the cooperative does not consider these profits as lost, but rather looks at price reductions simply as a means of distributing the gains from trade to its members.

Since the total gains from trade are limited by the volume of trade, the cooperative will produce better results for all of its members if, and only if, its annual volume of sales exceeds that of the monopolist. Whether or not this will occur depends upon the ability of the cooperative to finance a larger volume.

The simplest method for the cooperative to use in financing its activities is to choose among those quantities of output that would generate enough revenue to finance themselves. The upper bound of this set is that quantity at which the demand curve intersects the average-cost curve. In Figure A.1(a), this quantity is $\overline{Q}_A$. In Figure A.1(b), this figure is $\overline{Q}_B$.

Prove that the upper limit of the self-financing quantities is always greater than the quantity that maximizes the monopolists' profit.

Prove that in Figure A.1(a), the quantity that would maximize the *total* gains from trade is in the self-financing set.

Prove that in Figure A.1(b), the quantity that would maximize the total gains from trade is *not* in the self-financing set. How might this quantity be financed by the cooperative? A further discussion of this problem occurs in Chapter 10.

CHAPTER 2

Question 1

No, a competitive equilibrium may be pareto optimal even if some activities generate external benefits or costs. As long as "small" changes from the competitively determined levels of these externality-producing activities resulted in no change in the quantities of external benefits or costs, the competitive equilibrium may satisfy the conditions for pareto optimality. Recall that the conditions for pareto optimality imply that each activity be extended to the point at which the sum of the benefits derived by all individuals from undertaking an *additional* unit of the activity be just equal to the sum of all of the benefits from other activities that must be foregone (that is, the social marginal cost) in order to extend the activity under consideration. If, at the competitive equilibrium level of activities, the *marginal* social benefit of any activity is equal to the benefit received by the individual who undertakes that activity, and if its *marginal* social cost is equal to the benefits from other activities that are foregone by the individual who undertakes the activity in question, then the competitive equilibrium fulfills the necessary conditions for a pareto optimum.

To illustrate, the fact that my neighbor has a nicely kept yard increases the value of both his and my property. His yard work produces external benefits which I derive. However, given the extent of yard work which he has chosen *solely on the basis of its impact on the value of his own property*, I might very well receive no additional benefit if he were forced or induced to undertake additional yard work. That is, I receive benefits from some of his activity, but *at the margin,* the external benefits from his activity may be zero. Here the externality is irrelevant at the margin of decision, and there would be no possibility of a mutually profitable bribe being made to alter the outcome which was achieved through a pure market process.

Question 2

For the existence of a fire department to be valuable to an individual, he must be able to secure its services within a very short time after notifying it of a fire. That fire insurance rates rise steeply with distance from the nearest fire station is reflective of this fact. Therefore, the geographical "market area" of a fire station is quite small. Of further importance is the fact that most, if not all, of the costs of maintaining a fire station are invariant with respect to the density of the population it might serve in its market area. Providing service to a rural area with very low density would require a *total* cost almost as large as provision of service to a much more densely occupied suburb which occupied the same area. Consequently, the *average* cost of such service is much higher in rural than nonrural areas. Faced with quite high average costs, neither a private firm seeking profits, nor a collection of residents seeking fire protection may find the maintenance of a fire station a worthwhile activity.

As the density of the population increases, a private profit-making enterprise may realize sufficient demand at a price above average cost to secure a profit. Furthermore, given the declining average-cost characteristic of such service, a private firm could be assured of a virtual monopoly of such services. Just as in Question 3 of Chapter 1, the community could be better off if it organized its own fire protection services along the lines of a cooperative or volunteer department. Perhaps these potential gains via cooperative organization explain why one does not observe fire departments run as profit-making enterprises.

Note that a nonprofit enterprise such as a volunteer fire department may choose to exclude people from its services if they do not agree to share in the cost of providing those services. Indeed, unless it follows such exclusionary practice, it may find itself with too many free loaders to sustain the service. In areas that are not too densely settled, subscribers and supporters of a volunteer company may not be hurt if the company denies service to nonsupporters and would certainly gain (via a reduction in average cost) by an increased participating of the funding of the service. As the service area becomes more densely occupied, however, fire protection service generates external benefits by reducing the possibility of contagion. In other words, contributors to or supporters of the service will find the value of the services provided themselves reduced if those services are not also given nonsupporters. The advantages of reducing average cost to contributors combined with the externalities implied by a quite dense pattern of settlement will create pressure for such services to be publicly (that is, via taxes) financed (on equity grounds) and universally available (on efficiency grounds).

Question 3

An owner of a private forest must view the current cutting of trees as precluding his opportunity of capitalizing on the opportunity of cutting these same trees at some later date. The lost potential increase in the value of the tree will be treated by the owner of a private forest as a *cost* of cutting the tree at this point in time rather than at a later point in time. The benefit to the owner of cutting now rather than later comes from now having $x from the sale of the tree rather than waiting until some later point in time to receive $[x + v(t)] (where $v(t)$ is the increment in value as a result of delaying cutting until t periods from now). The magnitude of these benefits depends on what you could do with $x in the interim between now and period t. Only if the interest you could earn on $x available now and invested for t periods exceeded $v(t)$ for all t would you cut the tree now rather than wait until the tree has further matured. For very young trees, $v(t)$ is likely to exceed the possible accumulation of interest for t significantly greater than zero. That is, a private forester would only harvest trees that had matured sufficiently that their further *rate* of growth would be less than the rate of interest. If his forest contained trees of differing ages, he would almost never cut them all down in a given unit of time.

If one were logging a public forest along with many other loggers in the absence of any agreement or central control on cutting policy, you would not consider as an element of your costs the future increment in tree growth value foregone as a result of your own cutting. The reason is that unless there is a general cutting policy binding on all other cutters, you would have no assurance that *you* could capitalize on the tree growth if you left the tree uncut since another logger may cut it down. The cutting of a tree now rather than letting it grow further entails a *social* cost; but in this case, it appears to involve no *private* cost to the decision maker. As a consequence, each private cutter will cut any tree whose current selling price exceeds his cutting costs, *regardless* of the possible rate of growth of the tree. The public forest will be denuded of all, but the youngest trees and the total value of all the lumber producible by the forest will be less than if those trees whose rate of growth in value exceeded the interest rate were allowed to continue growing. (For a discussion of this kind of waste in another context, see H. S. Gordon, "The Economics of a Common-Property Resource: The Fishery," *Journal of Political Economy*, 1954, pp. 124–142.

Question 4

In an abstract sense (that is, assuming that one has been able to measure benefits and costs), the necessary condition for optimality is that, at the optimal level of pollution reduction, the sum over all pollutant receivers of the benefit of an additional increment of pollution reduction just equals the sum over all emitters of the costs of achieving an incremental reduction in pollution. The lower the incremental cost at any level of reduction, the greater will the optimal reduction be.

There are two kinds of costs in reducing pollution. First, there is the cost of administering a system which will monitor pollution reductions. Secondly, there is the cost in terms of reduced outputs of goods and services which must be incurred either to release resources for use in pollution-control devices or to reduce pollution without specific control devices or both. In our problem, the administrative costs are equal and, hence, irrelevant to a choice between taxes and standards. However, in all likelihood, any given level of pollution reduction could be achieved at a lower cost in terms of foregone output by using taxes rather than standards to induce the desired reduction in total pollution. To see this, consider the case where the target level of a 10-percent reduction in total emissions is achieved by standards which require *each* emitter to reduce his emissions by 10 percent. In all likelihood, there will be at least two emitters, A and B, who have different incremental costs of reducing their emissions. Suppose that A would save $1 million if he were allowed to increase his emissions above the standard by 10,000 pounds a year, while it would cost B only an additional $500,000 to reduce his emissions by 10,000 pounds below that required by the standard. Clearly, then, in principle, everyone could be made better off by allowing A to not reduce his pollution by 10 percent and inducing B to reduce his pollution by more than 10 percent. If A and B faced a uniform tax, this is exactly what would happen. Each would reduce his emissions until the incremental cost of further reductions exceeded the tax rate. Since B has a lower marginal cost of emission reduction than A, he would reduce emissions further than would A. More generally, all emitters would adjust emissions to the tax so that the marginal cost of emission reduction would be the same for all of them. But this is a necessary condition for minimizing the social cost of achieving any given level of pollution reduction. (Why?) Since the tax scheme minimizes the social cost of any given level of reduction, while the standards approach, in general, does not, the optimal level of reduction will be greater if a tax is used as the control instrument, than if standards are used.

While we have answered our question, in principle, what remains unanswered is how one would go about measuring the marginal benefits and costs of pollution reduction. The benefits are dependent upon the effects of pollution reduction. There is significant variation in pollution levels over space. Consequently, one might be able to establish statistical relations between differences in pollution levels and differences in the magnitude of various measures such as morbidity and mortality rates, rates of material decomposition, and so on. Numerous studies have been undertaken to investigate such relationships. Even knowing such effects, serious questions arise as to how to evaluate them. (See, for example, E. J. Mishan, "Loss of Life and Limb," *Cost-Benefit Analysis*, New York: Praeger, 1971, chs. 22–23.)

Unfortunately, the variations which produce these observable variations in pollution levels are not likely to be the kind that we shall observe if we impose pollution controls in a currently heavily polluted region. We do not, therefore, have the kinds of natural experiments that will enable us to estimate how much it will cost to achieve a given level of reduction in a particular region. In order to produce the relevant information, we shall most likely have to impose some controls and see what happens. The problem here is that the kinds of industrial adjustments which might be appropriate to one level of control might not be easily extended to another level. That is, such experimentation may be very wasteful. In the light of such a possibility, it is not at all clear to this writer what the appropriate path to pollution abatement would look like.

Question 5

A single individual has little incentive to sacrifice private goods in order to increase the supply of common property. Any commodity that is not a free good in the sense of free of opportunity cost, and that is given the legal status of common property will, therefore, tend to be undersupplied unless some collective decision is made for its provision. The question of which commodities ought (or ought not) to be given the legal status of common property, therefore, embodies the question of whether provision of the commodity ought (or ought not) to be determined by a political process.

Suppose a producer of ideas may be compensated for his work only if it has been specifically commissioned by a group or if he enters it in competition for a prize which the group offers. Neither the producer nor his sponsor can sell the ideas because, once they are produced, they legally become common property. For example, any group of people may get together and support an investigation of the relationship between particular interest groups and the funding of the political campaigns of the legislative sponsors of particular bills. This is true whether or not the results of such an investigation become common property. However, if the results must be made common property, then they cannot be resold. Consequently, the cost of producing the ideas which are incorporated in the investigative report (or more generally, the cost of producing any ideas) cannot be recouped through the sale of the report to the general public via a markup over transmission costs in the sales price of the report. This means that if the report is produced in written form, any and every publisher may reproduce the report without paying a royalty. Newspapers could reproduce the work without charge. If the report is presented on film, anyone and everyone may reproduce the report on their own film without charge, and so on. In such an environment, there would undoubtedly be some groups, organized on the basis of voluntary contributions, which would commission the production of ideas. (Public Interest Research Groups and Common Cause may represent prototypes of such groups. Patrons would represent another source of support for the arts.) However, the difficulty of forming such groups – of identifying individuals with a common interest in supporting a given intellectual endeavor, or type of endeavor, of reaching operational decisions about who and what to support and how the costs for that support are to be allocated over the group – is a formidable task. It is all the more formidable when one cannot use a market mechanism to elicit information and the threat of exclusion from benefits to induce individual contributions. But if ideas are made common property, the only alternative to the formation of such sponsoring groups is to have artistic and intellectual activity sponsored by the government. This raises the fundamental problem of censorship. Not every conceivable intellectual effort is worthy of support. But if a government refuses to fund some requests for support, it cannot avoid the appearance, and may not avoid the temptation, of censorship.

To summarize, giving ideas the legal status of common property eliminates the use of markets as devices to finance support for and allocate funds among intellectual endeavors. Without a market mechanism, either private sponsoring groups, which face a free-rider problem, or government, with the concomitant threat of censorship, must raise and distribute the funds to support such activity. In the realm of the production of ideas, every mode of social organization has some undesirable characteristics, and it may be that establishing a private market in ideas is the least undesirable mode of organization.

CHAPTER 3
Question 1
a. This can be proved by example

	Alternatives		
	A	B	C
a	2	0	1
b	1	2	0
c	0	1	2
Total	3	3	3

b. To win, an alternative must get at least 4 points. If it gets 6 points, then it is the most-preferred alternative for every voter and would be the majority choice. If it gets 5 points, it must get 2 points from two voters and hence would be the majority choice. If an alternative which gets only 4 points wins, either it is the most preferred by two voters and is the majority choice, or the remaining 5 points must be divided 3, 2 over the other issues. Assuming that A wins with 4 points and A is given 2 points by a, the following exhausts the possibilities.

	A	B	C		A	B	C		A	B	C		A	B	C
a	2	1	0		2	1	0		2	0	1		2	0	1
b	1	2	0		1	0	2		1	0	2		1	2	0
c	1	0	2		1	2	0		1	2	0		1	0	2

In each of these cases, A is the winner by majority rule also. By exchanging the row values of **a** for the row values of **b** or **c**, the same result will obtain. Similarly, if the column values of A are exchanged for the column values of B or C, these alternatives would be both the point and majority choices. Since these permutations exhaust all the possible point winners, we have shown that the point winner will always be the majority choice. (Question: Can you generalize this to N voters and M issues?)

c. The question assumes that B is adjacent to A, and C is adjacent to B. Hence ABC can be represented by points on a line.

```
____._____._____.___
    A        B       C
```

We know that whenever an alternative is most preferred by at least two voters, it wins by a majority. Under our restriction, this kind of majority choice will also be the point winner, since if one issues gets two 2's, no other issue can have more than 3 points. We need only verify, therefore, that if each individual has a different most-preferred alternative, then alternative B will win.

If B is the most-preferred alternative of one person, then it must receive 4 points according to our restriction. Furthermore, the person who assigns A 2 points must assign C zero points and, conversely, the person who assigns C 2 points must assign A zero points. A and C, therefore, get only 3 points each, and B is the point winner. Furthermore, since two of three individuals prefer B to A, and two of three also prefer B to C, B is also the majority choice.

d. The restriction implies that alternatives can be thought of as being placed in a single-dimensional ordering so that some sense can be given to the notion that alternative A is further away (in a nonpreferential sense) from a second alternative C than is a third alternative B. When issues involve alternative distributions of a fixed set of resources over a set of individuals, no single-dimensional ordering common to the perspective of each of the individuals would appear possible.

For a further discussion of issues raised by majority voting, see G. Tullock, *Toward a Mathematics of Politics*, Ann Arbor: University of Michigan Press, 1967, and Kenneth Arrow's review in *Public Choice*, Vol. 6, 1969.

Question 2

a. Since there is no way of dividing 3 among three parties such that each possible pair would get at least 2.5 units, some pair of communities would always be able to do better by forming a consolidation of only that pair than by joining with the third community in a fully integrated system. Therefore, one should expect that a fully integrated system will be rejected.

But a partially integrated system is not likely to be accepted either, since the excluded community could always offer a mutually profitable bribe to one of the other communities to join it in a partially integrated system. This is true no matter which community is excluded. Therefore, in the absence of inertia, the bargaining would be endless, and no system would be adopted.

b. If any pair could get only 1.5, then a complete consolidation would be profitable as long as the gains were divided in such a way that each community got at least 0.75 from belonging to the completely integrated system. Since the completely integrated system produces a savings of 3, which exceeds the minimum requirement by 0.75, the possibility will arise that the division of the savings will be affected by the bargaining skills of the respective communities. In the limit, one community could reap twice as much benefit as either of the others without destroying the common interest in a fully integrated system.

For a discussion of the prospects and problems of metropolitan areas, see Chapter 11.

Question 3

a. An individual's most-preferred level of expenditure will be that rate of expenditure at which the marginal benefit to him equals his marginal tax cost. Furthermore, given that the marginal tax cost to an individual is independent of the volume of expenditures in this problem, his preference order among alternative expenditure levels is single peaked. (Why?) Since each individual's preference order is single peaked, the majority choice of expenditure level will be the median of the most-preferred expenditure levels. The level at which A's marginal tax cost would equal his marginal benefit is to the right of K. The level at which B's marginal tax cost would equal his marginal benefit is at K. The level at which C's marginal benefit equals his marginal tax bill is J to the left of K. Therefore, K is the majority choice.

b. Pareto optimality requires that the sum of the marginal benefits be equal to the social marginal cost. S is the social marginal cost and is assumed constant with respect to output. At K the sum of the marginal benefits, as measured along the C curve, exceeds the marginal cost. Hence K is not pareto optimal. E is the pareto optimal level. (The D curve is found by *vertical* summation of the curves A', B', and C'. Why is it the vertical sum and not the horizontal?)

c. Suppose B's tax share was zero and A's was raised to make up the difference. Then either A or C's most-preferred choice would occupy the median position.

CHAPTER 4

Question 1

In order to choose between construction and rationing, we must determine, for any possible addition to the water supply system, the benefits and costs of such an addition. The costs can be measured directly from a knowledge of the nature and quantities of inputs required and their market prices. The benefits from the addition, conceptually, are the value of other goods and services that the users of the system would be willing to give up in order to secure that additional water. The practical problem is to estimate these benefits.

Consider an individual who, three years from now, would consume bundle A if sufficient additional capacity were available to avoid rationing and who would consume bundle B if water were rationed. In order to measure the benefit to this individual from avoiding rationing, we wish to calculate how much of all other goods we could take from this individual, given that he has $Q_0 + N$ rather than Q_0 units of water, without making him worse off than he would be if he had bundle B. If we knew his preference structure as represented by the indifference curves in Figure A.2, we could see immediately that this amount is AC. However, we generally cannot directly observe the preference map of an individual, but can only make inferences about it from our observations on the individual's behavior.

The theory of consumer demand tells us that if an individual is maximizing his utility subject to a budget constraint, then he will choose a bundle such that the value to him of the marginal unit of any particular good in terms of the other goods in the chosen bundle is just equal to the market price of that good. Since bundle B represents the bundle that would be chosen if water were rationed at a price P_0, P_0 is the measure of the marginal value of the quantity of water Q_0. Similarly, since bundle A contains all the water that would be purchased at a zero price, the marginal value of the quantity of water Q_{0+N} is zero. If we could calculate the value of each increment of water from Q_0 to Q_{0+N}, then the sum of these incremental values would approximate the (unobservable) amount AC.[1] We may work out this approximation by estimating the way the price of water varies as the quantity of water varies, holding real income constant; that is, estimate the equation $P_w = P(Q_w, P_{\text{all other things}}, \overline{M}/P_{\text{index}})$, where P_w is the price of water; $P_{\text{all other things}}$ is price index of all other things; P_{index} is a price index of all goods including water; and $\overline{M}$ is money income. The theoretical demand curve, which is being estimated, will be associated with the locus of points BA on the indifference map of our individual. For example, point B_1 contains Q_{0+1} units of water. We locate B_1 by rotating a

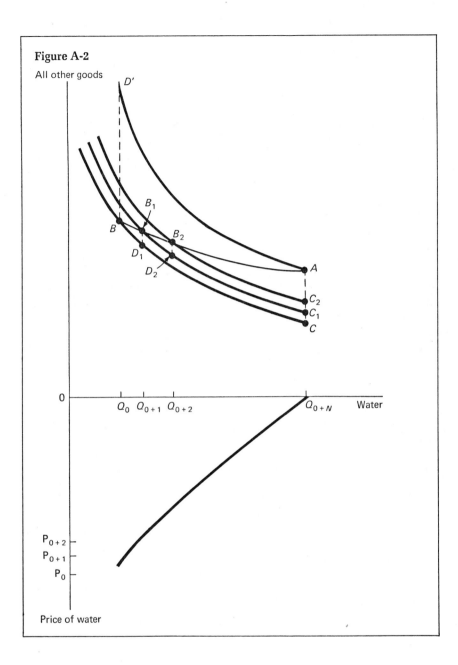

Figure A-2

price line through B until it is just tangent with an indifference curve containing Q_{0+1} units of water. Since the budget line was rotated through B, bundle B_1 costs no more than B. That is, our procedure holds real income M/P_{index} constant. The slope of this budget line is equal to the price of water in terms of all other goods. So we can associate the price P_{0+1} with the quantity Q_{0+1} in a price-quantity diagram. Furthermore, since P_{0+1} by inference is equal to the value of the (Q_{0+1}) unit of water, it must be equal to the (unobserved) measure of the value of the (Q_{0+1}) unit, B_1D_1. If the indifference curves are parallel, B_1D_1 will be just equal to CC_1.

We now repeat our procedure, rotating the budget line through B_1 until it is just tangent to point B_2, which has Q_{0+2} units of water. We can read off the price at which Q_{0+2} units will be purchased from the slope of our budget line, and we know by inference that this price must be equal to the (unobserved) measure of the value of the second increment in water, B_2D_2. Again, if the indifference curves are parallel, B_2D_2 will be just equal to C_1C_2.

By repeating our procedure, we shall trace out the entire curve BA and find its associated real-income-constant demand curve. The area under this demand curve from P_0 to 0 is equal to the sum of the values B_iD_i summed from i to 1 to N. If the indifference curves are parallel, this sum is equal to the sum of C_jC_{j+1} from $J = 0$ to $N - 1$, or equivalently to AC. This is why we can treat the area under the real-income-constant demand curve from $P = P_0$ to $P = 0$ as an approximate measure of the annual gross benefits from having sufficient water to avoid rationing.

Of course, the demand is likely to be growing over time so that the volume of annual benefits will also be growing. On the other hand, practically all of the costs of increasing the annual supply of water will be incurred at the time of construction. In order to compare this annual flow of benefits to a one-time increase in costs, it is necessary to convert the benefit stream into its present-value equivalent. To do this requires an estimate of the rate of return the community could earn on its resources if used elsewhere.

Question 2

a. If one specifies a specific target for a program to achieve, this target is better thought of as a constraint on the possible choice of a program than as an objective of the program. The objective is to choose among the possible programs the one that is "best" in some sense. Hence the objective may be to adopt the housing program that achieves the construction of 150,000 units at *least* cost, or with *maximum* dispersion among suburban communities, or in terms of some other evaluative criteria. Unless these criteria for selection of a program are stated, it is not possible for any one outside the department which is proposing the program to know why one program was selected rather than another. But without this knowledge, the programs of any department cannot be reviewed for effectiveness, and one of the purposes of program budgeting will be vitiated.

b. The ultimate objective of program budgeting is not simply to provide an outside review of the effectiveness with which each department is using the funds which it is allocated, but also to provide a guide to the allocation of funds among departments. In order to compare programs of different departments, it is necessary that some *common* measures are used in evaluating the benefits and costs. One important measure is the cost of capital. In order to assure that any project undertaken in any department is at least as profitable as every project rejected by other departments, it is necessary to evaluate the present value of the benefit streams of all projects by the same discount rate. This will occur if the budget director specifies the discount rate which is to be used.

Question 3

Efficient allocation of resources requires that the discount rate chosen to evaluate a given project reflect the social value of the opportunities which must be foregone if resources are devoted to the project under consideration. Since the budget constraint defines the set of potential projects with which a given project is competing for resources, a predetermined size of the national budget eliminates private projects as potential competitors for any public project. Consequently, under these conditions, the rate of return in the private sector would be *irrelevant* in evaluating a potential public project. Only if the total size of the government budget were not predetermined would the rate of return on private projects represent a measure of the foregone benefits from undertaking a public project.

CHAPTER 5

Question 1

a. The value of the taxes collected to maintain an armed force must, by definition, be equal to the cost of the resources required to maintain that force. The *real cost* of any resource devoted to a particular use is measured by the amount the owner of the resource would have to be compensated for willingly sacrificing the opportunity to use the resource elsewhere. This *real cost* exists independently of whether or not compensation is actually paid. It follows that the *total value* of the taxes collected to maintain an armed force is dependent only upon its size and composition, but is independent of the method by which the resources are diverted from other uses.

 The individual who *involuntarily* submits his labor services for use by the military is paying a portion of the tax required to cover the real cost of his services. This tax is simply the difference between what he is *actually* being paid as compensation and the compensation which would induce him to volunteer. When the draft is eliminated, the government will be forced to raise taxes from other sources to pay him a sufficient compensation to induce him to volunteer. But each dollar he is compensated reduces the tax in kind which the former conscriptee paid by $1. The total value of taxes collected remains *unchanged*, but its method of collection and the distribution of its burden have changed.

b. Yes. If a conscriptee can find a person who will, for a sum, agree to take his place, and if this sum is less than the conscriptee would be willing to pay in order to avoid military service, then the substitution of the volunteer for the conscriptee must reduce the real cost of the army. The reason is, while the military values the conscriptee's services equally with the volunteer's, in order to make it worthwhile for the conscriptee to have the volunteer take his place, the conscriptee must value his nonmilitary opportunities more than the volunteer does. Since the value of the nonmilitary opportunities foregone measures the real cost of the army, the substitution must reduce these real costs.

A direct implication of this argument is that an all-volunteer army can never cost more and will usually cost less than a conscripted army.

c. An indirect tax. The exempted categories induce people to change their occupational and marital service. The magnitude of this substitution effect may be judged by the change in the sex composition of public school teachers under age 30 between the first part of the decade of 1960–1970 and the second part.

Question 3

The existence of a stock market allows individuals to hedge their bets as to the directions in which the economy may move by holding a widely diversified portfolio. The economic rationale for a stock market is as an institution which facilitates gains from the specialization of physical capital without the necessity of tying its owner's fate to a single activity.

Just as there are gains from the specialization of capital, there are gains from the specialization of labor. However, if an individual is to become highly specialized (for example, to become an aeronautical engineer), he must also bear the risk of placing his investment in skills in a single asset, himself. There is no well-organized market in which an individual can sell shares in himself and buy shares in others. Consequently, the specialization of labor involves the concentration of risk upon the individual whose skills have become specialized. A progressive income tax can be viewed as a method for sharing the individual risks implicit in the specialization of labor. If all individuals prefer less to more risk, and if no one knew which specialties would be in unusually high demand and which would be in unusually low demand at the time the decision to institute a tax scheme was made, the risk-sharing aspect of a progressive income tax would be attractive to everyone.

Question 4

As the discussion in the text should make clear, there is no practical tax on activities that does not change the price system which one group of decision makers face relative to the price system which others face. The greater the difference in price systems, the more inefficient the allocation of resources. Indeed, the purpose of interfering in the "market" for pollution is to bring the "prices" which the emitters and receivers face more nearly into line. If this is accomplished by a tax on emissions, there is no fiscal need to interfere in other markets. However, the subsidy solution requires the government to interfere in other markets in order to finance the subsidy. This interference may widen the difference in the prices to which different decision makers respond, thereby reducing efficiency in one direction while attempting through the emission reduction subsidy to improve it in another. Of course, a judiciously chosen set of taxes might actually improve efficiency in these other markets. But, if this were possible, one need not wait upon the necessity of financing pollution abatement to make these corrective tax adjustments.

CHAPTER 6

Question 1

Forward shifting of any tax requires that the suppliers of the service which is being taxed reduce the volume of the service which they offer for sale. Suppliers will do this only if such a reduction leaves them with higher incomes than they could achieve by absorbing the tax and leaving their assets in place. If only some assets are taxed, then suppliers will find it profitable to move a sufficient volume of their assets into the untaxed sectors to reestablish equality of after-tax returns to capital in both the taxed and untaxed sectors. However, if the tax is *general*, there are no untaxed sectors to which the capital may move. Therefore, there would be no forward shifting of the tax. Furthermore, the ownership of property is more concentrated than claims to income from both property and labor services. Therefore, on an income basis, a *general* property tax would be progressive.

Question 2

Increased spatial concentration of economic activity requires an increase in the ratio of buildings to land. Removing the tax on buildings encourages a substitution of structural expense for expenditures on the site resulting in higher buildings occupying less ground space. To recoup the tax revenues through removal of the tax on structures, the city may increase the tax on the sites upon which the structures sit. Since a tax on land is fully capitalized in its selling price, it will not discourage the use of the site upon which it is placed. The combined effect of the two tax changes is to encourage more intensive use of land.

The tax on land has, as another effect, the reduction in the optimal time a land holder will take to convert site use from a less to a more intensive use. A land holder will delay converting a site to a more profitable use because once property is converted, its use (and rental stream) is fixed for some time. If he erects a three-story building on a vacant site, then he may not find it profitable at a later date to erect a five-story building on the same site. But if he builds the five-story building now, he will be worse off than if he built the three-story building. Consequently, he must decide whether to build the smaller building now or leave his land vacant so that he may build the five-story building later.

We can measure the benefit he derives from waiting one period before conversion by the difference between the value of his property if converted one period from now and its value if converted now.

Symbolically, $B(t) = V(t + 1) - V(t)$, where $V(x)$ is the difference at time x between the value of the vacant land and its value when converted to a use most appropriate to period x.

The cost of delaying conversion from period t to period $t + 1$ is composed of two parts. First, if the land is assessed at its value when placed in its highest-valued current use, the owner must pay taxes equal to $\lambda V(t)$, where λ is the rate of tax on the value of the gain which he could have if he converted at time t. Second, he loses the opportunity to sell that gain and secure an interest income of $rV(t)$ over the period from t to $t + 1$.

The holding costs, therefore, are represented by the equation

$$C(t) = (\lambda + r)V(t)$$

As long as $B(t) - C(t) > 0$, it pays him to wait another period before conversion. The optimal time to convert is when $B(T^*) - C(T^*) = V(T^* + 1) - V(T^*) - (\lambda + r)V(T^*) = 0$. This implies

$$\frac{V(T^* + 1) - V(T^*)}{V(T^*)} = \lambda + r$$

At the optimal time to convert the property, the rate of increase in the value of the property obtainable by waiting to convert to a more intensive use is equal to the sum of the tax plus interest rates.

Since building costs tend to rise more rapidly than the rentable square footage as the height of buildings increases, and the increase in land value as time passes is directly related to the increase in the optimal height of the building between possible conversion dates,

$$\frac{V(t + 1) - V(t)}{V(t)}$$

is likely to decline as time passes.

This means that if the tax rate λ is increased, the optimal time to convert is moved to a time in the less distant future where

$$\frac{V(t + 1) - V(t)}{V(t)}$$

is larger than at the previously optimal conversion date.

Question 3

As our discussion at the end of the chapter notes, because of the mobility of customers and capital and labor, any local tax will ultimately fall on owners of real estate. For purposes of tax administration, therefore, it makes good sense to simply use a real estate tax at the local level. The larger the geographic jurisdiction of a taxing body, the less elastic the supply of resources and the demand for products and the greater the opportunity to have the incidence of a tax fall on other groups within the economy.

Question 4

a. Individuals wish to maximize the after-tax yield on their investments (for any given level of risk). As a consequence, all bonds of a given risk class can be expected to have the same after-tax yield for any investor who holds more than one type of bond. (Why?) If the tax exemption on municipal bonds is removed, municipalities will have to offer larger yields on their bonds in order to remove the incentive investors would have to substitute corporate bonds for municipal bonds of the same risk class.

b. Since municipalities would face higher interest costs, they would have to raise their local tax rates and/or reduce their capital expenditures if the exemption were removed.

c. A holder of a municipal bond receives an annual dollar income which is fixed at the time the bond is issued. If the yield on municipals must rise when the tax exemption is removed, this will occur by a fall in the selling price of the bonds outstanding. This fall in market price obviously does not increase the before-tax *income* of current bond holders. The removal of the exemption, therefore, reduces the after-tax income of current bond-holders.

Since the downward market pressure on the price of municipals caused by the loss of exemption is removed when their price reaches the price of bonds of comparable riskiness, and since the exemption removal is likely to put upward pressure on these substitutes for municipal bonds, the possible before-tax yields available to a prospective municipal bond purchaser are no greater, and will generally be less, after the exemption is removed than when the exemption was in effect. Removal of the exemption, therefore, is likely to reduce the after-tax income of the average municipal bond buyer.

Question 5

Most assets do not have the character of bonds with fixed coupon rates. Many have the character of wine or trees, whose value grows with age. An important class of assets in this regard is that of resources whose supply is nonaugment-able and/or subject to depletion such as land and minerals whose value from one period to the next has the character of interest income, since the owner of such an asset could always sell it and invest the proceeds at interest if he wished rather than hold onto the asset and let it appreciate in value. If it is appropriate to treat interest received as ordinary taxable income, then it would seem appropriate to tax the implicit interest which accrues in the form of increases in capital value — independently of any change in the interest rate — at the same tax rate. However, in the United States, such accrued implicit interest is not taxed as it accumulates, only when the asset in which it is embodied is sold for a "capital gain." Even if the government received the same total number of tax dollars when the gain is realized as it would from an annual tax on the implicit interest income, the delay in the receipt of the tax reduces its value to the government.

CHAPTER 7
Question 1

The process of inflation leads to an increase in the cost of holding money. As the cost of holding money increases, individuals are led to choose a set of transactions which require smaller inventories of cash to effectively carry out than the set of transactions they would have chosen in the absence of inflation. The new transaction set must be no less costly (in terms of real profits and/or utility) than the set that would have been chosen in the absence of inflation; otherwise, it would have been chosen at the preinflation cost of holding money. To the extent that the new transaction set is more costly to make than the old set, the inflation has generated an excess burden.

To illustrate this point, consider the following problem. An individual receives a certain quantity of bonds worth \$R at the beginning of a period. He makes purchases of goods over the period whose value is equal to R. These purchases are spread out evenly over the period. To finance these purchases, the individual must sell off his bonds for cash. His problem is to choose the number of times he sells bonds. If the bonds bear interest, he will lose interest whenever he converts more bonds into cash then he actually needs to make payments. But since he is continuously making payments, he can avoid this interest loss only if he continuously sells off bonds. If there is a cost to making a transaction (a brokerage fee or the loss of time for other activities, and so on), a zero cash balance policy would involve an infinite transaction cost. The individual's problem, therefore, is to choose the optimal number of times to sell off bonds over the period. This number N will be such that the marginal cost of holding cash is just equal to the marginal cost of making transactions.

Formally, if some bonds are sold off N times during the period, then the individual sells off $H = R/N$ dollars worth of bonds each time he makes a bond transaction. Since he is continuously disbursing his cash, the average amount of cash he has on hand is $H/2 = R/2N$ dollars. If i is the bond rate of interest, holding this cash inventory costs him $iH/2 = iR/2N$ dollars. In addition, suppose it costs b dollars to make a transaction. Then the total cost of making his purchases over the period is

$$C = \frac{iR}{2N} + bN$$

This total cost is minimized by choosing an N at which

$$\frac{\Delta C}{\Delta N} = \frac{-iR}{2N^2} + b = 0$$

The optimal value of N is, therefore, given by

$$N^* = \sqrt{\frac{iR}{2b}}$$

Suppose the preinflation values of R, b, and i are R^0, b^0, i^0. Suppose now that inflation begins. This raises the values of R, b, and i. If r is the rate of inflation, the money value of R will be raised to $R^0(i + r)$. Similarly, the money value of b will be $b^0(i + r)$. But for reasons discussed in the text, the new rate of interest will be $i^0 + r$. If we compare the value of N^{*0} with the value of N^{*1}, we find that the inflation has raised the number of bond transactions we make to finance the same volume of real expenditures. Since these transactions involve real costs, the inflation raises the real cost of organizing trade.

CHAPTER 8
Question 1
If the government puts additional money into the system by substituting money for taxes, it will raise disposable income as a proportion of total income. Since consumption is positively related to disposable income, this substitution reduces the aggregate *rate* of saving out of total income. The difference between financing a deficit with new money and substituting new money for old bonds outstanding is that, in the first case, the infusion of new money reduces currently payable taxes, while in the second, the money infusion reduces a future stream of tax payments which would have been required to pay the interest on the bonds. If the same amount of new money were to be created via the deficit method as by the debt retirement method, then the present value of the tax reductions would be the same. However, from the point of view of the current generation's wealth, the effects of a cut in presently collected taxes are greater than the effect of a cut in the present value of future tax obligations. Consequently, we should expect a greater decline in the aggregate rate of saving if the money is injected into the system by cutting taxes than if the money is injected by retiring interest-bearing debt.

Question 3
In order that the government be able to sell its bonds, people must believe that it can meet its obligation to pay interest. Since the government can offer its taxing power as "security" on its bonds, the maximum size of the debt is set by the condition that its annual interest cost be no greater than GNP. In practice, one would expect that the maximum size of the debt be determined by an interest cost/GNP ratio substantially below 1.

For a fuller analysis, see E. D. Domar, "The Burden of the Debt and the National Income," *American Economic Review.* Dec. 1944.

CHAPTER 9
Question 1
a. For equilibrium in the commodity market, we must have

$$Y = E_p = C + I_p + G + (X - M)$$

or

$$Y = P\alpha - \beta T_0 + (\beta - \beta t) Y + P [\psi + v \cdot r] + P\bar{G} + P\bar{X} - zY$$

Simplifying, we get

$$Y = [P\alpha - \beta T_0 + P(\psi + v \cdot r) + P\bar{G} + P\bar{X}] \cdot \frac{1}{1 - \beta + \beta t + z}$$

b. The impact of a change in government spending on domestic money income is directly related to the size of the expression, $1/(1 - \beta + \beta T + z)$. Since the marginal propensity to import, z, is usually positive, the existence of the foreign sector tends to reduce the impact of changes in government spending on money income.

c. The smaller the domestic economy relative to the rest of the world, the more important is its foreign trade. But as the relative size of its foreign sector expands, the larger its marginal propensity to import is likely to be. As its marginal propensity to import increases, the less effective are variations in its own budget likely to be in controlling the level of aggregate demand in its economy.

Question 5

No. Suppose the government expenditure multiplier

$$\frac{dy}{dG} = \frac{1}{1 - \beta + \beta t + \dfrac{vk}{m}}$$

is positive and that the marginal tax rate $dT/dy = t$ exceeds 1. Then a reduction in the rate of government spending not only reduces aggregate demand, but also causes a reduction in tax revenues in excess of the reduction in government spending. Formally,

$$\Delta T = t\Delta Y = \frac{t}{1 - \beta + \beta t + \dfrac{vk}{m}} \cdot \Delta G$$

A sufficient condition for $\Delta T > \Delta G$ is $t > 1$ and

$$\frac{1}{1 - \beta + \beta t + \dfrac{vk}{m}} > 1$$

CHAPTER 11

Question 1

a. Figure A.3 reproduces Figure 11.1. Suppose community one chooses point A, and community two chooses point B. Their average output of desired goods is then Z, and their average production of waste is R. If each produced R units of waste, however, the average output would be $Z' > Z$. Geometrically, the average output and waste combination is at the midpoint of the chord connecting A and B. Given the assumption that waste rises more rapidly than output, the chord connecting any two points on the curve must always lie below the curve. Therefore, there is a point on the curve that lies above the midpoint of any chord. This point associates a higher level of output with a given level of waste than is associated with the two production points whose average waste production is represented by the midpoint of the chord.

b. This may be proved by contradiction. Suppose the rates of waste production differ. Then the rate at which community one can transform waste into goods differs from the rate community two can transform waste into goods (that is, the slope of the production-possibility frontier differs at points

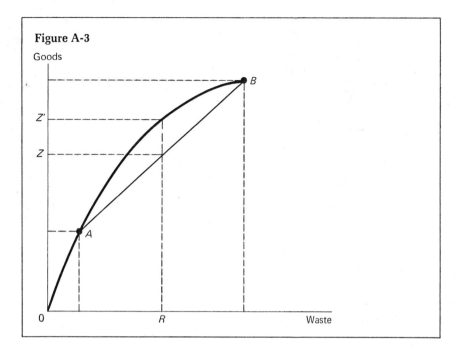

Figure A-3

A and B). By assumption of pareto optimality, the rate at which each community is just willing to substitute goods for waste is just equal to their respective rates of transformation of waste into goods. Since their rates of transformation differ, their rates of substitution differ. But whenever two groups have different rates of substitution for the *same commodities,* the distribution of commodities is not pareto optimal.

c. The above proof requires that waste produced in community one be indistinguishable in its physical properties from waste produced in community two. But if it is expensive to ship waste, or if, in the limit, it is not transportable, then the place where it is produced has economic significance. Waste in location one will be a different commodity from waste in location two.

Under these circumstances (nontransportability), the set of goods and environmental quality available to each community in its own location is independent of the set available to the other community. In other words, each community is stuck with its own garbage.

The disposal of waste destroys environmental amenities. The amenities provided by the environment are a public good. The control of the volume of waste disposal (and, given our assumptions, the volume of output) in a community is, therefore, a means of determining the volume of production of this public good. Pareto optimality requires that the sum over members of both communities of the rate of substitution of goods for environmental amenities available in a given community be equal to the rate at which environmental amenities can be transformed into goods in that community. If this summation condition is satisfied in both communities at the same production point or goods-waste disposal combination, then the sum of the rate of substitution of goods for environmental amenities in community one must equal the sum of the rate of substitution of goods for environment in community two. Since these sums depend on individual preferences, this equality could only exist under two conditions:

1. At the common production point the distribution over individuals of the rates of substitution should be identical in both communities. If they are not identical, then the rates of substitution of goods for environmental amenities in a given community summed over the members of that community will not equal the rates of substitution of goods for environmental amenities in the second community summed over members of the second community. But identity of distributions is inconsistent with communities having different preferences.

2. Individuals are willing to pay the same amount for waste reduction occurring in other communities as they are for waste reduction in their own community.

Question 2

When an individual decides to move from community B to community A, his decision is influenced primarily by the differences in the net benefits which he directly receives by living in A rather than B. He may realize that his presence in A will reduce the quality of public services in A because he will add to the congestion present in A's delivery systems. But the impact of the change in service quality on everyone else living in A is not directly relevant to his decision, since he cannot be made to pay a special fee in order to be allowed to enter A. If, on the other hand, he experienced a reduction in his cost of living in B, he may decide to continue to reside in B. One way the residents of community A can mitigate the increased congestion of their systems as the result of in-migration of (former) residents of B, therefore, is to take some of its own tax revenue and give it to community B. Community B may then reduce its own tax rates, thereby lowering the cost of living in B and reducing the migration flow from B to A.

(Question: When is it in the interest of community B to accept the revenue-sharing offer of community A? If whenever it is in the interest of B to refuse A's offer, is it possible to make the members of both A and B better off by having B offer to share its revenue with A?)

As long as we confine the problem to a migration between two locations, there is no apparent advantage to introducing a higher level of government through which those revenues to be shared are channeled. Suppose, however, that there were three communities A^1, A^2 and B, where both A^1 and A^2 were receiving in-migrants from B at the same rate. The addition of the third community drastically changes the nature of the problem of achieving an efficient distribution of population over locations. A^1 and A^2 may share a common interest in slowing the out-migration from B. But since any reduction in taxes in B affect A^1 and A^2 equally regardless of how the revenues channeled to B were divided between A^1 and A^2, communities A^1 and A^2 have a conflict of interest with respect to how the revenues channeled to B are to be divided between themselves. That is, with respect to A^1 and A^2, reduction in B's taxes may be considered a public good. Just as individuals may find it profitable to forego sovereignty with respect to public goods, so too communities may wish to have a higher level of government decide upon the revenue-sharing method to achieve a commonly desired goal.

Question 3

As we noted in the answer to Question 2, if the outsiders' interests are in reducing the cost of living in a particular community, then a revenue-sharing system, which places no restrictions on the recipient, is all that is required. (Prove that the reduction in the cost of living for the median voter in the recipient community is generally greater if no strings are attached to the intergovernmental grant than if strings are attached.) Conditions need to be attached to the grant in order to express outsiders' interests only if the outsiders have a concern for the kinds of activities pursued in the recipient community.

Notes

1. An alternative measure of the benefits from avoiding rationing is the amount of all other goods this individual would have to be given to make him as well-off with Q_0 units of water as we would be if he could have bundle A. This measure is BD in our diagram. If the indifference curves are vertically parallel, this second measure BD' would equal the first AC, no matter how large the implicit change in real income associated with the move from B to A. (If the indifference curves are parallel at given prices for all goods, what would happen to the proportion of income spent on water as income rose? Do you think you would actually observe this phenomena? If the proportion of income fell as income rose, which measure of the gain from avoiding rationing would be larger, BD' or AC?)

   For changes in the water supply that would imply a small change in real income, the difference between BD' and AC would be correspondingly small even if the indifference curves were not parallel. Furthermore, it can be shown that if the indifference curves are not parallel, the area under the real-income-constant demand curve would represent an estimate of the benefits that lies between BD' and AC, further justifying its use as an estimate of the benefits of having the additional water.

NAME INDEX

SUBJECT INDEX